Walking the Red Road

The Native American Path to Leading a Spiritual Life Every Day

Terri Jean

Adams Media Corporation
Avon, Massachusetts

This book is dedicated to my mother
for teaching me how to write, and to my
great-grandmother, Whitlatch, for all of
her inspiration and encouragement.

Published by Adams Media,
an F+W Publications Company
57 Littlefield Street, Avon, MA 02322. U.S.A.
www.adamsmedia.com

ISBN 13: 978-1-58062-849-5
ISBN 10: 1-58062-849-4

Printed in Canada.

J I H G

Library of Congress Cataloging-in-Publication Data
Jean, Terri.
365 days of walking the Red Road / by Terri Jean.
p.   cm.
Includes bibliographical references.
ISBN 1-58062-849-4
1. Indian philosophy--North America. 2. Indians of North America--Religion. 3. Calendars. I. Title: Three hundred sixty-five days of walking the Red Road. II. Title.
E98.P5 .J43   2002
299'.7--dc21   2002011341

Interior photographs courtesy of ©Corel, ©1999 PhotoDisc, Inc., and ©1998 Digital Stock Corp.

This book is available at quantity discounts for bulk purchases. For information, call 1-800-289-0963.

Acknowledgments

I would like to acknowledge the effort, energy, and education of the many people who believed in my work, my writing, and my convictions. To those family, friends, and mentors who supported me unconditionally, I appreciate your kindness, patience, and time. And to those who unselfishly chose to educate me on their Native history, issues, culture, and experiences, thank you. Without you, this book would not be possible.

Introduction

O' Great Spirit help me always to speak the truth quietly, to listen with an open mind when others speak, and to remember the peace that may be found in silence.

—CHEROKEE PRAYER

When one is walking the Red Road, one is living as instructed by the Creator. The person who walks the Red Road lives a life of truth and charity— values handed down generation to generation. Though the road is littered with obstacles, all can be overcome once internal balance is achieved and the soul is true to itself and to others.

This book is full of such values, and the inspirational speakers span hundreds of years of Native American history. Their philosophies are rich and full of feeling, articulating myriad emotions and cultural instruction. Each quote is a lesson; each speaker is a teacher. The 365 lessons ring with the same wisdom and strength now as they did the day they were spoken.

THE NORTHERN JOURNEY OF WINTER

White covers much of the earth during winter's harsh, cold months, representing the nourishing blanket that secures all of nature while it lies sleeping. Winter also represents elders and their final walks along the Red Road. Our grandparents are wise and the winter is silent. Therefore, the time of the North is a special time for storytelling. In olden times, children and adults would gather around a fire and hear the storyteller narrate legends and myths of their people. Storytellers orally teach the traditions of their people and keep alive the history of their tribe. The Chippewa call North "Waboose," which is depicted as a strong, powerful buffalo withstanding the effects of winter.

Direction: North
Season: Winter
Color: White

From the beginning there were drums, beating out world rhythm—the booming, never-failing tide on the beach; the four seasons, gliding smoothly, one from the other; when the birds come, when they go, the bear hibernating for his winter sleep. Unfathomable the way, yet all in perfect time. Watch the heartbeat in your wrist—a precise pulsing beat of life's Drum—with loss of timing you are ill.

—JIMALEE BURTON (HO-CHEE-NEE),
CHEROKEE, 1974

JANUARY

JANUARY ALGONQUIN MOON:
SUN-HAS-NOT-STRENGTH-TO-THAW MOON

Red Road Ethic 1
Honor the Great Spirit

Every element of creation expresses the Creator. Within each mountain, each stone, and each heart lies the Great Spirit. All are of the Creator, and each particle of the universe is equally deserving of respect and admiration. When looking upon a sunset, the trees, or even your worst enemy, you are looking at the Creator. Know this and give praise and prayer.

A wee child toddling in a wonder world, I prefer to their dogma my excursions into the natural gardens where the voice of the Great Spirit is heard in the twittering of birds, the rippling of mighty waters, and the sweet breathing of flowers. If this is Paganism, then at present, at least, I am a Pagan.

—ZITKALA-SA (GERTRUDE SIMMONS BONNIN OR RED BIRD), SIOUX AUTHOR AND ACTIVIST, 1876–1938

January 1

What is life? It is the flash of a firefly in the night. It is the breath of a buffalo in the wintertime. It is the little shadow which runs across the grass and loses itself in the sunset.

—CROWFOOT,
BLACKFOOT WARRIOR AND ORATOR,
1826–1890

On This Date in Native American History

January 1, 1802: Peter Jones, Mississauga (Ojibway), was born. He later became a Mississauga chief and Methodist missionary, traveling throughout Canada and the United States preaching the gospel and addressing Native issues.

January 2

I love a people who have always made me welcome to the best they had . . . who are honest without laws, who have no jails and no poor-houses . . . who never take the name of God in vain . . . who worship God without a Bible, and I believe God loves them also . . . who are free from religious animosities . . . who have never raised a hand against me, or stolen my property, where there is no law to punish either . . . who never fought a battle with white men except on their own ground . . . and Oh, how I love a people who don't live for the love of money!

—GEORGE CATLIN
AN AMERICAN NON-NATIVE ARTIST
OF THE 1830S, SPEAKING ABOUT THE
NATIVE PEOPLE HE HAD ENCOUNTERED

January 3

Did You Know?

The term "crossing over" is common among Native people today to refer to those who died or who are dying.

January 4

*Kindness is to use one's will to
guard one's speech and conduct
so as not to injure anyone.*

—ORAL TRADITIONAL
TEACHING OF THE OMAHA

On This Date in
Native American History

January 4, 1975: The Indian Self-
Determination and Education Assistance Act was passed by Congress to
encourage the development of tribal
educational services.

January 5

*The earth has received the
embrace of the sun and we
shall see the results of that love.*

—Hunkesni (Sitting Bull),
Hunkpapa Sioux, 1831-1890

A Native to Know

Handsome Lake, half brother of Cornplanter, was a spiritual prophet who stressed the importance of traditional religious ceremonies and preached a message that would later be known as the "Code of Handsome Lake." His spiritual messages were heard by many Iroquois people, who traveled for miles to hear him speak. Even after his death in 1815, his teachings continue through his followers and are now known as the Longhouse Religion.

January 6

Often in the stillness of the night when all nature seems asleep about me there comes a gentle rapping at the door of my heart. I open it and a voice inquires, "Pokagon, what of your people? What will their future be?" My answer is: "Mortal man has not the power to draw aside the veil of unborn time to tell the future of his race. That gift belongs of the Divine alone. But it is given to him to closely judge the future by the present, and the past."

—SIMON POKAGON,
POTAWATOMI, 1830–1899

January 7

Everything on the earth has a purpose, every disease an herb to cure it, and every person a mission. This is the Indian theory of existence.

—MOURNING DOVE
(CHRISTINE QUINTASKET), SALISH,
1888–1936

Did You Know?

"Alaska" is a Native word that means "the great country."

January 8

It is well to be good to women in the strength of our manhood because we must sit under their hands at both ends of our lives.

—HE DOG,
OGLALA SIOUX

Did You Know?

Beloved Woman is an important community figure among the Cherokee people. The wise woman bestowed this role acts as a one-woman legal counsel and judicial authority over all members of her tribe. Her word is law and all people must abide.

January 9

Civilization has been thrust upon me . . . and it has not added one whit to my love for truth, honesty, and generosity.

—LUTHER STANDING BEAR,
OGLALA SIOUX, 1868–1937

On This Date in Native American History

January 9, 1789: Treaty of Fort Harmar was signed.

January 10

The Great Spirit is in all things, he is in the air we breathe. The Great Spirit is our Father, but the Earth is our Mother. She nourishes us, that which we put into the ground she returns to us . . .

—BEDAGI (BIG THUNDER),
WABANAKÍ ALGONQUIN, 1900s

Did You Know?

The Talking Feather is a communication device used by various tribes to ensure a person's right to speak without interruption from others. The leader of the meeting would first hold the Talking Feather, and then pass it around the room or give it to those who requested a turn. The feather typically held a special meaning to that particular tribe, and it would be decorated with distinctive colors and symbols. In other tribal communities, a Talking Stick would be used in the same manner.

January 11

*I have already agreed to be there
and that is the same as if I gave you
my head and my heart . . . I won't
try to take back what I have said.
I will do as I told you I would.*

—WESTERN APACHE TRIBAL MEMBER

On This Date in
Native American History

January 11, 1972: The Reverend Harold Jones, a South Dakota Sioux, was made a bishop in the Episcopal Church. He was the first Native American Indian to hold this position.

January 12

*Honor the sacred. Honor the Earth—
our Mother. Honor the Elders. Honor
all with whom we share the Earth:
Four-legged, two-legged, winged ones,
swimmers, crawlers, plant and rock
people. Walk in balance and beauty.*

—ANONYMOUS NATIVE AMERICAN ELDER

Did You Know?

For many Native American tribes, certain colors hold specific and sacred meanings. For example, to the Cherokee, red and black are two Cardinal Colors worn at many ceremonies and dances. Red represents the east, and black the west. White is for south, while blue symbolizes north.

January 13

Among the Indians there have been no written laws. Customs handed down from generation to generation have been the only laws to guide them. Every one might act different from what was considered right, did he choose to do so, but such acts would bring upon him the censure of the Nation . . . This fear of the Nation's censure acted as a mighty band, binding all in one social, honorable compact.

—GEORGE COPWAY,
OJIBWAY CHIEF, 1818–1863

January 14

Why do you take by force what
you could obtain by love?

—WAHUNSONACOCK (POWHATAN),
POWHATAN, 1547–1622

On This Date in
Native American History

January 14, 1833: Reverend Samuel
Worcester was released from a Georgia
prison, after serving four years of hard
labor for speaking out against the mistreatment of Cherokee Indians.

Red Road Lesson 1
The Good Red Road

Originally, the term "The Red Road" or "The Good Red Road" was used by the Plains people to signify one's righteous relationship with their divinity.

When one walks the Red Road, one is living within the rules of the Creator, living a life of truth, friendship, respect, spirituality, and humanitarianism. Today, the phrase is shared by numerous people all over the world.

Creator of the world, Maker of all men; Lord of lords, my eyes fail me . . . for the sole desire [is] to know thee.

—INCA HYMN

January 15

Let us put our minds together and see what life will make for our children.

—HUNKESNI (SITTING BULL),
HUNKPAPA SIOUX, 1831–1890

A Native to Know

Sitting Bull, known as Tantanka-Iyotanka by his people, was a Hunkpapa Sioux holy man and follower of the Ghost Dance Religion who united his people and fought for survival on the northern plains. His courage was legendary and his tribal convictions made him a beloved and well-respected Native leader.

January 16

I hope the Great Heavenly Father, who will look down upon us, will give all the tribes His blessing, that we may go forth in peace and live in peace all our days, and that he will look down upon our children and finally lift us far above this earth; and that our Heavenly Father will look upon our children as His children, that all the tribes may be His children. And as we shake hands to-day upon this broad plain, we may forever live in peace.

—RED CLOUD (MAKHPIYA-LUTA),
OGLALA SIOUX CHIEF, LATE 19TH CENTURY

January 17

I cannot think that we are useless or God would not have created us.

—GOYATHLAY (GERONIMO),
APACHE MEDICINE MAN AND WAR CHIEF,
1829–1909

In Remembrance

Of Mangas Coloradas, Apache chief, who died on this date 1863.

January 18

We will bury the tomahawk in the earth.

—SAUK ADAGE MEANT
AS A PLEDGE OF PEACE

On This Date in
Native American History

January 18, 1800: The Peace Preservation
Act was passed.

January 19

We preferred hunting to a life of idleness on our reservation. At times we did not get enough to eat and we were not allowed to hunt. All we wanted was peace and to be let alone . . . I was not allowed to remain quiet. I was tired of fighting . . . I have spoken.

—CRAZY HORSE,
OGLALA SIOUX, ON HIS DEATHBED, 1877

January 20

*I will follow the white man's trail.
I will take him as my friend, but I
will not bend my back to his burdens.
I will be cunning as a coyote. I will
ask him to understand his ways, then
I will prepare the way for my children,
and their children. The Great Spirit
has shown me—a day will come when
they will outrun the white man in his
own shoes.*

—MANY HORSES

Did You Know?

That Appaloosa horses, though named
by Canadian-French explorers, were
developed by the Nez Perce Indians.

January 21

O Great Spirit whose voice I hear in the winds, I come to you as one of your many children. I need your strength and your wisdom. Make me strong not to be superior to my brother, but to be able to fight my greatest enemy: Myself.

—CHIEF DAN GEORGE,
COAST SALISH, 1899–1981

On This Date in
Native American History

January 21, 1969: Navajo Community College (now called Diné College), the first all-Indian-operated community college, opened.

January 22

The idea of full dress in preparation for a battle comes not from a belief that it will add to the fighting ability. The preparation is for death in case that should be the result of the conflict. Every Indian wants to look his best when he goes to meet the Great Spirit so the dressing up is done whether in imminent danger in an oncoming battle or a sickness or injury at times of peace.

—WOODEN LEG,
CHEYENNE WARRIOR AND TRIBAL JUDGE,
1858–1940

January 23

There is a dignity about the
social intercourse of old Indians
which reminds me of a stroll
through a winter forest.

—FREDERICK REMINGTON,
NON-NATIVE ARTIST AND SCULPTOR,
1861–1909

In Remembrance

January 23, 1870, at Marias River, Montana, the Baker Massacre, also called "the greatest slaughter of Indians ever made by United States troops," leaves 170 to 215 Indians dead in the snow. They are to be remembered.

January 24

A people without a history is
like wind on the buffalo grass.

—TETON SIOUX PROVERB

In Remembrance

Of Ira Hayes (of the Pima tribe), famous for raising the United States flag over Iwo Jima with fellow Marines during World War II. A bronze statue and postage stamp later commemorated the event. He died on January 24, 1955, at the age of 33. Bob Dylan immortalized him in the song "The Ballad of Ira Hayes."

January 25

The Great Spirit . . . made it to always change . . . sunlight to play . . . night to sleep . . . everything good.

—Flying Hawk,
Ogalala clan, 19th century

On This Date in
Native American History

January 25, 1968: The Mescalero Apaches were awarded $8.5 million from the United States Indian Claims Commission as compensation for land illegally ceded in the 1800s.

January 26

A Native to Know

Will Rogers, humorist/writer/actor, was born in Indian Territory (Oklahoma) in 1879. Speaking of his Native American heritage, he said, "My folks were Indian. Both my mother and father had Cherokee blood in them. [I was] born and raised in Indian Territory. 'Course we're not the American whose ancestors came over on the *Mayflower*, but they met 'em at the boat when they landed."

Famous for his commentaries and writings, he was known as the "Indian Cowboy" from the Cherokee Nation, and was one of the most popular entertainers of his time. In 1918 he went to Hollywood and starred in many features, becoming such a box office sensation that by 1934 he was voted the most popular male actor in Hollywood. Will Rogers also served as mayor of Beverly Hills, was instrumental in the presidential election of Franklin D. Roosevelt, and even rejected a nomination for governor of Oklahoma. He died in 1935 in a plane crash in Alaska.

January 27

I'm working for the Creation. I refuse to take part in its destruction.

—LEON SHANANDOAH,
IROQUOIS

In Remembrance

Of the Shoshone Indians who crossed over in the Battle of Bear River, January 27, 1863.

January 28

Children were encouraged to develop strict discipline and a high regard for sharing. When a girl picked her first berries and dug her first roots, they were given away to an elder so she would share her future success. When a child carried water for the home, an elder would give compliments, pretending to taste meat in water carried by a boy or berries in that of a girl. The child was encouraged not to be lazy and to grow straight like a sapling.

—MOURNING DOVE
(CHRISTINE QUINTASKET), SALISH,
1888–1936

January 29

All things in the world are two. In our minds we are two, good and evil. With our eyes we see two things, things that are fair and things that are ugly . . . We have the right hand that strikes and makes for evil, and we have the left hand full of kindness, near the heart. One foot may lead us to an evil way, the other foot may lead us to a good. So are all things two, all two.

—Letakots-Lesa
(Gray Eagle Chief), Pawnee,
19th century

January 30

I was born in Nature's wide domain! The trees were all that sheltered my infant limbs, the blue heavens all that covered me. I am one of Nature's children. I have always admired her.

—George Copway, Ojibway chief, 1818–1863

Did You Know?

Before the Europeans arrived in the Americas, more than 500 tribes (a collective group of 22 million people) inhabited what is now the United States.

January 31

There is no quiet place in the white man's cities, no place to hear the leaves of spring or the rustle of insect wings . . . the clatter only seems to insult the ears.

—CHIEF SEATTLE (SEATHL),
DUWAMISH-SUQUAMISH, 1785–1866

Did You Know?

The following 26 states are named after Native American words: Alabama, Alaska, Arizona, Arkansas, Connecticut, Idaho, Illinois, Indiana, Iowa, Kansas, Kentucky, Massachusetts, Michigan, Minnesota, Mississippi, Missouri, Nebraska, North Dakota, Ohio, Oklahoma, South Dakota, Tennessee, Texas, Utah, Wisconsin, and Wyoming.

FEBRUARY

FEBRUARY NORTHERN
ARAPAHO MOON:
FROST-SPARKLING-IN-THE-SUN MOON

Red Road Ethic 2
Honor Mother Nature

Mother Nature is not *for* us . . . she is *part* of us and we, like everything else that lives and breathes upon her, are her children. Your own direct connection with Mother Earth is to be encouraged daily. Paint her portraits, swim in her waters, tend to her flowers, stroll through her glorious forests, and care for her many children: all plants, people, and animals.

We must live according to her principles and choose not to pollute her body. The alternative is death to our mother—and death to her children.

The Great Spirit is our father, but the Earth is our mother. She nourishes us; that which we put into the ground she returns to us, and healing plants she gives us likewise. If we are wounded, we go to our mother and seek to lay the wounded part against her, to be healed.

—BEDAGI (BIG THUNDER), WABANAKÍ ALGONQUIN, 1900s

February 1

A Native to Know

Chief Joseph was a major celebrity during his lifetime. Born in what is now northeastern Oregon in 1840, he was the son of one of the first Nez Perce Christian converts, also named Joseph, who raised Chief Joseph to support peace with whites—until the government betrayed the elder Joseph and the Nez Perce. Chief Joseph succeeded his father's position in 1871. After several skirmishes and difficulties with the U.S. government, he became an eloquent speaker against injustice and inequality, and spoke in support of the freedom of the Native people.

February 2

Lose your temper and you lose a friend; lie and you lose yourself.

—HOPI ADAGE

Did You Know?

A mixture called "kinnikinnick" is typically smoked in peace pipes by Native people. Kinnikinnick is a mixture of various plants and herbs, including sage, white clover, bearberry leaves, and mullein leaves.

February 3

Will we let ourselves be destroyed in our turn without a struggle, give up our homes, our country bequeathed to us by the Great Spirit, the graves of our dead and everything that is dear and sacred to us? I know you will cry with me, "Never! Never!"

—TECUMSEH,
SHAWNEE, 1768–1813

Did You Know?

Traditionally, Native American heritage is handed down from the mother's side, even if both parents are Native American. If only the father is Native American, the Native American lineage is still followed. Some children today, though, follow both parents' lineage.

February 4

*All things are the works of the Great
Spirit. We should know that He is
within all things: the trees, the grasses,
the rivers, the mountains, and all the
four-legged animals, and the winged
peoples; and even more important, we
should understand that He is also
above all these things and peoples.*

—BLACK ELK,
OGLALA SIOUX, 1863–1950

February 5

There was never a better day to die.

—RED HORSE,
LAKOTA, 1876

Did You Know?

The word "Shaman" originated in Siberia, but today some Native tribes and many non-Natives, especially anthropologists, use this term to describe a Native American healer who dwells with the underworld, the supernatural, and the spirits. Individuals who are true shamans will not write a book or make a public appearance about their work, nor will they advertise their practice or speak of it in public. A shaman can only be found by word of mouth, and those who practice ancient customs are rare. They differ from Native healers, who often mix traditional medicine with unconventional methods and act more as a physician to the community.

February 6

What is gained from our inner nature is exact knowledge, which gives us a far-reaching outlook over the earth. The many powers of inner nature are hidden in everyone, and these are identified with Wakan-Tanka.

—BLUE THUNDER,
TETON SIOUX

Did You Know?

Many archaeologists and scholars claim that Native people may have inhabited the Americas as long as 70,000 years prior to non-Natives.

February 7

Then I was standing on the highest mountain of them all, and round about beneath me was the whole hoop of the world. And while I stood there I saw more than I can tell and I understood more than I saw; for I was seeing in a sacred manner the shapes of all things in the spirit, and the shape of all shapes as they must live together like one being . . . And I say the sacred hoop of my people was one of the many hoops that made one circle, wide as daylight and as starlight, and in the center grew one mighty flowering tree to shelter all the children of one mother and one father. And I saw that it was holy . . .

But anywhere is the center of the world.

—BLACK ELK,
OGLALA SIOUX, 1863–1950

February 8

I am not a child. I can think for myself. No man can think for me.

—Chief Joseph
(Hin-mah-too-yah-lat-kekt), Nez Perce,
1840–1904

On This Date in
Native American History

February 8, 1887: The Dawes Act, which caused American Indian groups to lose a collected 90 million acres of reservation land, was passed.

February 9

*Yigaquu osaniyu adanvto adadoligi
nigohilvi nasquv utloyasdi nihi
(May the Great Spirit's Blessings
Always Be with You).*

—CHEROKEE ADAGE

A Native to Know

Jay Silverheels was born May 26, 1912, on the Six Nations Reserve in Ontario, Canada, to a Mohawk Chief. Silverheels first worked as a stuntman in Hollywood films, and then as an actor in such movies as *Key Largo* (1948). In 1949, Silverheels landed his famous role as Tonto on the hit television show *The Lone Ranger,* which ran for eight years. In 1979, he became the first Native American awarded a star on Hollywood's Walk of Fame. Silverheels was inducted into the Hall of Honor of the First Americans in the Arts in 1998, 18 years after his death.

February 10

*To clothe a man falsely is
only to distress his spirit . . .*

—LUTHER STANDING BEAR,
OGLALA SIOUX, 1868–1937

On This Day in
Native American History

February 10, 1763: France ceded the
North American territory to England in
the Treaty of Paris, ending the French
and Indian War (1754–1763).

February 11

The reason Wakan Tanka does not make two birds . . . or two human beings exactly alike is because each is placed here . . . to be an independent individual to rely on himself.

—OKUTE, 19TH CENTURY

On This Date in Native American History

February 11, 1978: American Indian Movement leader Dennis Banks organized a five-month trek from California to Washington, D.C., to bring awareness to Native American issues. Thousands of people, representing 80 tribes, joined the walk, and they were met in Washington by thousands of supporters lining the city streets and sidewalks.

February 12

Teach your children that the ground beneath their feet is the ashes of our grandfathers. So that they will respect the land, tell your children that the earth is rich with the lives of our kin. Teach your children what we have taught our children—that the earth is our mother. Whatever befalls the earth, befalls the sons of the earth . . . This we know: all things are connected like the blood which unites one family.

—CHIEF SEATTLE (SEATHL),
DUWAMISH-SUQUAMISH, 1785–1866

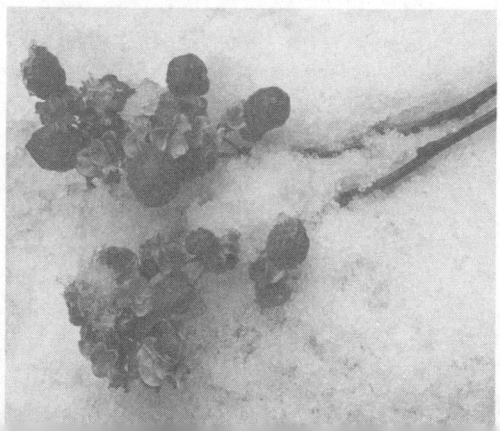

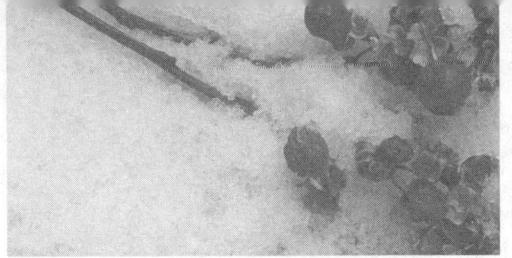

February 13

*You must stop your ears whenever you
are asked to sign a treaty selling your
home . . . This country holds your
father's body. Never sell the bones of
your father and your mother.*

—Old Chief Joseph (tu-eka-kas),
Nez Perce

On This Date in
Native American History

February 13, 1991: Graham Greene,
Oneida, was nominated for Best Supporting Actor by the Academy of Motion
Picture Arts and Sciences for his role in
the 1990 movie *Dances with Wolves*. He
later appeared in *Thunderheart* and *The
Green Mile*.

February 14

Great Spirit, you lived first,
and you are older than all need.

—BLACK ELK,
OGLALA SIOUX, 1863–1950

On This Date in
Native American History

February 14, 1986: The Smithsonian Institution's Museum of National History agreed to return skeletal remains of American Indians to those tribes with a verifiable lineage. The indigenous people have a burial custom and certain beliefs associated with those who passed on, and holding their ancestral remains is considered sacrilegious.

Red Road Lesson 2
Frybread and Community

Traditionally, frybread is a symbol of intertribal unity and community. It is a staple of powwows and, for many, family meals. The recipes can vary slightly. Here is one that's a personal favorite and is easy to prepare.

3 cups flour
1 tsp. salt
3 tsp. baking powder
1 cup milk
¼ cup warm water
Vegetable oil in deep fryer or
frying pan

1. Combine flour, salt, and baking powder in a large mixing bowl. Blend ingredients. Slowly stir in milk and knead dough until smooth, adding small amounts of warm water if mixture is too dry. Once dough is ready (when it is stiff and can be molded), cover with a cloth for 15 to 30 minutes.

2. Fill deep fryer or frying pan with oil, and heat until oil is very hot. Pinch off fist-size pieces of the frybread dough and flatten with your hands or with a rolling pin. Fry in the hot oil until golden brown on both sides (approximately 5 minutes). Drain on absorbent paper towels and serve.

Frybread dinner variations:

- Slice in half and serve with your favorite dip
- Use the frybread as the shell of your next taco dinner
- Spread peanut butter, cream cheese, or jelly onto your cooled bread
- Roll warm frybread in sugar for a special treat

Their wishes are our wishes and what we get I hope they will get.

—Running Antelope,
Sioux, speaking of friends and family

February 15

The Circle has healing power. In the Circle we are all equal. When in the Circle, no one is in front of you. No one is behind you. No one is above you. No one is below you. The Sacred Circle is designed to create unity. The Hoop of Life is also a circle. On this hoop there is a place for every species, every race, every tree, and every plant. It is this completeness of Life that must be respected in order to bring about health on this planet. To understand each other, as the ripples when a stone is tossed into the waters, the Circle starts small and grows . . . until it fills the whole lake.

—DAVE CHIEF, OGLALA LAKOTA, GRANDSON OF RED DOG/CRAZY HORSE'S BAND

February 16

*The ground on which we
stand is sacred ground.
It is the blood of our ancestors.*

—Chief Plenty Coups, Crow, 1848–1932

On This Date in
Native American History

February 16, 1835: Congress passed
the Indian Removal Act, initiating the
relocation of thousands of people.

February 17

Let the young men of this nation remember that idleness leads to poverty. Industry is honorable and leads to contentment.

—CHIEF JOHN ROSS, CHEROKEE, 1790–1866

In Remembrance

Of Geronimo, who died on February 17, 1909.

February 18

Out of the Indian approach to life there came a great freedom, an intense and absorbing respect for life, enriching faith in a Supreme Power, and principles of truth, honesty, generosity, equity, and brotherhood as a guide to mundane relations.

—LUTHER STANDING BEAR,
OGLALA SIOUX, 1868–1937

On This Date in Native American History

February 18, 1944: In an effort to introduce the beauty of the Native American culture to the people of New York City, and to raise funds for Native American charities, the Indian Confederation of American Indians staged a colorful powwow with dancers and participants representing more than 15 American Indian tribes.

February 19

Some of our chiefs make the claim that the land belongs to us. It is not what the Great Spirit told me. He told me that the lands belong to Him, that no people owns the land; that I was not to forget to tell this to the white people when I met them in council.

—KANAKUK, KICKAPOO, ADDRESSING GENERAL WILLIAM CLARK, 1827

Did You Know?

A medicine pipe is a sacred tool of Native tradition used to bring one closer to the Creator. The smoke acts as a communication device, bridging the two worlds.

February 20

The Kiowa braves have grown up from childhood, obtaining their medicine from the earth.

—SATANTA (WHITE BEAR),
KIOWA, 1830–1878

A Native to Know

Kiowa chief Satanta (Set'-tain-te) devoted himself to the preservation of the Kiowa way of life. He was an eloquent speaker whom the whites called the Orator of the Plains.

February 21

*If I have these and kept back the best
no one would believe I was in earnest.
I must give something that I really
value to show that my whole being
goes with the lesser gifts; therefore
I promise to give my body.*

—Chased-by-Bears,
Santee-Yanktonai Sioux, 1843–1915

In Remembrance

Of Walt Bresette, Red Cliff Chippewa, who died February 21, 1999, at the age of 51.

Bresette cofounded the Midwest Treaty Network and cowrote the book, *Walleye Warriors: An Effective Alliance Against Racism and for the Earth.*

February 22

A Native to Know

Wovoka woke the Native nations when he originated the Ghost Dance Religion in 1889. A prophet and spiritual leader, Wovoka believed there would one day be a time when all Indian people—those living and those who had died—would be reunited. In early 1890, the Ghost Dance Religion spread to many tribes throughout the West. Also in 1890, the Office of Indian Affairs outlawed the religion, arresting those who participated. After the death of Sitting Bull (arrested for suspicion of being a Ghost Dance leader), Big Foot and his band traveled to Wounded Knee where he and 300 other men, women, and children were killed. Despite the prohibitory law, practice of the Ghost Dance continued in secret until 1978.

February 23

*O ye people, be ye healed; Life anew
I bring unto ye. O ye people, be ye
healed; Life anew I bring unto ye.
Through the Father and all Do I thus.
Life anew I bring unto ye.*

—GOOD EAGLE (WANBLI-WASTE),
DAKOTA SIOUX, LATE 19TH CENTURY

In Remembrance

Of Quanah Parker, known as the last
free chief of the Comanche, who
crossed over today in 1911. He never
lost a battle to white troops and fought
passionately for the rights of his people.

February 24

*Whatever the gains,
whatever the loss, they are yours.*

—Five Wounds,
Nez Perce

A Native to Know

Novelist and poet N. Scott Momaday, born 1934, is considered one of the premier writers in the United States today. His books have achieved much literary success, and he won a Pulitzer Prize for his 1969 novel, *House Made of Dawn*. Momaday is a Kiowa and was raised on various Native reservations, and his writings reflect his love of his people, his culture, and his land. A graduate of Stanford University (with both a master's and doctoral degree), he created the Indian literature program at the University of California, in Berkeley.

February 25

We do not want riches.
We want peace and love.

—RED CLOUD (MAKHPIYA-LUTA),
OGLALA SIOUX, 1870

In Remembrance

Of those who died on February 25, 1643, in what is known as "The Slaughter of the Innocents." Considered one of the worst Native American slaughters in United States history, the massacre was the result of an order given by the director-general of New Netherlands to rid his territory of Indians. Several bands of tribes were exterminated and thousands of women, men, and children died.

February 26

The old Lakota was wise. He knew that man's heart away from nature becomes hard.

—Luther Standing Bear, Oglala Sioux, 1868–1937

Did You Know?

The largest reservation in the United States is the Navajo Indian Reservation (Utah, New Mexico, and Arizona) with nearly 3.5 million acres of land.

February 27

*We are contented to
let things remain as the
Great Spirit made them.*

—CHIEF JOSEPH
(HIN-MAH-TOO-YAH-LAT-KEKT),
NEZ PERCE, 1840–1904

On This Date in
Native American History

February 27, 1973: Wounded
Knee II erupted in South
Dakota.

February 28

Make everything straight and strong.

—DRAGGING CANOE,
CHICKAMAUGA TSALAGI

Did You Know?

There are many well-known Hollywood celebrities with claims to Native American lineage.

A few examples include A. Martinez, Brian Austin Green, Burt Reynolds, Carmen Electra, Cher, Chuck Norris, Della Reese, Elvis Presley, Heather Locklear, Hunter Tylo, James Earl Jones, James Garner, Johnny Cash, Johnny Depp, Jon Leguizamo, Kim Basinger, Bill Maher, Stephanie Kramer, Tommy Lee Jones, and Val Kilmer.

MARCH

MARCH CHEROKEE MOON:
"ANVHYI" OR STRAWBERRY MOON

*Spring—known as Sigun in Cree—
is upon us.*

Red Road Ethic 3
Search for Yourself, by Yourself

Do not allow others to make your path for you. It is *your* road and yours alone. Others may walk it *with* you, but no one can walk it *for* you. Accept yourself and your actions. Own your thoughts. Speak up when wrong, and apologize. Know your path at all times. To do this you must know yourself inside and out, accept your gifts as well as your shortcomings, and grow each day with honesty, integrity, compassion, faith, and brotherhood.

I have made myself what I am.

—TECUMSEH,
SHAWNEE, 1768–1813

March 1

*Sometimes dreams are
wiser than waking*

—Black Elk,
Oglala Sioux, 1863–1950

Did You Know?

The first Native American newspaper,
published in 1828, was the *Cherokee
Phoenix*.

March 2

When the Earth is sick, the animals will begin to disappear; when that happens, The Warriors of the Rainbow will come to save them.

—Chief Seattle (Seathl), Duwamish-Suquamish, 1785–1866

Did You Know?

Annie Dodge Wauneka, Navajo, received the Presidential Medal of Freedom Award in 1963 from President John F. Kennedy. The medal, granted to those who make outstanding contributions to peace, is the country's highest peacetime honor.

March 3

Let us look forward to the pleasing landscape of the future.

—CHIEF JOHN ROSS,
CHEROKEE, 1790–1866

A Native to Know

Simon Ortiz, Pueblo, won the Pushcart Prize for Poetry in 1981 for his collection entitled *From Sand Creek*. Ortiz holds a master's degree of fine arts and taught writing and literature at a number of colleges and universities.

March 4

The path of glory is rough and many gloomy hours obscure it. May the Great Spirit shed light on yours.

—BLACK HAWK,
SAUK, 1767–1838

Did You Know?

To many Native Americans, the term "bad medicine" means having a streak of bad luck, or that the spirits are working against them.

March 5

*Our land is everything to us . . .
I will tell you one of the things we
remember on our land. We
remember that our grandfathers
paid for it—with their lives.*

—WOODEN LEG,
CHEYENNE WARRIOR AND TRIBAL JUDGE,
1858–1940

Did You Know?

Through the centuries—and even today—there have been many female chieftains of various Native American tribal communities.

March 6

My friend, I am going to tell you the story of my life, as you wish; and if it were only the story of my life I think I would not tell it; for what is one man that he should make much of his winters, even when they bend him like a heavy snow? So many other men have lived and shall live that story, to be grass upon the hills.

—BLACK ELK,
OGLALA SIOUX, 1863–1950

A Native to Know

Black Elk was born in 1863 on the Little Powder River. When he was nine years old he received a vision that gave him a "special power," a power instrumental in his later becoming a prominent member of his tribe. A religious medicine man, he traveled the world and spoke to many about his beliefs and spirituality. In 1950, on the Pine Ridge Reservation, he crossed over.

March 7

There is one God looking down on us all. We are all children of one God. God is listening to me. The sun, the darkness, the winds, are all listening to what we now say.

—GOYATHLAY (GERONIMO),
APACHE MEDICINE MAN AND WAR CHIEF,
1829–1909

On This Date in
Native American History

March 7, 1934: Douglas Joseph Cardinal, Blackfoot, was born in Alberta, Canada. He is well known as a celebrated architect, and was commissioned in 1983 to design the Canadian Museum of Civilization building—a project worth over $90 million. In 1985 he was the chief architect of the National Museum of the American Indians project.

March 8

The soil you see is not ordinary soil—it is the dust of the blood, the flesh, and bones of our ancestors . . . You will have to dig through the surface before you can find nature's earth, as the upper portion is Crow. The land, as it is, is my blood and my dead; it is consecrated.

—SHES-HIS,
RENO CROW, LATE 19TH CENTURY

March 9

We do not walk alone.
Great Being walks beside us.
Know this and be grateful.

—POLINGAYSI QOYAWAYMA,
HOPI, BORN 1892

In Remembrance

Of the 90 innocent Christian Delaware Indians killed on March 9, 1782, in Gnadenhutten, Ohio.

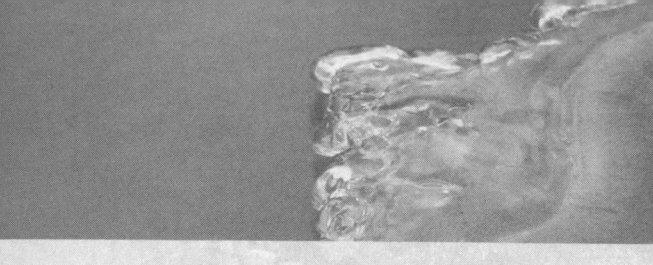

March 10

*Civilized people depend too much
on man-made printed pages.
I turn to the Great Spirit's book
which is the whole of his creation.*

—Tatanga Mani, 1871–1967

On This Date in
Native American History

March 10, 1861: Famed Mohawk poet E. Pauline Johnson was born to an English mother and a Mohawk father in Ontario at the Six Nations Reserve. She later published many works of poetry and novels including *The White Wampum* (1895) and *Canadian Born* (1903). She toured England, North America, and Canada reading her poetry in front of live audiences, and became highly acclaimed for her writing.

March 11

I never want to leave this country;
all my relatives are lying here in
the ground, and when I fall to pieces
I am going to fall to pieces here.

—WOLF NECKLACE,
PALOUSE

Did You Know?

A coup stick is a device used by Native Americans to strike an enemy, and it was a great achievement to strike the enemy without wounding them or without their knowledge of the presence of the person couping.

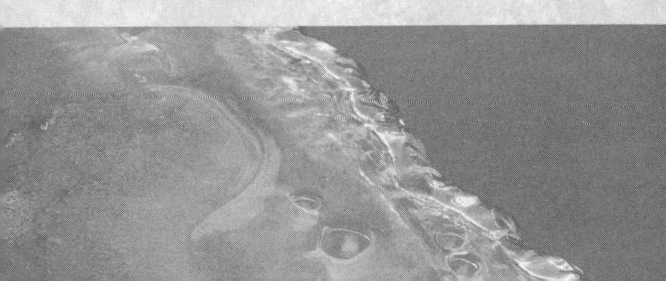

March 12

As a child I understood how to give;
I have forgotten this grace
since I became civilized.

—OHIYESA (CHARLES EASTMAN),
SANTEE SIOUX, 1858–1939

On This Date in
Native American History

March 12, 1880: Judge Elmer Dundy resolved that Native Americans are indeed "persons within the meaning of the law" and have the same rights as any other person. Until then, it was debated whether an Indian was a real person or an animal.

March 13

*To fight is to forget ourselves
as Indians in the world.*

—DR. CARLOS MONTEZUMA,
YAVAPAI

A Native to Know

Montezuma (II) is probably the most familiar figure in Aztec history. He led his people during the time of the Spanish conquest and was held hostage by Hernan Cortés for ransom until the 1520 Aztec revolt. Montezuma was stoned while talking to his people and died three days later.

March 14

Each man is good in His sight. It is not necessary for eagles to be crows.

—HUNKESNI (SITTING BULL),
HUNKPAPA SIOUX, 1831–1890

Did You Know?

The drum is one of the most important instruments used by the Native people. Often referred to as the "heartbeat of the people," the drum keeps order through rhythm, especially when dancing.

Red Road Lesson 3
The Many Names of the Great Spirit

The Great Spirit is the name given to the life force radiating from all creation. This energy is called many things by many different people: the Creator, A'wonawil'onas (Zuni), Wankan-Tankan (Sioux), God, Tirawa (Pawnee), Great Mystery, and Grandfather.

We may quarrel with men about things on Earth, but we never quarrel about the Great Spirit.

—CHIEF JOSEPH
(HIN-MAH-TOO-YAH-LAT-KEKT), NEZ PERCE,
1840–1904

March 15

I have noticed in my life that all men have a liking for some special animal, tree, plant, or spot of earth. If men would pay more attention for these preferences and seek what is best to do in order to make themselves worthy of that toward which they are so attracted, they might have dreams which would purify their lives. Let a man decide upon his favorite animal and make a study of it, learning its innocent ways. Let him learn to understand its sounds and motions. The animals want to communicate with man, but Wakan Tanka does not intend they shall do so directly—man must do the greater part in securing an understanding.

—BRAVE BUFFALO,
TETON SIOUX, LATE 19TH CENTURY

March 16

When we lift our hands we signify our dependence on the Great Spirit.

—BLACKFOOT,
MOUNTAIN CROW LEADER

A Native to Know

Notah Begay III, born in New Mexico, 1972, is the first Native American Indian to join the PGA Tour. Begay is Navajo, San Felipe, and Isleta—all tribes from the southwestern United States. Former teammate Tiger Woods said Begay is "happy to represent the Native American people, and in some regards, be a role model."

March 17

When we Indians kill meat, we eat it all up. When we dig roots, we make little holes. When we build houses, we make little holes. When we burn grass for grasshoppers, we don't ruin things. We shake down acorns and pine nuts. We don't chop down the trees. We only use dead wood. But the White people plow up the ground, pull down the trees, kill everything . . . the White people pay no attention . . . How can the spirit of the earth like the White man? . . . everywhere the White man has touched it, it is sore.

—WINTU WOMAN,
19TH CENTURY

March 18

I have always taught you
that a liar is not worthy of
being considered a man . . .

—Stung Arm

Did You Know?

The portrait on the U.S. buffalo nickels, sculpted in 1911, is said to be the composite of three Native Americans: Iron Tail, Big Tree, and Two Moons.

March 19

I am poor and naked but I am the chief of a nation. We do not want riches but we do want to train our children right. Riches would do us no good. We could not take them with us to the other world. We do not want riches. We want peace and love.

—RED CLOUD (MAKHPIYA-LUTA), OGLALA SIOUX CHIEF, 1822–1909

On This Date in Native American History

March 19, 1827: Cherokee author, journalist, and activist John Rillin Ridge was born.

March 20

*O Great Spirit, help me never
judge another until I have walked
two weeks in his moccasins.*

—Edwin Laughing Fox

Did You Know?

In 1774, Thomas Paine studied the Iroquois Confederacy, culture, and language in order to further his education in democratic government.

March 21

The Kiowa braves have grown up from childhood, obtaining their medicine from the earth.

—Satank,
Kiowa, c. 1810–1871

Did You Know?

There are many common foods that are of Native American origin. A few are pumpkin, zucchini, squash, sweet potatoes, peanuts, maple syrup, and hot chocolate.

March 22

*Our bare feet are conscious of the
sympathetic touch of our ancestors
as we walk over this Earth.*

—CHIEF SEATTLE (SEATHL),
DUWAMISH-SUQUAMISH, 1785–1866

Did You Know?

A Shaman is generally a person who
uses healing practices to treat and prevent illnesses associated with negative
spirits, while medicine men and medicine women treat illnesses caused by
both natural and supernatural forces.

March 23

We do not take up the
warpath without a just cause
and honest purpose.

A Native to Know

Pushmataha was a Choctaw chief who kept peace with the U.S. government, even when it meant siding against such influential men as Tecumseh. His services to the government earned him the rank of U.S. brigadier general, and when he died in 1824, he was buried with full U.S. military honors.

March 24

Misfortunes do not flourish
particularly in our path.
They grow everywhere.

—BLACK ELK,
OGLALA SIOUX, 1863–1950

Did You Know?

Several games were played by Native people prior to 1492, including badminton, field hockey, cat's cradle, darts, lacrosse, and spinning tops.

March 25

While living I want to live well. I know I have to die sometime, but even if the heavens were to fall on me, I want to do what is right. I think I am a good man . . . There is one God looking down on us all. We are all children of the one God. God is listening to me. The sun, the darkness, the winds, are all listening to what we now say.

—GOYATHLAY (GERONIMO),
APACHE MEDICINE MAN AND WAR CHIEF,
TO GENERAL GEORGE CROOK DURING
A PEACE CONFERENCE, MARCH 25, 1886

March 26

*Neither anger nor fear shall
find lodging in your mind.*

—DEKANAWIDAH,
IROQUOIS, C. 1300

On This Date in
Native American History

March 26, 1839: The Trail of Tears
ended.

March 27

If we could have spared more,
we would have given more . . .

—Canassatego,
Onondaga

On This Date in
Native American History

March 27, 1973: At the Academy Awards
presentation, Marlon Brando protested
the mistreatment of American Indians.

March 28

*The Great Spirit will not punish
us for what we do not know.*

—RED JACKET (SAGOYEWATHA),
SENECA, C. 1752–1830

Did You Know?

The totem pole has been a part of the
Alaskan tribes' history for centuries.
Carved from a column of wood, the
pole depicts various animal and mythological symbols important to the individual, family, and/or tribe.

March 29

To the Indian, words that are true sink deep into his heart where they remain; he never forgets them.

—FOUR GUNS

Did You Know?

In 1744 Benjamin Franklin sought the advice of Chief Canassatego on how to unite the American colonies into one confederacy.

March 30

Why don't you talk and go straight and all will be well?

—BLACK KETTLE,
SOUTHERN CHEYENNE CHIEF

A Native to Know

There are few personal details known about Black Kettle, a Southern Cheyenne chief, but what is known about him is legendary. He was an eloquent speaker, a dedicated leader, and a consistent champion of his people.

March 31

Your feet shall be as swift as forked lightning; your arm shall be as the thunderbolt, and your soul fearless.

—METHOATASKE

Did You Know?

A medicine bag, or medicine bundle, is carried by many Native people to hold sacred objects—such as stones, animal talons, totem, sacred herbs, or other prized possessions. It is worn on their body and kept close to them at all times. These items protect the individual and are used during sacred ceremonies or events. A "totem" is an object (animal, plant, etc.) that an individual is intimately related to. The person has a bond with this item, and uses it for prayer or to draw strength from during times of need.

THE EASTERN
JOURNEY OF SPRING

Yellow is the color of Mother Earth's sunsets, and the color of spring. The east is the direction of a new day, of new beginnings, and of first light. Spring is the perfect time to start new projects, raise your own vegetables and herbs, and to overcome challenges such as kicking bad habits.

Direction: East
Season: Spring
Color: Yellow

*My heart is filled with joy, when
I see you here, as the brook fills
with water when the snows melt in
the spring, and I feel glad, as the
ponies are when the fresh grass starts
in the beginning of the year.*

—TEN BEARS,
YAMPARIKA COMANCHE

APRIL

APRIL MOHAWK MOON:
ONERAHTOKHA: THE BUDDING TIME

Red Road Ethic 4
Community Code of Conduct

Treat the guests in your home with much consideration. Serve them the best food, give them the best bed, and treat them with respect. Honor the thoughts, wishes, and words of others. Never interrupt another or mock or mimic them. Allow each person the right to freedom of opinion. Respect that opinion. Never speak ill of others. As you travel along life's road never harm anyone, nor cause anyone to feel sad. On the contrary, if at any time you can make a person happy, do so.

Even as you desire good treatment, so render it.

—HANDSOME LAKE,
SENECA, c. 1735–1815

April 1

Naturally the Indian has many noble qualities. He is the very embodiment of courage. Indeed, at times he seems insensible to fear. If he is cruel and revengeful, it is because he is outlawed and his companion is the wild beast.

—N. G. TAYLOR,
U.S. COMMISSIONER, 1868

A Native to Know

Norval Morrisseau (Copper Thunderbird) was born on March 14, 1932, on Sand Point Ojibway Reserve in Ontario. An accomplished artist, he founded an art school in Canada, the Woodland School, has exhibited more than 40 one-man shows (many in France), received the prestigious Order of Canada Medal in 1978, and was elected to the Royal Canadian Academy of the Arts. In 1989 he became the only Canadian painter asked to exhibit in the Paris French Revolution Bicentennial.

April 2

You must speak straight so that your words may go as sunlight to our hearts.

—COCHISE,
CHIRICAHUA APACHE TRIBAL LEADER,
1812–1874

A Native to Know

Cochise was chief of the Chiricahua Apache and known for his intelligence and strategic strength. U.S. Cavalry soldiers referred to him as "The Serpent."

April 3

That hand is not the color of your hand, but if I pierce it I shall feel pain. The blood that will follow from mine will be the same color as yours. The Great Spirit made us both.

—LUTHER STANDING BEAR,
OGLALA SIOUX, 1868–1937

On This Date in
Native American History

April 3, 1994: In New Mexico, artist Charlene Teters closed her controversial exhibit "It Was Only an Indian: Native American Stereotypes."

April 4

*My forefathers were warriors.
Their son is a warrior. From
them I take my existence, from
my tribe I take nothing. I am
the maker of my own fortune.*

—TECUMSEH,
SHAWNEE, 1768–1813

On This Date in
Native American History

April 4, 1991: According to the U.S. census, 1,959,234 American Indians live in the United States.

April 5

*Men must be born
and reborn to belong.*

—LUTHER STANDING BEAR,
OGLALA SIOUX, 1868–1937

A Native to Know

Poet and novelist Sherman Alexie, born in 1966 and brought up on a Spokane Indian Reservation, has won several awards for his writing, including the National Endowment for the Arts Poetry Fellowship in 1992. With more than 200 published poems and stories, he is best known for the book *The Lone Ranger and Tonto Fistfight in Heaven* (1993).

April 6

*My words make haste to
reach your ears, harken to them.*

—GARANGULA,
ONONDAGA, 1684

Did You Know?

To the Haudenosaunee, the symbol of
arrows bundled together signifies unity
and brotherhood among Native nations.

April 7

A Native to Know

Cory Witherill (born 1971), Navajo, holds the distinction of being the most successful Native American race car driver in history. Witherill has raced several times in the PPG Dayton Indy Lights Championship, and in 2001 raced his first Indianapolis 500.

April 8

*Stand fast and remain united
and all will soon be well.*

—CHIEF JOHN ROSS,
CHEROKEE, 1790–1866

Did You Know?

There are hundreds of words in the American English language borrowed from or influenced by indigenous languages. Here are just a few: chocolate, tomato, llama, caribou, moose, persimmon, opossum, raccoon, muskrat, skunk, pecan, puma, caucus, kayak, toboggan, hickory, squash, hooch, chipmunk, woodchuck, and bayou.

April 9

Hoka hey! Follow me! Follow me!
Today is a good day to fight,
today is a good day to die!

—Crazy Horse,
Oglala-Brulé Sioux, June 1876

A Native to Know

Crazy Horse, Oglala-Brulé Sioux, was born east of the sacred Black Hills in 1842. He later became the war leader of an Oglala subgroup, the Teton Sioux, and was involved in several skirmishes including the Battle of the Little Bighorn. He surrendered in 1877 and was then killed.

April 10

*The Earth and myself
are of one mind.*

—Chief Joseph
(Hin-mah-too-yah-lat-kekt), Nez
Perce, 1840–1904

Did You Know?

A potlatch is a lavish ceremonial feast of the Northwest Coast tribal communities where extravagant gifts are exchanged between host and attendees.

April 11

Convince the world by your character that Indians are not as they have been shown.

—CHIEF JOHN ROSS, CHEROKEE, 1790–1866

**On This Date in
Native American History**

April 11, 1968: The American Indian Civil Rights Act was passed by the U.S. Congress.

April 12

*Never has the earth been so lovely
nor the sun so bright, as today . . .*

—NIKINAPI

A Native to Know

Sequoyah (1770–1843), Cherokee, developed a syllabary for the Cherokee language and opened many new doors for his fellow people. It took Sequoyah 12 years to finish his work, and he will be remembered as one of the only people in world history to create an entire syllabary on his own.

April 13

Savages we call them, because their manners differ from ours, which we think the perfection of civility; they think the same of theirs. Perhaps, if we could examine the manners of different nations with impartiality, we should find no people so rude as to be without any rules of politeness; nor any so polite, as not to have some remains of rudeness . . . The politeness of these savages in conversation is indeed carried to excess, since it does not permit them to contradict, or deny the truth of what is asserted in their presence. By this means they indeed avoid disputes, but then it becomes difficult to know their minds, or what impression you make upon them. The missionaries who have attempted to convert them to Christianity, all complain of this as one of the great difficulties of their mission. The Indians hear with patience the truths of the Gospel explained to them, and give their usual tokens of assent and approbation; you would think they were convinced. No such matter. It is mere civility.

—Benjamin Franklin, 1783

April 14

In all your official acts, self-interest shall be cast aside. You shall look and listen to the welfare of the whole people and have always in view, not only the present but the coming generations— the unborn of the future Nation.

—DEKAWIDAH, CHEROKEE, 1720

Red Road Lesson 4
The Tree of Life

The Tree of Life represents all that is life, encompassing all that exists upon the planet. When we walk the Red Road, our journey ends under the protection of this Tree. It causes the rhythm of the world to continue year after year, and with each cycle, fruit nourishes those who stand under her boughs. The roots dig deep into history. Those dedicated to this energy know the value of all beings, tend to Mother Earth, and live an honorable life in honor of the spirit of the ancient Tree.

The white man is too far removed from America's formative processes. The roots of the tree of his life have not yet grasped the rock and soil. . . . But for the Indian, the spirit of the land is still vested . . . When the Indian has forgotten the music of his forefathers, when the sound of the tom-tom is no more, when the memory of his heroes is no longer told in story . . . he will be dead.

—LUTHER STANDING BEAR,
OGLALA SIOUX CHIEF, 1905–1939

April 15

. . . for the Indian the spirit of the land is still vested; it will be until other men are able to divine and meet its rhythm.

—Luther Standing Bear,
Oglala Sioux, 1868–1937

Did You Know?

Helen Hunt Jackson (1830–1885) was a novelist whose controversial work included a novel exploring the U.S. government's mistreatment of Native Americans. *A Century of Dishonor* detailed the government's role in violating treaties and violating basic human rights. Published in 1881, her revolutionary book created quite a sensation and even today is still in print.

April 16

*Listen or your tongue
will keep you deaf.*

—NATIVE AMERICAN PROVERB

Did You Know?

Lacrosse is a game with Native American origins, though the actual name stems from a French priest who, in 1705, saw Algonquin Indians playing the sport and thought the webbed sticks resembled a bishop's cross. The sticks and the game were eventually renamed lacrosse.

April 17

Teach us the road to travel,
and we will not
depart from it forever.

—SATANK,
KIOWA, C. 1810–1871

On This Date in
Native American History

April 17, 1680: Catherine, Mohawk, died. She was the first American Indian to become a Catholic nun.

April 18

You must not hurt anybody or do harm to anyone. You must not fight but do right always.

—Wovoka (Jack Wilson), Paiute spiritual leader, c. 1856–1932

A Native to Know

One of the most well known Native leaders of Ohio is Chief Tarhe (the Crane). In 1794 the Wyandot leader was involved in the Battle of Fallen Timbers and fought for the rights and land of his people. In the War of 1812, at the age of 70, Tarhe led his warriors into battle. He was known by whites and Indians alike as a noble man.

April 19

The monitor within my breasts has taught me the will of the Great Spirit . . .

—SENACHWINE,
POTAWATOMI

On This Date in
Native American History

April 19, 1907: Canadian long-distance runner Tom Longboat, Onondaga, won the Boston Marathon.

April 20

. . . I have seen that in any great undertaking it is not enough for a man to depend simply upon himself.

—LONE MAN (ISNA-LA-WICA), TETON SIOUX, LATE 19TH CENTURY

Did You Know?

Nevada was first known as the Washoe Territory, named after the Washoe Indians.

April 21

Take only memories,
leave nothing but footprints.

—Chief Seattle (Seathl),
Duwamish-Suquamish, 1785–1866

A Native to Know

Maria Martinez is considered one of the greatest American Indian potters of the 20th century. Born in 1886, she worked with archaeologists in 1907 and copied work of pottery found at excavations. She is most famous for her black-on-white pottery, a tradition passed to her daughter.

April 22

It is important to understand that there are many different ways of seeing the world and expressing the wisdom of Native belief . . . No one voice speaks for all voices . . .

—JOSEPH BRUCHAC,
FROM HIS BOOK *NATIVE WISDOM*

Did You Know?

Robbie Robertson, best known for being a member of the 1970s group The Band, connected with his Native American roots after the 1994 television documentary *Music for the Native Americans.* His songs, for the documentary, a mix of rock, cutting-edge sounds, and Native chants and myths, are well received both by Native people and non-Natives.

April 23

Abuse no one and no living thing, for abuse turns the wise ones to fools and robs the spirit of its vision. When it comes your time to die, be not like those whose hearts are filled with fear of death, so that when their time comes they weep and pray for a little more time to live their lives over again in a different way. Sing your death song and die like a hero going home.

—TECUMSEH,
SHAWNEE, 1768–1813

April 24

I beg you now to believe this, all miserable as we seem in your eyes, we consider ourselves nevertheless much happier than thou, in that we are very content with the little that we have . . . Thou deceivest thyselves greatly if thou thinkest to persuade us that thy country is better than ours.

—GASPESIAN CHIEF, 1676

Did You Know?

The term "Eskimo"—which means "the eater of raw flesh"—is considered derogatory by many Alaskan Natives. The preferred term is "Inuit."

April 25

A child believes that only the action of someone who is unfriendly can cause pain.

—Chased-by-Bears,
Santee-Yanktonai Sioux, 1843–1915

Did You Know?

Traditional Hopi have a specific procedure for naming their children. The first 20 days following birth, mother and child stay in an isolated room hidden from the sun. After the 20 days, the child is presented to the sun to be blessed and is given several names. One name is the childhood name; other names will be decided later as the child grows, changes, and evolves.

April 26

When you arise in the morning,
give thanks for the morning light,
for your life and strength. Give
thanks for your food and the joy of
living. If you see no reason for giving
thanks, the fault lies in yourself.

—TECUMSEH,
SHAWNEE, 1768–1813

April 27

*Take the best of the white man's road,
pick it up and take it with you. That
which is bad leave alone, cast it away.
Take the best of the old Indian ways—
always keep them. They have been
proven for thousands of years. Do not
let them die.*

—ATTRIBUTED TO HUNKESNI (SITTING BULL),
HUNKPAPA SIOUX, 1831–1890

April 28

The American Indian is of the soil, whether it be the region of forests, plains, pueblos, or mesas. He fits into the landscape, for the hand that fashioned the continent also fashioned the man for his surroundings. He once grew as naturally as the wild sunflowers, he belongs just as the buffalo belonged . . .

—LUTHER STANDING BEAR,
OGLALA SIOUX, 1868–1937

April 29

They could not capture me except under a white flag. They cannot hold me except with a chain.

—OSCEOLA, SEMINOLE, MADE PRISONER OF WAR WHILE UNDER A FLAG OF TRUCE. HE DIED IN HIS PRISON CELL IN 1838.

Did You Know?

Indigenous peoples have been making baskets for thousands of years out of grasses, reeds, and sticks. And today, basketmaking is still a strong art practiced by many tribes, including the Hopi, Ute, and Shoshone.

April 30

We concealed nothing.
We came not secretly nor in the night.
We came in open day.

—MANGAS COLORADAS,
APACHE, 1797–1863

In Remembrance

Of those 144 defenseless Aravaipa
Apache Indians who were murdered
by an angry mob on April 30, 1871, at
Camp Grant.

Red Road Ethic 5
Banish Fear from Your Life

Fear stunts your soul and limits the amount of road needed to travel to reach the Tree of Life, and to know the Great Spirit. Fear is nonbeneficial and leads to an unbalanced mind, body, and spirit. To banish fear you must know your path and trust yourself—and the world around you. With trust comes confidence. Self-confidence banishes fear.

I fear no man,
and I depend on the Great Spirit.

—KONDIARONK,
HURON, LATE 17TH CENTURY

MAY

May 1

Together the two paths form a north-south road, the good Red Road. This is your spiritual path, the one where you will be happiest.

—MEDICINE HAWK,
COUNCIL CHIEF OF THE
SHADOWLIGHT MEDICINE CLAN

Did You Know?

In all Native American languages still spoken today, there is no word for "religion." Native people do not consider their beliefs one of religion. There is no fixed dogma or a list of written rules. There is only an understanding that one is to seek one's own path and live right with nature and right with the world.

May 2

We like our religion,
and do not want another.

—RED JACKET (SAGOYEWATHA),
SENECA, 1811

Did You Know?

There is often a set protocol for how to search for wild plants for medicinal uses.

Often the rules include showing respect and thanking the plant for its sacrifice.

May 3

*We shall live as brothers as long as sun
and moon shine in the sky. We have a
broad path to walk. If the Indian sleep
and the Yengeesman come, he pass
and do not harm to the Indian. If
Yengeesman sleep in path, the Indian
pass and do him no harm. Indian say,
"He's Yengees; he loves sleep."*

—TAMMANY,
DELAWARE CHIEF, 1682

May 4

*Given the proper incentive,
no mountain, it seems, is too
high to climb, no current too swift
to swim, if one is a Cherokee.*

—GRACE STEELE WOODWARD,
AUTHOR

On This Date in
Native American History

May 4, 1999: Sacagawea and her infant child were chosen to appear on the new golden United States dollar coin.

May 5

We don't have gold temples in this lake, but we have a sign of a living God to whom we pray—the living trees, the evergreen and spruce and the beautiful flowers and the beautiful rocks and the lake itself . . . We are taking that water to give us strength so we can gain in knowledge and wisdom . . . That is the reason this Blue Lake is so important to us.

—THE 1961 ASSOCIATION ON AMERICAN INDIAN AFFAIRS TAOS SPOKESMAN

May 6

Where I am, I build my house;
and where I build my house,
all things come to it.

—OSAGE INDIAN PROVERB

Did You Know?

Native American people were forbidden to legally practice the Ghost Dance until 1978.

May 7

When we use water in the sweat lodge we should think of Wakan-Tanka who is always flowing, giving His power and life to everything; we should even be as water which is lower than all things, yet stronger than the rocks.

—BLACK ELK,
OGLALA SIOUX, 1863–1950

May 8

It has come to me through the bushes that you are not yet all united; take time and become united . . .

—BIG BEAR

Did You Know?

The terms "Grandfather" and "Grandmother" are used to show respect to an elder, whether or not they are related by blood.

May 9

*Just what Power is I cannot explain,
for it is beyond my comprehension.
Those who seek it go alone that they
may be tested for worthiness. It is a
gift to be bestowed not only for
virtue but for prayer and courage.*

—VICTORIO,
MIMBRES APACHE, 1820–1880

Did You Know?

In Native American tradition, there are two basic categories of songs: those written by people, and songs given to an individual through visions or dreams.

May 10

Is there not something worthy of per-petuation in our Indian spirit of democracy, where Earth, our mother, was free to all, and no one sought to impoverish or enslave his neighbor?

—OHIYESA (CHARLES EASTMAN), SANTEE SIOUX, 1858–1939

A Native to Know

Ohiyesa, of the Eastern Woodland Santee Sioux, was born in 1858 and raised traditionally with his Woodland Sioux grandmother in southwestern Minnesota until he was 15. He was later educated at Dartmouth and then Boston University Medical School, where he delivered the graduation address to his fellow classmates. Ohiyesa is well known today for his writing, storytelling, essays, and lectures.

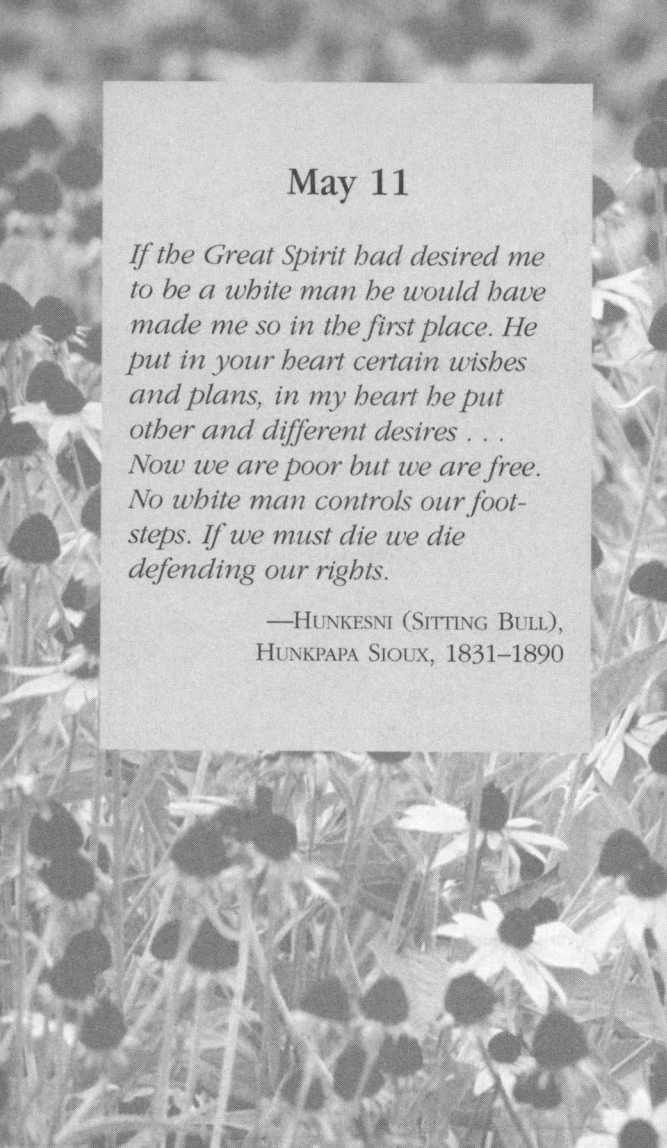

May 11

If the Great Spirit had desired me to be a white man he would have made me so in the first place. He put in your heart certain wishes and plans, in my heart he put other and different desires . . . Now we are poor but we are free. No white man controls our footsteps. If we must die we die defending our rights.

—HUNKESNI (SITTING BULL),
HUNKPAPA SIOUX, 1831–1890

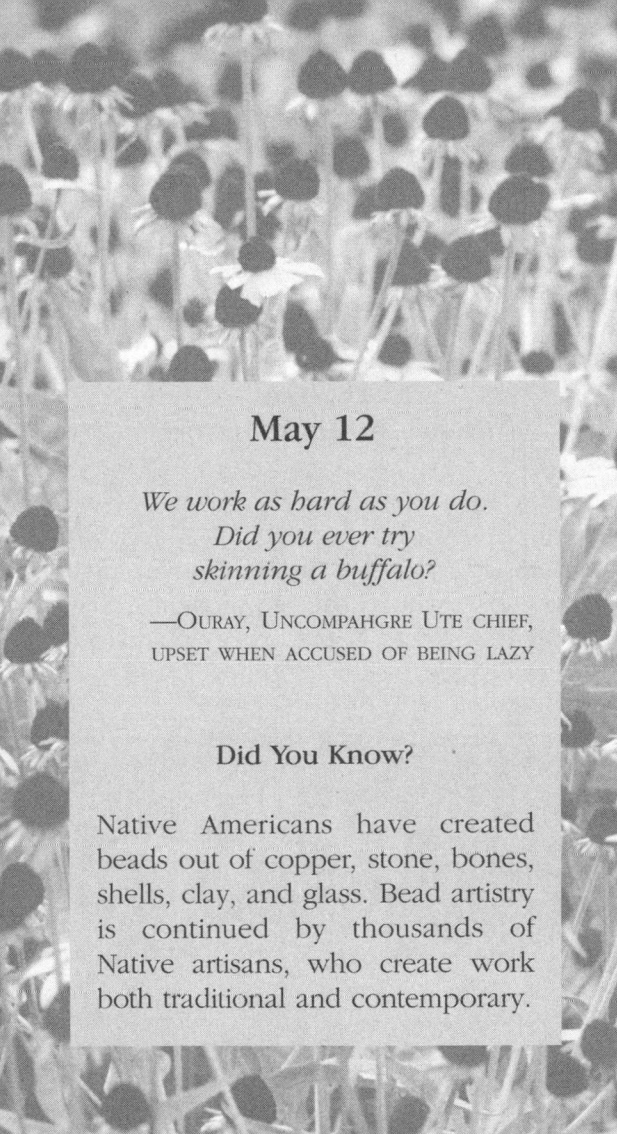

May 12

*We work as hard as you do.
Did you ever try
skinning a buffalo?*

—OURAY, UNCOMPAHGRE UTE CHIEF,
UPSET WHEN ACCUSED OF BEING LAZY

Did You Know?

Native Americans have created beads out of copper, stone, bones, shells, clay, and glass. Bead artistry is continued by thousands of Native artisans, who create work both traditional and contemporary.

May 13

Let us look forward to the pleasing landscape of the future.

—CHIEF JOHN ROSS,
CHEROKEE, 1790–1866

On This Date in
Native American History

May 13, 1916: "Indian Day" was recognized by the Society of American Indians (a group of non-Native supporters), who wished to recognize the plight of the Native people and to honor their legacy.

May 14

Training began with children who were taught to sit still and enjoy it. They were taught to use their organs of smell, to look when there was apparently nothing to see, and to listen intently when all seemingly was quiet. A child that cannot sit still is a half-developed child.

—Luther Standing Bear,
Oglala Sioux, 1868–1937

Did You Know?

Activist and artist Charlene Teters is called the "Rosa Parks" of the American Indians for her controversial work and exhibits (such as the exhibit "It Was Only an Indian"), which speak out against stereotyping Native people in the media, for commercial purposes, and in sports mascots. Her activism was made into a documentary entitled *In Whose Honor*. She is known as one of today's most respected Native leaders.

Red Road Lesson 5
The Medicine Wheel

The Medicine Wheel is the symbol of all creation. This ancient emblem represents all of life's forces. The Medicine Wheel explains our existence It tells what is true and what is needed to live.

The Medicine Wheel, is divided into four parts. Those four parts represent the whole of the person, the whole of the Creator, or the whole of the universe. A Medicine Wheel representing life would include birth/death, childhood, adulthood, and old age.

The Wheel may symbolize "self"— spiritual, emotional, physical, and mental. If a person lacks one aspect of the wheel, or one section is sick or lagging, the Medicine Wheel will remain unbalanced and the self will not be whole. Once the area is mended, the self can focus on its path.

Humankind has not woven the web of life. We are but one thread within it. Whatever we do to the web, we do to ourselves. All things are bound together.

—CHIEF SEATTLE (SEATHL), DUWAMISH-SUQUAMISH, 1785–1866

May 15

*The chastisement of God is worse
than any physical pain or sickness.*

—Rosalio Moises,
Yaqui

On This Date in
Native American History

May 15, 1978: Having their federal
tribe recognition stripped from them
years before, which officially deter-
mined the Modoc, Wyandot, Peoria,
and Ottawa Indian tribes of Oklahoma
extinct (according to the United States
government), their status as a living
and breathing tribe was reinstated.

May 16

It is the general belief of the Indians that after a man dies his spirit is somewhere on the earth or in the sky. We do not know exactly where, but we are sure that his spirit still lives. So it is with Wakan tanka. We believe that he is everywhere yet he is to us as the spirits of our friends whose voices we can not hear.

—CHASED-BY-BEARS,
SANTEE-YANKTONAI SIOUX, 1843–1915

May 17

Let the person I serve express his thanks according to his own bringing up and his sense of humor.

—Ohiyesa (Charles Eastman),
Santee Sioux, 1858–1939

Did You Know?

One of the most persistent stereotypes of the Native American Indians relates to tipis. Contrary to popular opinion, the tipi was not home to all Native Americans prior to—and following—the settlement of the white man. In fact, it was primarily used by the Plains people, who needed a sturdy home that could be torn down and packed rather quickly.

May 18

Great Spirit, Great Spirit, my Grand-father, all over the earth the faces of living things are all alike. Look upon these faces of children without number and with children in their arms that they may face the winds and walk the good road to the day of quiet.

—BLACK ELK, OGLALA SIOUX, 1863–1950

Did You Know?

Since before 2000 B.C., Native peoples have used tobacco during ceremonies and sacred rituals, and as an offering to the Earth or Earth's Creator or to other spiritual beings. Traditionally, the herb may have been smoked in a pipe during council meeting, or, for tribes such as the Ojibway, it may have been used prior to a vision quest. Often, smoking tobacco prefaced a tribal action. The people did not move forward, nor would an important decision be made, without first using tobacco to clear the mind and to consult the spirits.

May 19

If the white man wants to live in peace with the Indian, he can live in peace . . . Treat all men alike. Give them all the same law. Give them all an even chance to live and grow. All men were made by the same Great Spirit Chief. They are all brothers.

—CHIEF JOSEPH
(HIN-MAH-TOO-YAH-LAT-KEKT), NEZ PERCE,
1840–1904

May 20

*While living I want to live well.
I know I have to die sometime, but
even if the heavens were to fall on me
I want to do what is right . . .*

—GOYATHLAY (GERONIMO),
APACHE MEDICINE MAN AND WAR CHIEF,
1829–1909

On This Date in
Native American History

May 20, 1972: 21,000 acres from the Gifford Pinchot National Forest were returned to the Yakima Indians of Washington state by President Richard M. Nixon.

May 21

Much has been said of the want of what you term "civilization" among the Indians. Many proposals have been made to adopt your laws, your religion, your manners, and your customs. We would be better pleased with beholding the good effects of these doctrines in your own practices, than with hearing you talk about them. You say, "Why do not the Indians till the ground and live as we do?" May we not ask with equal propriety, "Why do not the white people hunt and live as we do?"

—OLD TASSEL,
CHEROKEE

May 22

When temptation comes, I don't say, "Yes," and I don't say, "No." I say, "Later." I just keep walking the Red Road—down the middle. When you're in the middle, you don't go to either extreme. You allow both sides to exist.

—Dr. A. C. Ross (Ehanamani), Lakota

Did You Know?

Dreamcatchers are not supposed to be placed around car mirrors. They serve a cultural importance that places them only above one's bed, where one sleeps.

May 23

Good words do not last long unless they amount to something. Words do not pay for my dead people. Words do not pay for my country, now overrun by white men. They do not protect my father's grave. They do not pay for all my horses and cattle. Good words will not give me back my children. Good words will not make good the promise of your War Chief. Good words will not give my people good health and stop them from dying. Good words will not get my people a home where they can live in peace and take care of themselves. I am tired of talk that comes to nothing. It makes my heart sick when I remember all the good words and all the broken promises. There has been too much talking by men who had no right to talk.

—CHIEF JOSEPH
(HIN-MAH-TOO-YAH-LAT-KEKT), NEZ PERCE,
1840–1904

May 24

Friendship between two persons depends upon the patience of one.

A Native to Know

Colorado Senator Ben Nighthorse Campbell was born in 1933 to a Northern Cheyenne mother and a Portuguese father. Raised in California, he is the first Native American Indian to serve in the U.S. Senate in more than 60 years. Campbell serves on the Indian Affairs Committee, and is also a published author, rancher, and jewelry designer.

May 25

From Wakan-Tanka, the Great Mystery, comes all power. It is from Wakan-Tanka that the holy man has wisdom and the power to heal and make holy charms. Man knows that all healing plants are given by Wankan-Tanka, therefore they are holy. So too is the buffalo holy, because it is the gift of Wakan-Tanka.

—FLAT IRON,
OGLALA SIOUX, LATE 19TH CENTURY

May 26

*The Black Hills are the house
of gold for our Indians.
We watch it to get rich.*

—LITTLE BEAR

Did You Know?

For many indigenous tribes, it was a common practice to sing a song—called a Death Chant—while dying. Kiowa leader Satank sang his death song in 1871 to show that he knew he was about to cross over.

May 27

My father, you have made promises to me and to my children. If the promises had been made by a person of no standing, I should not be surprised to see the promises fail. But you, who are so great in riches and in power, I am astonished that I do not see your fulfilled promises. I would have been better pleased if you had never made such promises, than that you should have made them and not performed them . . .

—Shinguaconse (Little Pine)

May 28

Listen to all the teachers in the woods. Watch the trees, the animals and all living things—you'll learn more from them than from books.

—JOE COYHIS,
STOCKBRIDGE-MUNSEE

Did You Know?

The bald eagle, the national symbol of the United States, was first the symbol of the Iroquois Nation.

May 29

That is the way with us Indians,
goods and earth are not equal.
Goods are for using the earth.

—Yellow Serpent

Did You Know?

"Alabama" means "I am one who works the land, harvests food from it" in Choctaw.

May 30

His brave warriors will be with us,
a bristling wall of strength.

—Chief Seattle (Seathl),
Duwamish-Suquamish, 1785–1866

A Native to Know

Chief Seattle was born near Puget Sound in 1785. He was well known for his beliefs in peace, friendship, and love of the land. A strong advocate of his people, Chief Seattle is considered one of the most beloved Native leaders of all time.

May 31

I believe much trouble would be saved if we opened our hearts more. I will tell you in my way how the Indian sees things. The white man has more words to tell you how they look to him, but it does not require many words to speak the truth.

—CHIEF JOSEPH
(HIN-MAH-TOO-YAH-LAT-KEKT), NEZ PERCE,
1840–1904

Red Road Ethic 6
Respect

Respect is to be given for all beings placed upon this earth by the Creator.

Respect is to be given to elders, who are rich with wisdom.

Respect one's privacy, thoughts, and wishes.

Respect human siblings by only speaking of their good qualities.

Respect one's personal space and belongings.

Respect another's spiritual path and do not judge their choices.

Trouble no one about their religion; respect others in their view, and demand that they respect yours. Love your life, perfect your life, and beautify all things in your life. Seek to make your life long and its purpose in the service of your people. Prepare a noble death song for the day when you go over the great divide. Always give a word or a sign of salute when meeting or passing a friend, even a stranger, when in a lonely place. Show respect to all people and bow to no one . . .

—TECUMSEH, SHAWNEE, 1768–1813

JUNE

JUNE POTAWATOMI MOON:
MONTH OF THE TURTLE

*Summer—known as Cohattayough
in Powhatan—is upon us.*

June 1

I know of no species of plant, bird, or animal that were exterminated until the coming of the white man. The white man considered natural animal life upon this continent, as "pests." There is no word in the Lakota vocabulary with the English meaning of this word . . . [the Indian] was . . . kin to all living things and he gave to all creatures equal rights with himself. [To the white man] the worth and right to live were his. Forests were mowed down, the buffalo were exterminated, the beaver driven to extinction and his wonderfully constructed dams dynamited. Springs, streams, and lakes that lived no longer ago than my boyhood have dried, and a whole people harassed to degradation and death. The white man has become the symbol of extinction for all things natural to this continent. Between him and the animal there is no rapport.

—Luther Standing Bear,
Oglala Sioux, 1868–1937

June 2

Last night I saw the sun set for the last time, and its light shine upon the tree tops, and the land, and the water, that I am never to look upon again.

—MENEWA, CREEK,
PRIOR TO HIS FORCED MARCH WESTWARD IN 1836

On This Date in
Native American History

June 2, 1924: All American Indians were granted U.S. citizenship.

June 3

My father went on talking to me in a low voice. This is how our people always talk to their children, so low and quiet, the child thinks he is dreaming. But he never forgets.

—MARIA CHONA, PAPAGO

On This Date in Native American History

June 3, 1948: Korczak Ziolkowski began his prodigious task of sculpting the Crazy Horse Monument from a mountain near Mount Rushmore, South Dakota.

June 4

Wolf I am, Everything . . .
in darkness will be good . . .
In light because Maheo . . .
Whenever I search Protects us
. . . Wherever I run Ea ea ea ho.

—Song of a Cheyenne scout

June 5

The Great Spirit first made the world, and next the flying animals, and found all things good and prosperous—He is immortal and everlasting. After finishing the flying animals, He came down on earth, and there stood. Then He made different kinds of trees and weeds of all sorts, and people of every kind. He made the spring and other seasons, and the weather suitable for planting . . . When the Great Spirit had made the earth and its animals, He went into the great lakes, where He breathed as easily as anywhere else and then made the different kinds of fish . . . He is the cause of all things that exist, and it is very wicked to go against His will . . . Some of us now keep the seventh day; but I wish to quit it, for the Great Spirit made it for others, but not for the Indians, who are out everyday to attend to their business.

—CORNPLANTER,
SENECA, 1736–1836

June 6

These were not our ways. We kept the laws we made and lived our religion. We have never been able to understand the white man, who fools nobody but himself.

—CHIEF PLENTY COUPS,
CROW, 1848–1932

On This Date in
Native American History

June 6, 1971: Forty American Indians protested for rights atop Mount Rushmore National Memorial.

June 7

Indian names were either character-istic nicknames given in a playful spirit, deed names, birth names, or such as have a religious and symbolic meaning . . . A man of forcible character, with a fine war record, usually bears the name of the buffalo or bear, lightning or some dread natural force. Another of more peaceful nature may be called Swift Bird or Blue Sky . . .

—Ohiyesa (Charles Eastman),
Santee Sioux, 1858–1939

In Remembrance

Of Chief Seattle, who crossed over on June 7, 1866.

June 8

We are part fire, and part dream.
We are the physical mirroring of
Miaheyyun, the Total Universe, upon
this earth, our Mother. We are here to
experience. We are a movement of
hand within millions of seasons, a
wink of touching within millions and
millions of sun fires. And we speak with
the Mirroring of the Sun. The wind is
the Spirit of these things. The force of
the natural things of this world are
brought together within the whirlwind.

—FIRE DOG,
CHEYENNE

In Remembrance

Of Chief Cochise, who crossed over on
June 8, 1874.

June 9

In the beginning of all things, wisdom and knowledge were with the animals, for Tirawa, the One Above, did not speak directly to man. He sent certain animals to tell men that he showed himself through the beast, and that from them, and from the stars and the sun and moon should man learn . . . all things tell of Tirawa.

—LETAKOTS-LESA (GRAY EAGLE CHIEF), PAWNEE, 19TH CENTURY

June 10

American Indians share a history rich in diversity, integrity, culture, and tradition. It is also rich in tragedy, deceit, and genocide. As the world learns of these atrocities and cries out for justice for all people everywhere, no human being should ever have to fear for his or her life because of their political or religious beliefs. We are in this together, my friends, the rich, the poor, the red, white, black, brown, and yellow. We share responsibility for Mother Earth and those who live and breathe upon her. Never forget that.

—LEONARD PELTIER,
NATIVE AMERICAN RIGHTS ACTIVIST

June 11

The Native vision, the gift of seeing truly, with wonder and delight into the natural world, is informed by a certain attitude of reverence and respect. It is a matter of extrasensory as well as sensory perception. In addition to the eye, it involves the intelligence, the instinct, and the imagination. It is the perception not only of objects and forms but also of essences and ideals.

—N. Scott Momaday,
Kiowa, 1934–

On This Date in
Native American History

June 11, 1971: The 19-month occupation of Alcatraz Island ended when the last of the protesting American Indians—six men, five children, and four women—were removed by federal marshals.

June 12

*There is a dignity about the
social intercourse of old Indians
which reminds me of a stroll
through a winter forest.*

—COCHISE

*Do you know or can you believe that
sometimes the idea obtrudes . . .
whether it has been well that I have
sought civilization with its bothersome
concomitants and whether it would
not be better even now to return to
the darkness and most sacred wilds
(if any such can be found) of our
country and there to vegetate and
expire silently, happily and forgotten
as do the birds of the air and the
beasts of the field. The thought is a
happy one but perhaps impracticable.*

—ELY S. PARKER,
SENECA-IROQUOIS, 1828–1895

June 13

So I know that it is a good thing I am going to do; and because no good thing can be done by any man alone, I will first make an offering and send a voice to the spirit world, that it may help me to be true. See I fill this sacred pipe with the bark of the red willow; but before we smoke it you must see how it is made and what it means. These four ribbons hanging here on the stem are the four quarters of the universe. The black one is for the west where the thunder beings live to send us rain; the white one for the north, whence comes the great white cleansing wind; the red one for the east, whence springs the light and where the morning star lives to give men wisdom; the yellow for the south, whence comes the summer and the power to grow.

—BLACK ELK,
OGLALA SIOUX, 1863–1950

June 14

Do not grieve. Misfortunes will happen to the wisest and best of men. Death will come and always out of season. It is the command of the Great Spirit, and all nations and people must obey. What is past and cannot be prevented should not be grieved for . . . Misfortunes do not flourish particularly in our path. They grow everywhere.

—Omaha chief Big Elk,
in a funeral speech for
Black Buffalo, heroic Indian leader,
delivered June 14, 1815,
at a great council at Portage des Sioux.

Red Road Lesson 6
Four Sacred Medicines

Though all plants are purposeful and important, four plants are sacred:

1. Tobacco is used in the offering of prayer to the Great Spirit. The smoke contains the prayers that are then lifted skyward.

2. Cedar purifies; good fortune will come your way if you carry cedar in your shoes.

3. Sage cleans the body and repels negative energy.

4. Sweetgrass also purifies and is carried for positive.

So I know that it is a good thing I am going to do; and because no good thing can be done by any man alone, I will first make an offering and send a voice to the spirit world that it may help me to be true. See, I fill this sacred pipe with the bark of the red willow; but before we smoke it you must see what it means. These four ribbons hanging here on the stem are the four quarters of the universe.

—BLACK ELK, OGLALA SIOUX, 1863–1950

June 15

My friends, how desperately do we need to be loved and to love. Love is something you and I must have. We must have it because our spirit feeds upon it. We must have it because without it we become weak and faint. Without love our self-esteem weakens. Without it our courage fails. Without love we can no longer look out confidently at the world. We turn inward and begin to feed upon our own personalities, and little by little we destroy ourselves. With it we are creative. With it we march tirelessly. With it, and with it alone, we are able to sacrifice for others.

—CHIEF DAN GEORGE,
COAST SALISH, 1899–1981

June 16

During the first year a newly married couple discovers whether they can agree with each other and can be happy—if not, they part, and look for other partners. If we were to live together and disagree, we should be as foolish as the whites. No indiscretion can banish a woman from her parental lodge. It makes no difference how many children she may bring home; she is always welcome. The kettle is over the fire to feed them.

—BLACK ELK,
OGLALA SIOUX, 1863–1950

June 17

The Indians were religious from the first moments of life. From the moment of the mother's recognition that she had conceived the mother's spiritual influence was supremely important. . . . Silence and isolation are the rule of life for the expectant mother. She wanders prayerful in the stillness of great woods, and to her poetic mind the imminent birth of her child prefigures the advent of a hero. And when the day of days in her life dawns—the day in which there is to be a new life, the miracle of whose making has been entrusted to her—she seeks no human aid. She has been trained and prepared in body and mind for this. Childbirth is best met alone, where no curious embarrass her, where all nature says to her spirit: "It's love! It's love! The fulfilling of life!" She feels the endearing warmth of it and hears its soft breathing. It is still a part of herself, and no look of a lover could be sweeter than its deep, trusting gaze.

—OHIYESA (CHARLES EASTMAN),
SANTEE SIOUX, 1858–1939

June 18

My breath—this is what I call my song, for it is just as necessary to me to sing as it is to me to breathe. I will sing this song, a song that is strong . . . Songs are thoughts, sung out with the breath when people are moved by great forces and ordinary speech no longer suffices. Man is moved just like the ice floe sailing here and there out in the current. His thoughts are driven by a flowing force when he feels joy, when he feels sorrow. Thoughts can wash over him like a flood, making his blood come in gasps, then it will happen that we, who always think we are small, will feel still smaller. And we will fear to use words. But it will happen that the words we need will come of themselves. When the words we want to use shoot up of themselves—we get a new song.

—ORPINGALIK, NETSILINGMUIT

June 19

We do not worship the Great Spirit as the white people do, but we believe that the forms of worship are indifferent to the Great Spirit.

—Red Jacket (Sagoyewatha), Seneca, 1811

Did You Know?

Indigenous cultures often had birth rituals that involved where the child was born, how the child was born, what was done with the umbilical cord, and the rules that were set for the first few weeks of the child's life. These rules and rituals were to ensure the safety of the mother, and also the safety, success, and luck of the child and of the entire family.

June 20

Oh, the comfort, the inexpressible comfort of feeling safe with a person, having neither to weigh thoughts . . . but pouring them all out, just as they are, chaff and grain together, certain that a faithful hand will take and sift them, keep what is worth keeping, and with a breath of kindness, blow the rest away.

—Anonymous Shoshone tribal member

June 21

The Great Spirit told me to tell the Indians that he had made them, and made the world that he placed them on to do good, not evil.

—Tenskwatawa (The Prophet),
Shawnee, 1808

On This Date in
Native American History

June 21, 1968: Nearly 100 American Indians demonstrated outside the Bureau of Indian Affairs to show their support for the Poor People's Campaign in Washington, D.C., which was conceived and organized by Martin Luther King Jr.

June 22

*The land known as the Black Hills
is considered by the Indians as
the center of their land.*

—RUNNING ANTELOPE,
FOLLOWING LT. COL. GEORGE A. CUSTER'S
1874 BLACK HILLS GOLD EXPEDITION

Did You Know?

The 1828 *Cherokee Phoenix,* the first American Indian newspaper, was published in both Cherokee and English.

June 23

A warrior who had more than needed would make a feast. He went around and invited the old and needy. The man who could thank the food, some worthy old medicine man or warrior said, "Look to the old, they are worthy of old age. They have seen their days and proven themselves. With the help of the Great Spirit they have attained a ripe old age. At this age the old can predict or give knowledge or wisdom whatever it is: it is so. At the end is a cane. You and your family shall get to where the cane is.

—BLACK ELK,
OGLALA SIOUX, 1863–1950

June 24

Your religious calling was written on plates of stone by the flaming finger of an angry God. Our religion was established by the traditions of our ancestors, the dreams of our elders that are given to them in the silent hours of night by the Great Spirit.

—Chief White Cloud, Iowa

A Native to Know

Carol Geddes, Inland Tlingit, was born in a small Yukon village in 1945. She is best known for the more than 20 movies she has produced, including the highly acclaimed *Doctor, Lawyer, Indian Chief* (1986) which won an award at the 1988 National Educational Film and Video Festival.

June 25

When I was a young man I went to a medicine-man for advice concerning my future. The medicine-man said: "I have not much to tell you except to help you understand this earth on which you live . . . If a man is to succeed on the hunt or the warpath he must not be governed by his inclination but by an understanding of the ways of animals and of his natural surroundings, gained through close observation. The earth is large, and on it live many animals. The earth is under the protection of something which at times becomes visible to the eye."

—LONE MAN (ISNA-LA-WICA),
TETON SIOUX, LATE 19TH CENTURY

June 26

I believe that ancient tribal cultures have important lessons to teach the rest of the world about the interconnectedness of all living things and the simple fact that our very existence is dependent upon the natural world we are rapidly destroying.

—Wilma Mankiller,
first woman elected
Cherokee deputy chief, 1991

June 27

*He who is present at a wrongdoing
and lifts not a hand to prevent it,
is as guilty as the wrongdoers.*

—ESTAMAZA, OMAHA, 1818–1888

Did You Know?

The Arawak people of the Lesser Antilles developed a language just for females after many women were captured and enslaved, and the men killed.

June 28

We believed in a power that was higher than all people and all the created world, and we called this power the Man-Above. We believed in some power in the world that governed everything that grew, and we called this power Mother-Earth. We believed in the power of the Sun, of the Night-Sun or Moon, of the Morning Star, and of the Four Old Men who direct the winds and the rains and the seasons and give us the breath of life. We believed that everything created is holy and has some party of the power that is over all.

—CARL SWEEZY,
ARAPAHO, 1881–1953

June 29

*Though we are powerful and
strong, and we know how to fight,
we do not wish to fight.*

—CHEROKEE ADAGE

Did You Know?

"Arkansas" means "land of the south
wind people" in Sioux.

June 30

I appeal to any white man to say if he ever entered Logan's cabin hungry, and he gave him not meat; if he ever came cold and naked, and he clothed him not. During the course of the last long and bloody war, Logan remained idle in his cabin, an advocate for peace.

—Chief Logan (Tahgahjute), Cayuga, about 1774

THE SOUTHERN JOURNEY OF SUMMER

Green is a common color for summer. It represents the lush grass and the emerald fullness of nature's forest. Summer is warm, comforting, and a time to relax and enjoy the sunshine. It's a perfect opportunity to build community ties and participate in summer solstice events such as bonfires and cookouts. South is representative of living willfully, passionately, and with love.

Direction: South
Season: Summer
Color: Green

Great Spirit, Great Spirit, my Grandfather, all over the earth the faces of living things are all alike . . . Look upon these faces of children without number and with children in their arms, that they may face the winds and walk the good road to the day of the quiet.

—BLACK ELK,
OGLALA SIOUX, 1863–1950

JULY

JULY ZUNI MOON:
MOON WHEN LIMBS OF TREES
ARE BROKEN BY FRUIT

Red Road Ethic 7
Speak the Truth

Speak only the truth and do right always. You are what you say . . . and what you say needs to be honest, forthright, and of your own personal belief. Without truth you cannot achieve inner balance—balance within yourself, with other beings, with Mother Earth, and with the Creator.

Good words do not last long until they amount to something.

—CHIEF JOSEPH
(HIN-MAH-TOO-YAH-LAT-KEKT), NEZ PERCE,
1840–1904

July 1

The man who sat on the ground in his tipi meditating on life and its meaning, accepting the kinship of all creatures and acknowledging unity with the universe of things, was infusing into his being the true essence of civilization.

—LUTHER STANDING BEAR, OGLALA SIOUX, 1868–1937

July 2

I was going around the world with the clouds when God spoke to my thought and told me to . . . be at peace with all.

—COCHISE,
CHIRICAHUA APACHE TRIBAL LEADER,
1812–1874

Did You Know?

"Illinois" means "men" or "warriors" in Algonquin.

July 3

Indians . . . know better how to live . . . Nobody can be in good health if he does not have all the time fresh air, sunshine and good water.

—CHIEF FLYING HAWK,
OGLALA SIOUX, 1852–1931

Did You Know?

The majority of Native Americans are of mixed heritage. A "full-blooded" Indian is very rare. Native people may have European, Asian, or African blood in their lineage. Others mix with other Native nationalities, some of which are not federally recognized.

July 4

*The traditions of our people are
handed down from father to son.
The Chief is considered to be the most
learned, and the leader of the tribe.
The Doctor, however, is thought to have
more inspiration. He is supposed to be
in communion with spirits . . . He
cures the sick by the laying of hands,
and prayers and incantations and
heavenly songs. He infuses new life
into the patient, and performs most
wonderful feats of skill in his practice
. . . He clothes himself in the skins of
young innocent animals, such as the
fawn, and decorates himself with the
plumage of harmless birds, such as the
dove and hummingbird . . .*

—SARAH WINNEMUCCA,
PAIUTE, 1844–1891

July 5

Flowers are for our souls to enjoy; not for our bodies to wear. Leave them alone and they will live out their lives and reproduce themselves as the Great Gardener intended.

—Sioux adage

Did You Know?

Tribal women play an important and respected role in their communities. Women and men had specific duties, and their roles in the tribe are valued. Women's duties are not degrading, nor are they considered an easier task.

July 6

You sent for us; we came . . .

—Tall Bull (Hotoakhihoois),
Cheyenne leader

Did You Know?
Indian Pledge of Allegiance

I pledge allegiance to my Tribe,
to the democratic principles of the
Republic
and to the individual freedoms
borrowed from the Iroquois and
Choctaw Confederacies,
as incorporated in the United States
Constitution,
so that my forefathers
shall not have died in vain.

This pledge was first presented in
1993 during the opening address of the
National Congress of American Indian
Tribal-States Relations Panel in Nevada.

July 7

*. . . if we cut ourselves, the blood will
be red—and so with the whites it is the
same, though their skin be white . . .
I am of another nation, when I speak
you do not understand me. When you
speak, I do not understand you.*

—Spokan Gary,
Middle Spokan chief, 1811–1892

Did You Know?

Ancient Native people had no written
language but did keep tribal records via
symbols inscribed on stone, bark, hide,
and pottery. Many of these inscriptions
still survive today.

July 8

*We have reason to glory in the
achievements of our ancestors.*

—O NO'SA

On This Date in
Native American History

July 8, 1970: President Richard M. Nixon
promised new services to Native people
and a strengthening of their community.
He then returned the sacred land of
Blue Lake to the Taos Pueblo Indians.

July 9

*One does not sell the
land people walk on.*

—CRAZY HORSE,
SEPTEMBER 23, 1875

Did You Know?

Warbonnets were worn by many of the
Plains tribes prior to setting off for battle.

July 10

When a man does a piece of work which is admired by all we say that it is wonderful; but when we see the changes of day and night, the sun, the moon, and the stars in the sky, and the changing seasons upon the earth, with their ripening fruits, anyone must realize that it is the work of someone more powerful than man.

—CHASED-BY-BEARS,
SANTEE-YANKTONAI SIOUX, 1843–1915

July 11

"Ea Nigada Qusdi Idadadvhn"
(all my relations in creation)

—C<small>HEROKEE</small> ADAGE

On This Date in
Native American History

July 11, 1968: The American Indian Movement (AIM) was founded in Minneapolis, Minnesota.

July 12

Once I was in Victoria, and I saw a very large house. They told me it was a bank and that the white men place their money there to be taken care of, and that by and by they got it back with interest. We are Indians and we have no such bank; but when we have plenty of money or blankets, we give them away to other chiefs and people, and by and by they return them with interest, and our hearts feel good. Our way of giving is our bank.

—CHIEF MAQUINNA,
NOOTKA

July 13

You ask me to plow the ground. Shall I take a knife and tear my mother's bosom? Then when I die she will not take me to her bosom to rest. You ask me to dig for stones! Shall I dig under her skin for bones? Then when I die I cannot enter her body to be born again. You ask me to cut grass and make hay and sell it and be rich like white men, but how dare I cut my mother's hair? I want my people to stay with me here. All the dead men will come to life again. Their spirits will come to their bodies again. We must wait here in the homes of our fathers and be ready to meet them in the bosom of our mother.

—WOVOKA (JACK WILSON), PAIUTE SPIRITUAL LEADER, C. 1856–1932

July 14

Do not wrong or hate your neighbor;
for it is not he that you wrong;
you wrong yourself.

—SHAWNEE SAYING

Did You Know?

Native people of yesterday lived off the entire buffalo. They ate the meat, tongue, liver, and ribs, and boiled the hooves as glue. Sinew was dried and split for bow strings, the bladder was used as a water jug, the skull was adornment, and the hide was used for clothing, blankets, shields, and shelter.

Red Road Lesson 7
The Circle

The Circle is an ancient symbol that represents eternity and life of all beings upon Mother Earth. The almighty sun is round, Mother Earth is round, and the cycle of life—from birth to death/rebirth—is also round. It represents unification and fulfillment, and is a powerful visual tool of the Medicine Wheel.

You have noticed that everything an Indian does is in a circle, and that is because the Power of the World always works in circles, and everything tries to be round . . . The Sky is round, and I have heard that the earth is round like a ball, and so are all the stars. The wind, in its greatest power, whirls. Birds make their nest in circles, for theirs is the same religion as ours . . . Even the seasons form a great circle in their changing, and always come back again to where they were. The life of a man is a circle from childhood to childhood, and so it is in everything where power moves.

—BLACK ELK, OGLALA SIOUX, 1863–1950

July 15

Brother, you say there is but one way to worship and serve the Great Spirit. If there is but one religion, why do you white people differ so much about it? Why not all agreed, as you can all read the Book?

—RED JACKET (SAGOYEWATHA),
SENECA, C. 1752–1830

A Native to Know

Seneca Chief Red Jacket was born in present-day New York near Seneca Lake in 1752. When asked about his being a warrior, he replied, "A warrior? I am an orator. I was born an orator!" Red Jacket, called this because he usually wore a red military jacket given to him by a British army acquaintance, was gifted in speech and in his ability to deal peacefully with non-Natives. Many of his speeches have been recorded and remembered.

July 16

In all your official acts, self-interest shall be cast aside. You shall look and listen to the welfare of the whole people and have always in view, not only the present but the coming generations— the unborn of the future Nation.

—DEKANAWIDAH,
IROQUOIS, C. 1300

Did You Know?

You must never refer to Native dress as a "costume," especially at special exhibits and powwows. This term is considered offensive. The proper term is "outfit" or "dress."

July 17

There were many whites, who,
after having tried it, expressed a
preference for the free but
hazardous life of savagery to the
more restrained life of civilization . . .

—ALEXANDER HENRY,
A YOUNG AMERICAN TRADER, WHO LIVED
AMONG THE INDIANS IN 1763 AND 1764

Did You Know?

"Michigan" comes from the Chippewa
word meaning "great water."

July 18

The wind that gave our grandfather his first breath also receives his last sigh. And the wind must also give our children the spirit of life.

—CHIEF SEATTLE (SEATHL),
DUWAMISH-SUQUAMISH, 1785–1866

Did You Know?

In the 19th century, many tipis were painted, and their designs would be handed down from generation to generation.

July 19

In the last place . . . we are bound . . . to watch for each other's preservation.

—CANASSATEGO,
ONONDAGA, 1742

On This Date in Native American History

July 19, 1881: When he surrendered in Dakota Territory, Sitting Bull said, "Let it be recorded that I am the last man of my people to lay down my gun."

July 20

When a man does a piece of work which is admired by all we say that it is wonderful; but when we see the changes of day and night, the sun, the moon, and the stars in the sky, and the changing seasons upon the earth, with their ripening fruits, anyone must realize that it is the work of someone more powerful than man.

—CHASED-BY-BEARS,
SANTEE-YANKTONAI SIOUX,
1843–1915

July 21

Walk on a rainbow trail,
walk on a trail of song,
and all about you will be beauty.
There is a way out of every dark mist,
over a rainbow trail.

—Navajo song

July 22

There are many secrets which the Great Mystery will disclose only to the most worthy. Only those who seek him [in] fasting and in solitude will receive his signs.

—UNCHEEDAH,
SANTEE SIOUX

A Native to Know

Pauline Johnson was a Mohawk poet born to an English mother and a Mohawk chief father in 1861 at the Six Nations Reserve in Ontario. Her first book of poetry was published in 1895; she later successfully toured the Americas giving readings, and published five additional works.

July 23

We acknowledge first the goodness of Wankan Tanka . . . we are sure his spirit lives.

—CHASED-BY-BEARS, SANTEE-YANKTONAI SIOUX, 1843–1915

On This Date in Native American History

July 23, 1999: Nearly 900 bands of Native nations met at the Assembly of First Nations and the National Congress of American Indians to build an alliance between indigenous people in Canada, the United States, Mexico, and South America.

July 24

They speak of the mysteries of the light of day by which the earth and all living things that dwell thereon are influenced.

—PLAYFUL CALF

On This Date in
Native American History

July 24, 1977: A 200-year-old debate between Comanche and Ute nations regarding hunting rights was officially settled. More than 2,000 members participated in a traditional ceremony that included smoking a peace pipe.

July 25

There are no such things as emptiness in the world. Even in the sky there were no vacant places. Everywhere there was life, visible and invisible, and every object possessed something that would be good for us to have also—even to the stones . . . The world teemed with life and wisdom; there was no complete solitude for the Lakota.

—LUTHER STANDING BEAR,
OGLALA SIOUX, 1868–1937

July 26

*We believed in one God, the Great
Spirit. We believed in our own kind of
Ten Commandments. And we behaved
as though we believed in them.*

—VINE DELORIA SR., YANKTON SIOUX,
1901–1990

A NATIVE MISSIONARY PRIEST ON SOUTH
DAKOTA INDIAN RESERVATIONS, VINE DELORIA
SR. WAS INSTRUMENTAL IN HIS ADVOCACY WORK
FOR NATIVE PEOPLE. VINE DELORIA JR. WROTE
CUSTER DIED FOR YOUR SINS AND *GOD IS RED.*

July 27

Almost every evening a myth, or a true story of some deed done in the past, was narrated by one of the parents or grandparents, while the boy listened with parted lips and glistening eyes . . .

—OHIYESA (CHARLES EASTMAN),
SANTEE SIOUX, 1858–1939

Did You Know?

To the Haudenosaunee, the eagle is the protector of peace, sitting upon the Tree of Peace to sound alarm when danger is near.

July 28

*Oh, Eagle, come with wings
outspread in sunny skies.
Oh, Eagle, come and bring us peace,
thy gentle peace.
Oh, Eagle, come and give new life
to us who pray.
Remember the circle of the sky, the
stars, and the brown eagle,
the great life of the Sun,
the young within the nest.
Remember the sacredness of things.*

—Pawnee prayer

Did You Know?

Often, in speech, prayer, or song, Native Americans may give praise to the Great Spirit and to all Native relations including the two-legged, four-legged, and winged ones. This is common practice, since most Native beliefs center around the fact that all living beings are brothers and sisters, and all are equal in the eyes of the Creator.

July 29

Our fathers gave us many laws, which they had learned from their fathers. Those laws were good. They told us to treat all men as they treated us, that we should never be the first to break a bargain, that it was a disgrace to tell a lie, that we should only speak the truth . . .

—CHIEF JOSEPH (HIN-MAH-TOO-YAH-LAT-KEKT), NEZ PERCE, 1840–1904

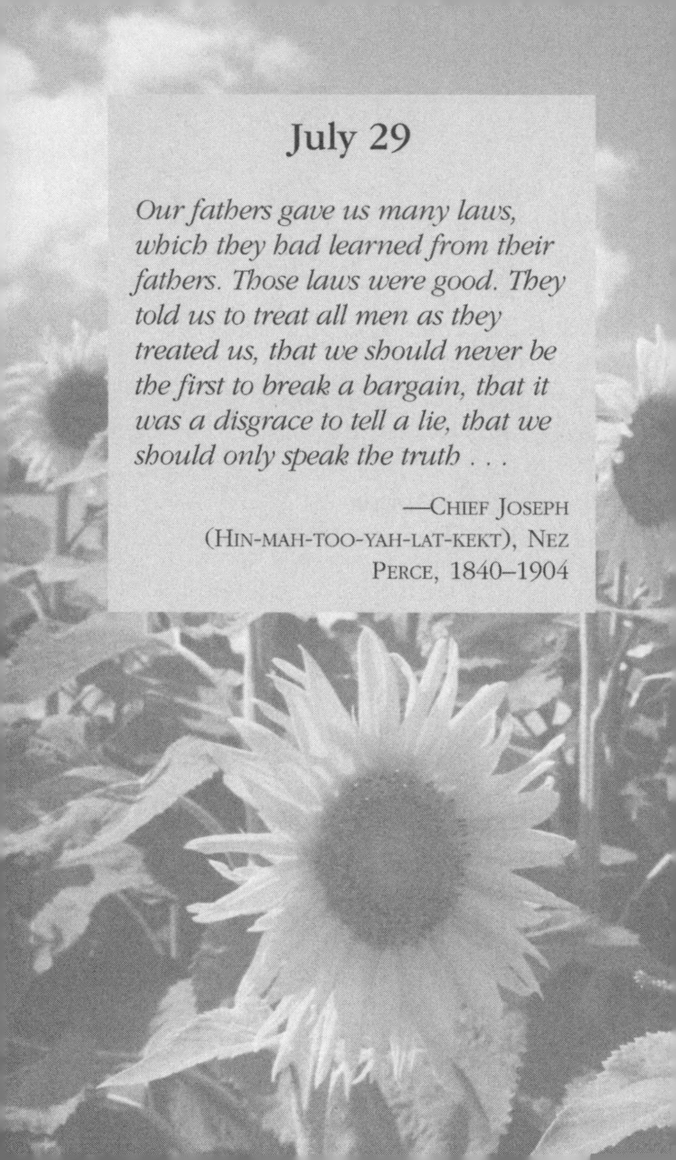

July 30

We do not know what may happen today, but let us act as though we were the Seven Stars (Big Dipper) in the sky that live forever. Go with me as far as you can, and I will go with you while there is breath in my body.

—CHIEF PLENTY COUPS, CROW, 1848–1932

Did You Know?

The word "squaw" is considered extremely derogatory to Native women and should *never* be used in their presence or in reference to them.

July 31

Just what Power is I cannot explain,
for it is beyond my comprehension.
Those who seek it go alone that they
may be tested for worthiness. It is a gift
to be bestowed not only for virtue but
for prayer and courage.

—VICTORIO,
MIMBRES APACHE, 1820–1880

A Native to Know

Victorio was chief of the Ojo Caliente Apache and at one time served under Apache Mangas Coloradas. Victorio was an adamant fighter for his people and used physical force when necessary. It took an army of more than 2,000 soldiers to defeat the brilliant strategist and his people, numbering fewer than 200.

August

August Hopi Moon:
Paamuya: Joyful Moon

Red Road Ethic 8
Reject Materialism

When one is materialistic, one is not right with the Red Road. To value and appreciate what you have and to know that you are loved and safe under the limbs of the Tree of Life is to reject materialism and to live a life of virtue and appreciation. Materialism only fills your heart with envy and greed, while appreciation breeds contentment, balance, and true happiness.

. . . These are my young men. I am their Chief. Look among them and see if you can find among them who are rich. They are all poor because they are all honest.

—RED DOG,
OGLALA SIOUX, 1870

August 1

What is man without the beasts? If all the beasts were gone, men would die from great loneliness of spirit, for whatever happens to the beasts also happens to man. All things are connected. Whatever befalls the earth befalls the children of the earth.

—CHIEF SEATTLE (SEATHL),
DUWAMISH-SUQUAMISH, 1785–1866

Did You Know?

"Oklahoma" is a Choctaw word meaning "Red Men."

August 2

Each one must learn for himself the highest wisdom. It cannot be taught in words.

—SMOWHALA, WANAPUM

Did You Know?

Most Native nations have two or more names for their tribe. One was given to them by Europeans, while the second is the people's original tribal name, which had a specific meaning. Here are a few tribal names and their meanings:

Apache:	Enemy
Cayuga:	People at the mucky land
Cherokee:	People of different speech
Fox:	Red Earth People
Hopi:	Peaceful Ones
Lakota:	Friend
Omaha:	Upstream people or people going against the current
Powhatan:	Falls in a current of water
Yuki:	Stranger

August 3

The Crow country is good country. The Great Spirit has put it exactly in the right place; while you are in it you fare well; whenever you go out of it, which ever way you travel, you fare worse . . . There is no country like Crow country.

—ARAPOOSH,
CROW, 1833

On This Date in
Native American History

August 3, 1990: November was officially declared "National American Indian Heritage Month" by Congress.

August 4

The Cherokee lives as a natural part of his environment and strives to complement it, not subdue or dominate it. It's an Indian philosophy that is playing an increasing role in everyone's life now that we realize that natural resources are limited and imbalance between man's technology and nature is perilously close to disaster.

—HUEY P. LONG,
CHEROKEE

August 5

Men die but live again in the real world of Wakan-Tanka, where there is nothing but the spirits of all things; and this true life we may know here on earth if we purify our bodies and minds thus coming closer to Wakan-Tanka who is all-purity.

—BLACK ELK,
OGLALA SIOUX, 1863–1950

In Remembrance

Of Lower Brulé Sioux leader Spotted Tail, who crossed over on August 5, 1881, at the age of 68.

August 6

There is a special magic and holiness about the girl and woman. There are the bringers of life to the people, and the teachers of the little children.

—SWEET MEDICINE,
CHEYENNE

On This Date in
Native American History

August 6, 1975: President Gerald Ford signed into law an act granting non-English-speaking citizens, including American Indians, the right to vote in more than one language.

August 7

We must truly honor what is past,
when we seek in our changed
conditions to attain the same
proficiency that our fathers showed in
their day and in their lives.

—"OLD KEYAM" (EDWARD AHENAKEW),
PLAINS CREE

On This Date in
Native American History

August 7, 1969: Louis Bruce, a Mohawk-Oglala-Sioux Indian from New York, was appointed to the position of Commissioner of Indian Affairs by President Richard M. Nixon and Walter Hickel, Secretary of the Interior. Bruce was the third American Indian to be appointed to this position; the other two were Robert Bennett and Ely Parker.

August 8

The more you know the more you will trust and the less you will fear.

—Ojibway adage

Did You Know?

A powwow was originally an event held during springtime to celebrate the upcoming season of life, birth, fruition, and renewal. Communities would gather together to sing, conduct religious ceremonies, dance, and connect with friends and family. Today, powwows are an important part of tribal unity, perseverance, and renewal, and are held at all times of the year. Some powwows including singing and competitive dancing, and have food and artwork for sale.

August 9

The lands of the planet call to humankind for redemption. But it is a redemption of sanity, not a supernatural reclamation project at the end of history. The planet itself calls to the other living species for relief. Religion cannot be kept within the bounds of sermons and scriptures. It is a force in and of itself and it calls for the integration of lands and peoples in harmonious unity. The land waits for those who can discern their rhythms. The peculiar genius of each continent—each river valley, the rugged mountains, the placid lakes—all call for relief from the constant burden of exploitation.

—VINE DELORIA JR., LAKOTA,
1973, FROM HIS BOOK *GOD IS RED*

August 10

Look twice at a two-faced man.

—CHIEF JOSEPH (HIN-MAH-TOO-YAH-LAT-KEKT),
NEZ PERCE, 1840–1904

Did You Know?

The medicine pole used by the Mandans (Plains) was similar to the totem pole used by the northwestern tribes. The medicine pole included various animal symbols, which brought power or good energy to the family and/or community.

August 11

*If you do bad things your children
will follow you and do the same.
If you want to raise good children,
be decent yourself.*

—CHRIS,
MESCALERO APACHE

On This Date in
Native American History

August 11, 1978: Congress enacted the
American Indian Religious Freedom
Act, which lifted the ban from many
Native American religious ceremonies,
including the legendary Ghost Dance.

August 12

Every struggle, whether won or lost, strengthens us for the next to come. It is not good for people to have an easy life. They become weak and inefficient when they cease to struggle. Some need a series of defeats before developing the strength and courage to win a victory.

—VICTORIO,
MIMBRES APACHE, 1820–1880

August 13

I shall not speak with fear and trembling. I have never injured you, and innocence can feel no fear.

—BLACK THUNDER, FOX

Did You Know?

Music and singing were a vital element in Native American culture. People chanted and played instruments made from animal hides and bone.

August 14

When the hearts of the givers are filled with hate, their gifts are small.

—CHIEF PLENTY COUPS,
CROW, 1848–1932

On This Date in
Native American History

August 14, 1982: Navajo servicemen who relayed messages that could not be deciphered by the Japanese during World War II were honored by President Ronald Reagan, who declared today National Navajo Code Talkers Day.

Red Road Lesson 8

How to Say "I Love You"

Here is how you can say "I love you" in eight different Native American languages.

Cheyenne	*Nemehotâtse*
Chickasaw	*Chiholloli*
Hawaiian	*Aloha I'a Au Oe*
Hopi	*Nu' umi unangwa'ta*
Mohawk	*Konoronhkwa*
Navaho	*Ayor anosh'ni*
Ojibway	*Gi zah gin*
Zuni	*Tom ho' ichema*

Love is something you and I must have. We must have it because our spirit feeds upon it.

—Chief Dan George,
Coast Salish, 1899–1981

August 15

My people were wise. They never neglected the young or failed to keep before them deeds done by illustrious men of the tribe. Our teachers were willing and thorough. They were our grandfathers, fathers, or uncles. All were quick to praise excellence without speaking a word that might break the spirit of a boy who might be less capable than others. The boy who failed at any lesson got only more lessons, more care, until he was as far as he could go.

—CHIEF PLENTY COUPS,
CROW, 1848–1932

August 16

The smarter a man is the more he needs God to protect him from thinking he knows everything.

—George Webb, Pima,
author of the 1959 book
A Pima Remembers

Did You Know?

In 1881, President Chester Arthur authorized official rules forbidding "rites, customs . . . contrary to civilization." And all Native dances, traditional rituals, and spiritual rites also were forbidden.

August 17

Experience is the wisest teacher . . .

—PLEASANT PORTER,
CREEK, 1840–1907

Did You Know?

"Metis" is a term used to classify a group of people of mixed blood, primarily Indian and French.

August 18

Free yourself from negative influence. Negative thoughts are the old habits that gnaw at the roots of the soul.

—Moses Shongo,
Seneca

A Native to Know

Mabel McKay, Long Valley Cache Creek Pomo basketmaker, prophet, and physician, was born in California in 1907. She became one of the best known traditional basketmakers of her time, and was the last weaver to create such traditional work. Prior to her death in 1993, she taught basketmaking at universities and to her own people. Her work is showcased in numerous collections throughout the United States and in Europe.

August 19

My father, you see us as we are. We are poor. We have but few blankets and little clothing. The great father who made us and gave us this land to live upon, made the buffalo and other game to afford us sustenance; their meat is our only food; with their skins we clothe ourselves and build our lodges. They are our only means of life—food, fuel, and clothing . . . We hear a great trail is to be made through our country. We do not know what this is for; we do not understand it, but we think it will scare away the buffalo.

—OLD BRAVE, ASSINIBOIN,
SPEAKING TO GOVERNOR ISSAC STEVENS, 1853

August 20

It is in peace only that our women and children can enjoy happiness, and increase in numbers.

—CHIEF JOHN ROSS,
CHEROKEE, 1790–1866

On This Date in
Native American History

August 20, 1994: Miracle, the first white female buffalo calf in over a century, was born in Janesville, Wisconsin, to non-Native ranchers. The birth of a white buffalo calf was prophesied by Native people generations ago, and she is seen as a sign of tribal unity and peace by believers all across the country. Thousands pilgrimage to see her, and Miracle received worldwide media attention.

August 21

One has to face fear or
forever run from it.

—HAWK,
CROW

On This Date in
Native American History

August 21, 1861: Cherokee Principal
Chief John Ross spoke to his people
about remaining neutral with both
sides in the American Civil War: "While
ready and willing to defend our fire-
sides, let us not make war wantonly
against the authority of the United or
Confederate States, but avoid a conflict
with either, and remain strictly on our
own soil."

August 22

*If you have one hundred people
who live together, and if each one
cares for the rest, there is one mind.*

—SHINING ARROWS,
CROW

On This Date in
Native American History

August 22, 1810: Tecumseh embarked
on a journey to protect his people, fight
for their property rights, and build a
confederacy among his fellow Indians.

August 23

*The white man thinks
with his head—the Indian
thinks with his heart.*

—JIMALEE BURTON
(HO-CHEE-NEE), CHEROKEE

On This Date in
Native American History

August 23, 1886: Geronimo, the great Chihuahua Apache leader, surrendered to General Nelson A. Miles and agreed to give up arms and live on a reservation, in peace, for the remainder of his days.

August 24

I do not want to settle down in the houses you would build for us. I love to roam over the wild prairies. There I am free and happy. When we sit down, we grow pale and die.

—Satanta (White Bear),
Kiowa, 1830–1878

Did You Know?

Native American spirituality is primarily rooted in the personal experience with nature. Each person is to nurture his or her own path, to form his or her own connections and attachments.

August 25

It is a truth, a melancholy truth, that the good things which men do are often buried in the ground, while their evil deeds are stripped naked and exposed to the world.

—BLACK THUNDER,
FOX

Did You Know?

Just like other cultures, Native Americans had their own explanations of how and why they—and the Earth—were created, and by whom. Many claim their tribal birth from the womb of Mother Earth, while others give credit to animals or mythological beings.

August 26

In you, as in all men, are natural powers. You have a will. Learn to use it. Make it work for you. Sharpen your senses as you sharpen your knife . . . We can give you nothing. You already possess everything necessary to become great.

—LEGENDARY DWARF CHIEF, CROW

Did You Know?

There were 13 basic housing structures used by Native people: Chickee, Igloo, Pit House, Tipi, Wickiup, Pueblo, Hogan, Wattle and Daub, Longhouse, Wigwam, Plank House, Lean-to, and Earthlodge.

August 27

. . . An Indian who is as bad as a white man could not live in our nation; he would be put to death and eaten by the wolves. The white men are bad schoolmasters; they carry false looks and deal in false actions; they smile in the face of the poor Indian to cheat him; they shake him by the hand to gain his confidence, to make him drunk, to deceive him, to ruin his wife . . . Black Hawk is a true Indian, and disdains to cry like a woman. He feels for his wife, his children and his friends. But he does not care for himself. He cares for his nation, and the Indians. They will suffer. He laments their fate . . . Farewell, my nation! . . . He can do no more. He is near his end. His sun is setting, and will rise no more. Farewell to Black Hawk!

—BLACK HAWK,
FROM HIS SPEECH TO J. M. STREET,
AUGUST 27, 1832

August 28

The color of the skin makes no difference; what is good and just for one is good and just for the other.

—White Shield, Arikara

Did You Know?

If an eagle feather falls from a dancer's outfit during a dance or powwow, the event stops and a ceremony is quickly performed to restore the feather's power.

August 29

In every human heart there is a deep spiritual hunger for an abiding belief in some future existence. Such a faith stabilizes character, and many of our young people have no such anchor for their souls.

—THOMAS WILDCAT ALFORD, SHAWNEE, 1930

On This Date in Native American History

August 29, 1911: Ishi, the last Yana Indian, was found hiding in Oroville, California.

August 30

Wowienke he iyotam wowa sake (Truth is power).

—LAKOTA ADAGE

Did You Know?

There is an old belief among Native people that 90 percent of all illnesses come from bad feelings, guilt, or negative energy.

August 31

. . . The Earth is our Mother. From her we get our life . . . and our ability to live. It is our responsibility to care for our Mother, and in caring for our Mother, we care for ourselves. Women, all females are the manifestation of Mother Earth in human form. We are her daughters and in my cultural instructions—Minobimaatisiiwin—we are to care for her. I am taught to live in respect for Mother Earth. In Indigenous societies, we are told that Natural Law is the highest law, higher than the law made by nations, states, municipalities and the world bank. That one would do well to live in accordance with Natural Law, with those of our Mother. And in respect for our Mother Earth of our relations— indinawaymuguni took.

—WINONA LADUKE, OF THE MISSISSIPPI BAND OF THE ANISHINAABE OF THE WHITE EARTH RESERVATION, MINNESOTA, AND A CANDIDATE FOR VICE PRESIDENT IN 2000 UNDER THE GREEN PARTY TICKET, SPEAKING TO AN ASSEMBLY AT THE INDIGENOUS WOMEN'S NETWORK IN BEIJING, CHINA

SEPTEMBER

SEPTEMBER TEWA PUEBLO MOON:
MOON WHEN THE CORN IS TAKEN IN

*Autumn—also known as Pahcotai
in Shawnee—is upon us.*

Red Road Ethic 9
Seek Wisdom

Those who are wise have lived a lifetime with ears open and a willingness to not only experience truth, but to pursue it as well.

Wisdom is gained by:

Listening to your elders. They have walked a longer path than you.

Seeking all that is true. Wisdom lies within honesty, not deception.

Realizing that education is never-ending. Even death is a final lesson.

Learning from Mother Nature. Her wisdom is infinite.

The greatest obstacle to the internal nature is the mind. If it relies on logic such as the white man's mind, the domain of the inner nature is inaccessible. The simple fact is man does not challenge the wisdom of the Holy Mystery.

—Turtleheart, Teton Sioux

September 1

Whenever the white man treats the Indian as they treat each other, then we will have no more wars. We shall all be alike—brothers or one father and one another, with one sky above us and one country around us, and one government for all.

—CHIEF JOSEPH
(HIN-MAH-TOO-YAH-LAT-KEKT) NEZ PERCE,
1840–1904

Did You Know?

Inuit women used to tattoo their faces to enhance their beauty and to signify their readiness to marry.

September 2

The people were put upon this world to learn of themselves and of their brothers and sisters. We are these People. We are the Fallen Star. Our laws of men change with our understanding of them. Only the laws of the Spirit remain always the same.

—WHITE WOLF,
CROW

Did You Know?

Fall harvest festivals, feasts, and giving-thanks celebrations have been a part of Native tradition for thousands of years.

September 3

If an Apache had allowed his aged parents to suffer for food or shelter, if he had neglected or abused the sick, if he had profaned our religion, or had been unfaithful, he might be banished from the tribe.

—GOYATHLAY (GERONIMO),
APACHE MEDICINE MAN AND WAR CHIEF,
1829–1909

In Remembrance

On this day in 1783, an entire Brulé village was massacred by 1,300 soldiers avenging the death of 30 soldiers who were killed for murdering Conquering Bear, the Brulé chief, during an argument over livestock.

September 4

He gains success and avoids failure by learning how others succeeded or failed, and without trouble to himself.

—CROW TEACHING

Did You Know?

The Plains tribes would lay their dead on elevated platforms or in treetops so the bodies would be close to the Great Spirit and safe from preying animals.

September 5

Finish what you begin.
Those who leave things half
done get boils on their heads.
Do you want boils on your head?

—Sevenka Qoyawayma,
Hopi, 1964

In Remembrance

Of Crazy Horse, who died September 5, 1877, at Fort Robinson, Nebraska.

September 6

There are four ways in which you may go, if you are going somewhere. The first is to go immediately on first thought. That is not right. Think about it. This will make it the second way. Then think about it a third time, but don't go away yet. Then on the fourth consideration, go and it will be all right. Thus you will be safe. Sometimes wait a day in between considerations of your problems.

—DIABLO,
WHITE MOUNTAIN APACHE, 1942

September 7

For an important marriage the chief presided, aided by his wife. He passed a pipe around the room so each could share a smoke in common. In this way families were publically united to banish any past or future disagreement and thus stood as "one united." The chief then gave the couple an oration of his advice, pointing out the good characteristics of each, and then offered his congratulations to them for a happy future.

—MOURNING DOVE (CHRISTINE QUINTASKET), SALISH, 1888–1936

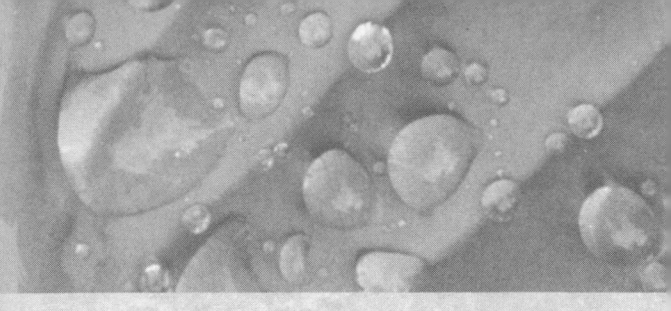

September 8

But if the vision was true and mighty, and I know, it is true and mighty yet; for such things are of the spirit, and it is in the darkness of their eyes that men get lost.

—BLACK ELK,
OGLALA SIOUX, 1863–1950

On This Date in
Native American History

September 8, 1565: The first permanent European colony was established at St. Augustine, Florida, in what will eventually become the United States of America.

September 9

The Indian believes profoundly in silence—the sign of a perfect equilibrium. Silence is the absolute poise or balance of body, mind and spirit. The man who preserves his selfhood is ever calm and unshaken by the storms of existence . . . What are the fruits of silence? They are self-control, true courage or endurance, patience, dignity, and reverence. Silence is the cornerstone of character.

—OHIYESA (CHARLES EASTMAN), SANTEE SIOUX, 1858–1939

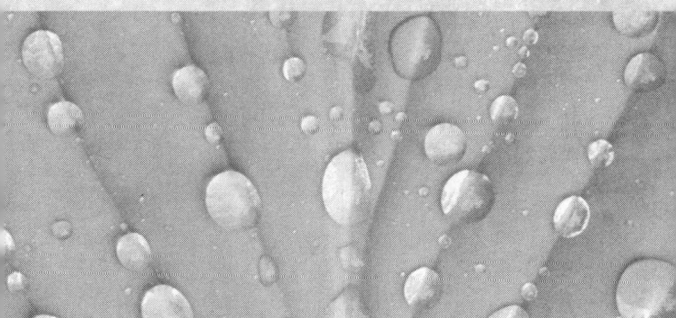

September 10

*The frog does not drink up
the pond in which he lives.*

—TETON SIOUX PROVERB

Did You Know?

Cotton cloth was first invented by American Indians.

September 11

*The honor of the people lies in
the moccasin tracks of the women . . .
No people goes down until their
women are weak and dishonored,
or dead upon the ground.*

—Anonymous male Sioux

Did You Know?

A give-away is a common custom among many Native nations. Unlike other cultures where a person is given gifts for their accomplishments, many Native societies believe gifts are given by the person being honored. The more revered they are, the more they give. For some, the chief was the poorest person in the community.

September 12

We cannot reap happiness while wallowing in the mire of immaturity, because immaturity fosters emotional chaos, self-degradation, and depravity.

—Moses Shongo,
Seneca

On This Date in
Native American History

September 12, 1962: Ojibway artist Norval Morrisseau exhibited his now-famous paintings at the Pollock Gallery (Toronto) for the very first time.

September 13

*So live your life that the fear of
death can never enter your heart.*

—Tecumseh,
Shawnee, 1768–1813

On This Date in
Native American History

*The American have not yet defeated us
by land; neither are we sure that they
have done so by water; we therefore,
wish to remain here, and fight our
enemy, if they should make an appearance. If they defeat us, we will then
retreat with our father.*

*You have got the arms and ammuni-
tion which our great father sent for his
red children. If you have an idea of
going away, give them to us, and you
may go and welcome.*

—Tecumseh, Shawnee,
speaking to Colonel Henry Proctor,
who wanted Tecumseh and his people
to retreat with the British into Canada,
September 13, 1813

September 14

When you see a new trail or a footprint you do not know, follow it to the point of knowing.

—UNCHEEDAH,
SANTEE SIOUX

On This Date in
Native American History

September 14, 1972: Noted golfer, Notah Begay III, the very first Native American Indian to join a PGA Tour, was born.

Red Road Lesson 9
The Moon

The moon, referred to as Grandmother Moon by various American Indian people, pertains to female fertility, night activities, dreams, and, for most, lunar calendars and weather.

It is necessary to not only learn about the moon as a celestial entity, but to also celebrate her rotations, rhythms, and importance to the world as a whole. Be sure to gaze upon her full face each month and memorialize her grand beauty. Use this time to reflect on your life, and to plan for your future.

My father explained this to me. "All things in this world," he said, "have souls or spirits. The sky has a spirit, the clouds have spirits; the sun and moon have spirits; so have animals, trees, grass, water, stones—everything."

—EDWARD GOODBIRD,
HIDATSA, 1914

September 15

Have patience.
All things change in due time.
Wishing cannot bring autumn
glory nor cause winter to cease.

—GINALY-LI, CHEROKEE

Did You Know?

Tribes often have two names. One is the name they call themselves, and the second is the name the non–Native Indians called them (and usually, still use when referring to them). Below are just a few alternative tribal names:

Common name	Tribal name
Anadarko	Nadaco
Cayuga	Kweniogwen
Cherokee	Tsalagi
Crow	Absaroke
Iowa	Pahodja
Kickapoo	Kiwigapawa
Lumbee	Cheraw
Navajo	Dineh
Shawnee	Savannah

September 16

Every part of this Earth is sacred to my people, every shining pine needle, every sandy shore, every mist in the dark woods, every meadow, every humming insect . . .

—CHIEF SEATTLE (SEATHL), DUWAMISH-SUQUAMISH, 1785–1866

Did You Know?

Interested in attending a powwow? There are basic guidelines:

Listen to the Master of Ceremonies.

Remove your hat, and stand when others do.

Seats inside the circles are reserved for performers.

Do not dress "like an Indian" or mimic the Native people.

Do not touch a person's regalia (outfit) without permission.

If you are asked to dance by an elder, do so. Saying no is disrespectful.

Pick up your trash.

Support the people via donations or by purchasing items at vending areas.

September 17

*It is senseless to fight when
you cannot hope to win.*

—GOYATHLAY (GERONIMO),
APACHE MEDICINE MAN AND WAR
CHIEF, 1829–1909

Did You Know?

The American Indian Historical
Society was founded in 1964 to
educate the public about
Native American people and
culture.

September 18

The entire Creation still follows . . . Instructions of Life. The Tree, the fruits, they never fail. They never make a mistake to bring their fruits in their season. The animals never make a mistake. They still live as they were created. Among the Creation . . . Life, the circle, a measurement with no beginning and no ending.

—PHILLIP DEERE, MUSKOGEE-CREEK, 1977

September 19

Guard your tongue in youth, and in age you may mature a thought that will be of service to your people.

—WABASHA,
MDEWAKANTON SIOUX, 19TH CENTURY

Did You Know?

A community college in San Francisco, California, was named Ohlone College in 1967 in honor of the Ohlone Indians, who once resided on the land the school is occupying.

September 20

To "make medicine" is to engage upon a special period of fasting, thanksgiving, prayer and self-denial, even of self-torture. The procedure is entirely a devotional exercise. The purpose is to subdue the passions of the flesh and to improve the spiritual self. The bodily abstinence and the mental concentration upon lofty thoughts cleanses both the body and the soul and puts them into or keeps them in health. Then the individual mind gets closer toward conformity with the mind of the Great Medicine above us.

—WOODEN LEG,
CHEYENNE, LATE 19TH CENTURY

September 21

*Why would you devote yourselves,
your women, and your
children to destruction?*

—Between the Logs,
Wyandot, about 1812

Did You Know?

A sweat lodge is a ceremonial building made of twigs, animal hides, and/or tree bark, and is used for purification purposes. Water is poured over hot rocks and the construction captures and holds steam much like a sauna. Sweat lodges were common in Native American cultures and are still used today.

September 22

You say that you are sent to instruct us how to worship the Great Spirit agreeably to his mind; and if we do not take hold of the religion which you white people teach we shall be unhappy hereafter? You say that you are right, and we are lost. How do you know this to be true? We understand that your religion is written in a book. If it was intended for us as well as for you, why has not the Great Spirit given it to us; and not only to us, but why did he not give our forefathers the knowledge of that book, with the means of understanding it rightly?

—RED JACKET (SAGOYEWATHA),
SENECA, ABOUT 1790

September 23

No talk is ever given without first indicating your humility. "I am an ignorant man; I am a poor man . . ."—all the talks start this way. "I don't know nearly as much as you men sitting around here, but I would like to offer my humble opinion . . ."—and then he'll knock you down with logic and wisdom.

—ALLEN QUETONE,
KIOWA, 1974

September 24

Death will come, and always comes out of season. It is the command of the Great Spirit, and all nations and people must obey.

—Black Elk,
Oglala Sioux, 1863–1950

Did You Know?

For more than 4,000 years, Inuits in the Arctic have trained dogs to pull loaded sleds.

September 25

There are the springs of the Great Spirit . . . To bathe in them gives new life; to drink them cures every bodily ill.

—ARAPAHO INDIAN GUIDE

Did You Know?

A "pahos" is a prayer stick, or prayer feathers, used by the Hopi. Pahos are used during prayer and taken to sacred shrines, and are ritually smudged.

September 26

The many moons and sunny days we have lived here will long be remembered by us. The Great Spirit has smiled upon us and made us glad. But we have agreed to go. We go to a country we know little of. Our home will be beyond a great river on the way to the setting sun. We will build our wigwams there in another land . . . The men we leave here in possession of these lands cannot say Keokuk or his people ever took up the tomahawk . . . In peace we bid you goodbye . . . If you come see us, we will gladly welcome you.

—Keokuk, a Sauk tribal leader, who signed a number of treaties with the United States government giving it various tracts of land in exchange for reservation land and necessities for his people. This speech was given when his people were told they would have to relocate west of the Mississippi River, September 26, 1833

September 27

God Almighty has made us all.

—RED CLOUD (MAKHPIYA-LUTA),
OGLALA SIOUX CHIEF

Did You Know?

In 1923, John Levi became the first Native American to be named to the All-America football team.

September 28

We respected our old people above all others in the tribe. To live to be so old they must have been brave and strong, and good fighters, and we aspired to be like them. We never allowed our old people to want for anything . . . We looked upon our old people as demigods of a kind, we loved them deeply. They were all our fathers.

—Buffalo Child Long Lance, 1890–1932

September 29

If an innocent man doesn't get angry, he'll live a long while. A guilty man will get sick because of bad thoughts, a bad conscience.

—TRADITIONAL HOPI TEACHING

A Native to Know

Abenaki filmmaker Alanis Obomsawin was born in 1932 and raised on the Odanak Abenaki Reserve in Quebec. She first became a singer, and then an actress, and then turned to documentary filmmaking. Her film, *Kanehsatake: 270 Years of Resistance*, won several international awards.

September 30

We were taught to believe that the Great Spirit sees and hears everything, and that he never forgets; that hereafter he will give every man a spirit-home according to his deserts . . . This I believe, and all my people believe the same.

—CHIEF JOSEPH
(HIN-MAH-TOO-YAH-LAT-KEKT) NEZ PERCE,
1840–1904

A Native to Know

He received a vision as a young boy and saw that the buffalo would be destroyed, and so would the Crow way of life. He was an honored warrior and quickly rose to the rank of chief. Chief Plenty Coups is considered the last chief to gain the status of "chief" in the traditional Crow manner.

THE WESTERN JOURNEY OF AUTUMN

Autumn is a time for introspection, harvest, and thankfulness. As the growing season comes to an end, we look to the west, the direction of sundown, and know that the blackness of winter is approaching. Use this time to reflect, to remember our past and those who crossed over before us. Autumn is also for sharing, for donating time and money to charity, and for forgiving those who need forgiveness. Set aside grievances and focus on tomorrow.

Direction: West
Season: Autumn
Color: Black

Of all the animals the horse is the best friend of the Indian, for without it he could not go on long journeys. A horse is the Indian's most valuable piece of property. If an Indian wishes to gain something, he promises that if the horse will help him he will paint it with native dye, that all may see that help has come to him through the aid of his horse.

—BRAVE BUFFALO,
TETON SIOUX, LATE 19TH CENTURY

OCTOBER

OCTOBER PASSAMAQUODDY MOON:
HARVEST MOON

Red Road Ethic 10
Practice Forgiveness

Your journey upon the Red Road will be filled with acts requiring forgiveness—forgiveness of others and forgiveness of yourself. Mindfully practice this incredible act of humanity and the Red Road will be an easy path to follow. Also, absolution breeds the same in others. Be quick to forgive and others will grant you the same kindness.

Indians love their friends and kindred, and treat them with kindness.

—CORNPLANTER,
SENECA, 1736–1836

October 1

Peace . . . comes within the souls of men when they realize their relationship, their oneness, with the universe and all its powers, and when they realize that at the center of the Universe dwells Wakan-Tanka, and that this center is really everywhere, it is within each of us.

—BLACK ELK,
OGLALA SIOUX, 1863–1950

On This Date in
Native American History

October 1, 1969: Parents of American Indian children attempted to enroll their children in a desegregated school in South Carolina. Federal marshals and school officials forced the families to exit the premises or be faced with criminal charges.

October 2

God said he was the Father and the
Earth was the Mother of mankind;
that nature was the law; that the ani-
mals and fish and plants obeyed
nature and that man only was sinful.
This is the old law.

—SMOWHALA,
WANAPUM

On This Date in
Native American History

October 2, 1978: The Federal Acknow-
ledgment of Indian Tribes Act was
passed through Congress. The purpose
of the legislation is to acknowledge the
actual existence of certain American
Indian tribes within the United States.

October 3

I wonder if the ground has anything to say? I wonder if the ground is listening to what is said? I wonder if the ground would come alive and what is on it? Though I hear what the ground says. The ground says, It is the Great Spirit that placed me here. The Great Spirit tells me to take care of the Indians, to feel them aright. The Great Spirit appointed the roots to feed the Indians on. The water says the same thing. The Great Spirit directs me, Feed the Indians well. The grass says the same thing, Feed the Indians well. The ground, water and grass say, The Great Spirit has given us names. We have these names and hold these names. The ground says, The Great Spirit has placed me here to produce all that grows on me, trees and fruit. The same way the ground says, It was from me man was made. The Great Spirit, in placing men on the Earth, desired them to take good care of the ground and do each other no harm . . .

—CHIEF YOUNG, CAYUSE, 1855

October 4

*There is something that whispers
to me it would be prudent to
listen to offers of peace.*

—LITTLE TURTLE,
MIAMI, 1794

A Native to Know

Little Turtle was born in Indiana in 1752 but was raised in Ohio. He was a brave warrior and became leader of the Miamis by 1790. He struggled with the whites and tried to secure his land for his people, and even united with the Wyandots, Shawnees, and Delawares. But after the Battle of Fallen Timbers, he opted to fight for peace, not war.

October 5

*Too many have strayed from the path
shown to us by the Great Spirit.*

—SEQUICHIE GRANDFATHER

In Remembrance

Of Tecumseh, the great Shawnee tribal
leader, who worked to forge an alliance
among Native Americans to fight for
land and basic rights of their people. He
died on October 5, 1813, in battle with
U.S. forces.

October 6

It is better for us to die like warriors than to diminish away by inches. The cause of the red men is just, and I hope that the [Creator] who governs everything will favor us.

—CORNSTALK,
SHAWNEE, 1700s

Did You Know?

"Connecticut" is from the Mohican word meaning "long river place."

October 7

*The chastisement of God is worse
than any physical pain or sickness.*

—Rosalio Moises,
Yaqui

Did You Know?

Virginia Rosemyre, Gabrielino-Serrano,
was an accomplished artist and produced several hundred oil paintings in
her lifetime. She lived from 1875 to 1921.

October 8

Do not speak of evil, for it creates curiosity in the minds of the young.

—Lakota Sioux proverb

Did You Know?

More than 8,000 Indians served in World War I, 25,000 in World War II, 41,000 in Vietnam, and 24,000 in Operation Desert Storm.

October 9

Walk the good road . . . Be dutiful,
respectful, gentle and modest . . .
Be strong with the warm,
strong heart of the earth.

—ANONYMOUS MALE SIOUX

On This Date in
Native American History

October 9, 1813: Major Thomas Rowland described the death of Tecumseh at the battle of the Thames: "There was something so majestic, so dignified, and yet so mild, in his countenance as he lay stretched on the ground, where a few minutes before he rallied his men to the fight, that while gazing on him with admiration and pity, I forgot he was a savage. He had such a countenance as I shall never forget. He had received a wound in the arm, and had it bound up, before he received the mortal wound."

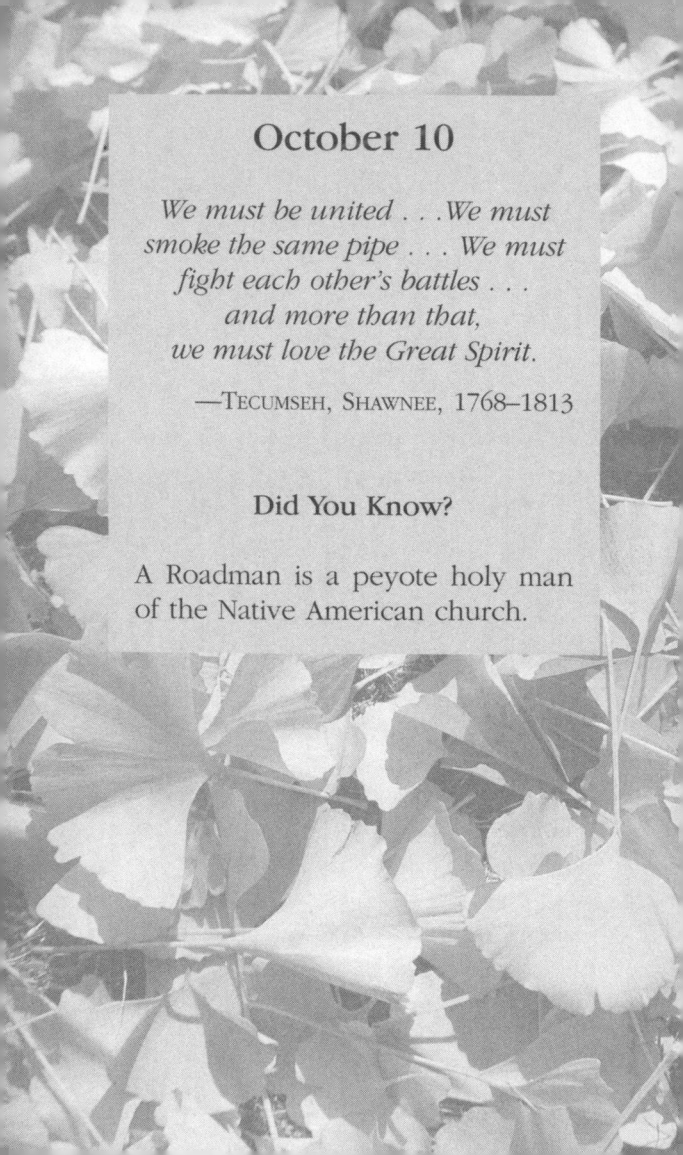

October 10

*We must be united . . .We must
smoke the same pipe . . . We must
fight each other's battles . . .
and more than that,
we must love the Great Spirit.*

—TECUMSEH, SHAWNEE, 1768–1813

Did You Know?

A Roadman is a peyote holy man
of the Native American church.

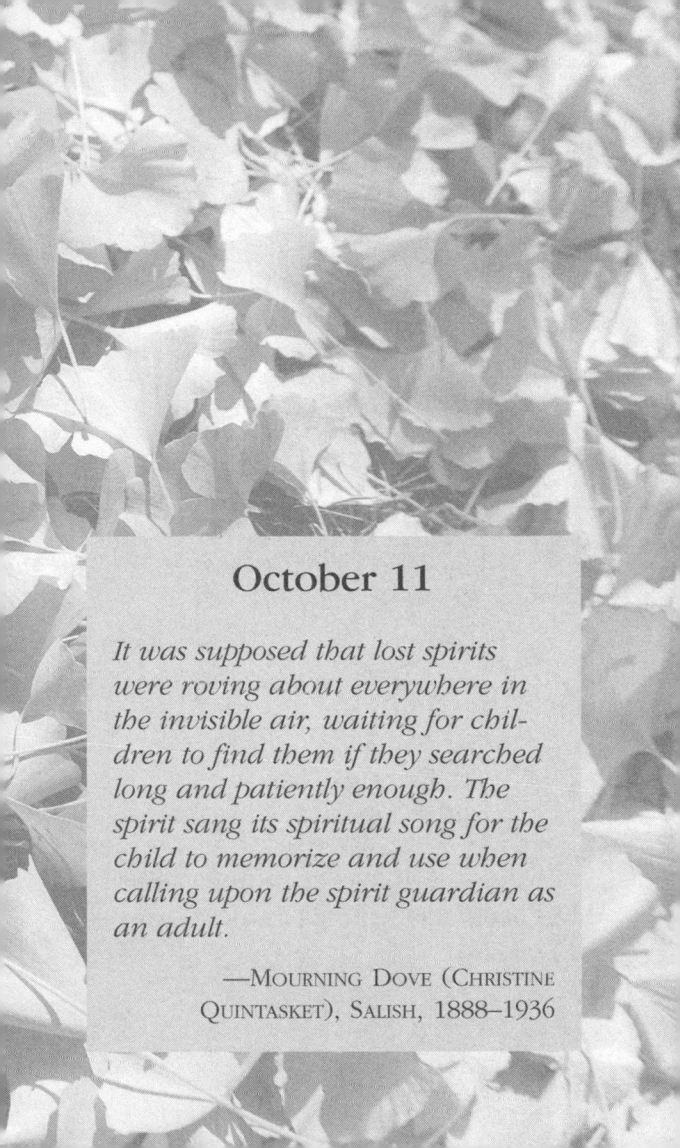

October 11

It was supposed that lost spirits were roving about everywhere in the invisible air, waiting for children to find them if they searched long and patiently enough. The spirit sang its spiritual song for the child to memorize and use when calling upon the spirit guardian as an adult.

—MOURNING DOVE (CHRISTINE QUINTASKET), SALISH, 1888–1936

October 12

Your mind must never be like a tipi.
Leave the entrance flap open so that
the fresh air can enter and clear out
the smoke of confusion.

—CHIEF EAGLE,
TETON SIOUX

On This Date in
Native American History

October 12, 1492: Christopher Columbus accidentally lands in the Bahamas.

October 13

We may misunderstand,
but we do not misexperience.

—Vine Deloria Jr.,
Lakota, Standing Rock Sioux

A Native to Know

Cree musician Buffy Sainte-Marie was raised by a Micmac couple in Canada. She was world-famous by the 1970s for her singing and songwriting, especially protest songs like "Now That the Buffalo's Gone."

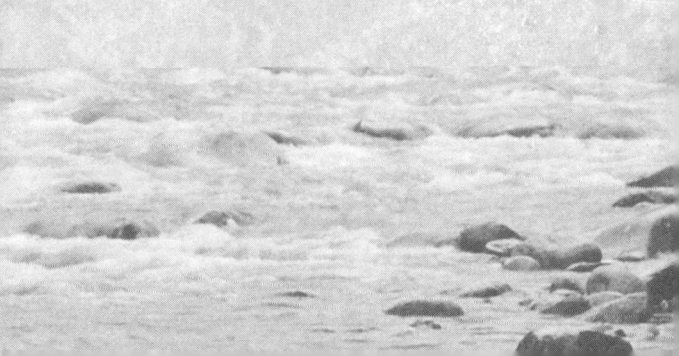

October 14

The song of the bird in the open tree is the one that brings true music to the ear, while that of the one in the cage is but a sad imitation.

—"Old Keyam" (Edward Ahenakew),
Plains Cree

On This Date in
Native American History

October 14, 1964: Billy Mills, Sioux, won the Olympic Gold Medal for the 10,000-meter run in record time—28 minutes and 24.04 seconds—in Tokyo. With his victory came much publicity and distinction. In the 100-year history of the Olympic games, Mills was the first Native American Indian to win the event.

Red Road Lesson 10
Turtle Island

Northern America has been called Turtle Island by many Native tribes for generations. The reference stems from a belief that the continent was placed upon the Great Turtle's back. Drawings of North America often depict the land as a turtle, and some use the tortoise as a representation of their tribes.

Indians love their friends and kindred, and treat them with kindness.

—CORNPLANTER,
SENECA, 1736–1836

October 15

In our language there is no word to say inferior or superiority or equality because we are all equal . . .

—ALANIS OBOMSAWIN,
ABENAKI

On This Date in
Native American History

October 15, 1925: *The Vanishing American*, a controversial motion picture exploring the mismanagement and corruption of reservations and how this affects the American Indian, premiered in New York City. This sympathetic view of indigenous people was not completely well received by the American public, and many debated not only the condition of the American Indian, but also what should be done with them.

October 16

I can tell my children that the way to get honor is to go to work and be good men and women.

—CHIEF RUNNING BIRD,
KIOWA

Did You Know?

When a young hunter killed his first deer, seal, buffalo, or other large animal meant for consumption, the community usually held a special ceremony in his honor.

October 17

Certain small ways and observances sometimes have connection with large and more profound ideas.

—LUTHER STANDING BEAR, OGLALA SIOUX, 1868–1937

A Native to Know

Pretty Shield, Crow, was born in 1857. She became an important medicine woman and an outspoken advocate for her people's traditional way of life.

October 18

I'm the only one who's responsible for my soul, if I don't do the right thing here. I'm at fault, not him, not the church, not that mountain over there or the sun. This is the way they teach Indian religion. No one is going to influence you, no one is going to bring you up to your grave, but yourself.

—ALEX SALUSKIN,
YAKIMA, 1970

October 19

There are no Indians
left now but me . . .

—HUNKESNI (SITTING BULL),
SAID IN ANGER TO HIS PEOPLE FOR TURNING
OVER 10 MILLION ACRES OF RESERVATION LAND
TO THE U.S. GOVERNMENT IN 1889

On This Date in
Native American History

October 19, 1984: An amendment to the Indian Education Act of 1972 called, The Indian Education Amendment, was enacted, promising to improve educational standards of Native American children by extending programs and allowing Indian tribes to engage in a policy of self-determination.

October 20

*I went up to heaven and saw the Great
Spirit and all the people who had died
a long time ago. The Great Spirit told
me to come back and tell my people
they must be good and love one
another, and not fight, steal, or lie.*

—WOVOKA (JACK WILSON),
PAIUTE SPIRITUAL LEADER, 1889

On This Date in
Native American History

October 20, 1876: Satanta (White Bear)
spoke to representatives of the United
States government at Medicine Lodge
Creek. Satanta spoke of the right to raise
his children as he was raised. He asked
not to be placed on a reservation, and
said, "I have heard that you intend to
settle us on a reservation. I don't want to
settle. I love to roam over the prairies.
When we settle down we grow pale
and die." Satanta was later imprisoned
for alleged participation in murderous
raids on white frontiersmen—he committed suicide in prison in 1878.

October 21

*When [I was] a child, my mother
taught me . . . to kneel and pray
to Usen for strength, health,
wisdom, and protection.*

—GOYATHLAY (GERONIMO),
APACHE MEDICINE MAN AND WAR CHIEF,
1829–1909

A Native to Know

Wilma Mankiller was elected the first
female deputy chief of the Cherokees
in 1983. She was involved in the Alcatraz occupation of 1969, has taught at
Dartmouth College, and has written
her memoir.

October 22

An Indian respects a brave man,
but he despises a coward.
He loves a straight tongue,
but he hates a forked tongue.

—CHIEF JOSEPH,
NEZ PERCE, 1879

On This Date in
Native American History

October 22, 1844: Metis leader Louis Riel Jr. was born.

October 23

To give up when all is against you is a sign of being weak and cowardly.

—CHIEF EAGLE,
TETON SIOUX

In Remembrance

Of Chief Ten Bears, a great leader of the Yamparika Comanches, who died on October 23, 1872, following a trip to Washington, D.C., to discuss peace between his people and the United States.

October 24

My son, you are now flesh and bone of our bone. By the ceremony performed this day, every drop of white blood was washed from your veins; you were taken into the Shawnee nation . . . you were adopted into a great family.

—BLACK FISH, SHAWNEE, AT THE TRIBAL ADOPTION OF DANIEL BOONE, 1778

October 25

Standards of conduct were just as rigid as the laws of any other people, but force seldom was used to enforce good conduct. Each person was his own judge. Deceitfulness was a crime. We lived according to our own standards and principles, not for what others might think of us.

—Thomas Wildcat Alford, Shawnee

October 26

We believe that the spirit pervades all creation and that every creature possesses a soul in some degree, though not necessarily a soul conscious of itself. The tree, the waterfall, the grizzly bear, each is an embodied Force, and as such an object of reverence.

—OHIYESA (CHARLES EASTMAN),
SANTEE SIOUX, 1858–1939

October 27

We ask every lover of justice, is it right that a great and powerful government should, year by year, continue to demand cessions of land from weaker and dependent people, under the plea of securing homes for the homeless?

—Delegates of the Choctaw and Chickasaw Nation, about 1895

October 28

When this pipe touches your lip, may it operate as a blessing upon all my tribe. May the smoke rise like a cloud, and carry away with it all the animosities which have arisen between us.

—BLACK THUNDER,
FOX

On This Date in
Native American History

October 28, 1871: In Edmonton, Alberta, Canada, indigenous people began a six-month sit-in at the Indian Affairs Office to protest the harsh conditions for children at reservation schools.

October 29

Marriage among my people was like traveling in a canoe. The man sat in front and paddled the canoe. The woman sat in the stern, but she steered.

—ANONYMOUS

Did You Know?

The dreamcatcher is an easily recognizable piece of Native Americana. There are two kinds of dreamcatchers. The first, for children, will include feathers and is made from willow so that it will eventually fall apart (representing the child growing out of childhood). The adult dreamcatcher is usually made with a center feather and beads. It is made of woven fiber and will last longer.

All dreamcatchers have some type of representation of the four directions as well as a spider's web, and will be made from all-natural material. The dreamcatcher is *only* to be placed on the wall above the bed of the person the dreamcatcher was made for. It must be made from hand.

October 30

I am the Maker of heaven and earth, the trees, lakes, rivers, and all things else. I am the Maker of Mankind; and because I love you, you must do my will . . .

—Pontiac, Ottawa tribe, repeating what the Great Spirit told him in 1763

On This Date in Native American History

October 30, 1990: Congress enacted the Native American Languages Act, admitting that ". . . there is a widespread practice of treating Native American languages as if they were anachronisms . . . there is a lack of clear, comprehensive, and consistent Federal policy on treatment of Native American languages which has often resulted in acts of suppression and extermination of Native American languages and cultures . . . in conflict with the United States policy of self-determination for Native Americans."

October 31

Brother: We are of the same opinion with the people of the United States; you consider yourselves as independent people; we, as the original inhabitants of this country, and sovereigns of the soil, look upon ourselves as equally independent, and free as any other nation or nations. This country was give to us by the Great Spirit above; we wish to enjoy it

—THAYENDANEGEA (JOSEPH BRANT), MOHAWK, AT A COUNCIL WITH WHITES, 1794

NOVEMBER

NOVEMBER WISHRAM MOON:
SNOWY-MOUNTAINS-IN-
THE-MORNING MOON

Red Road Ethic 11
Practice Optimism

It is easy to live within the shadow of fear, procrastination, and pessimism. But these are bad habits and stumbling blocks that keep you from experiencing life, the Red Road, and the Great Spirit. It is well known to the Native people that optimism is the key to good health. Worry makes you sick—as do bad thoughts. Replace them with happiness and optimism and you shall live a long, healthy life.

Oh hear me, Grandfather, and help us, that our generation in the future will live and walk the good road with the flowering stick of success. Also, the pipe of peace, we will offer it as we walk the good road to success. Hear me, and hear our plea . . .

—BLACK ELK,
OGLALA SIOUX, 1863–1950

November 1

*My heart laughs with joy
because I am in your presence.*

—CHITMACHAS CHIEF

On This Date in
Native American History

November 1, 1972: Hundreds of Indian activists banded together in protest at the Sioux Rosebud Reservation.

November 2

All life was injustice . . . Lightning found the good man and the bad; sickness carried no respect for virtue, and luck flitted around like the spring butterfly. It is good to learn this in the days of mother's milk.

—Bad Arm,
Sioux, 1862

Did You Know?

November is American Indian Heritage Month.

November 3

A Native to Know

Billy Mills, Oglala Sioux, was born June 30, 1938, in South Dakota. He is known for his outstanding long-distance running abilities and his accomplishments at the 1964 Summer Olympic games in Japan. Mills entered the 10,000-meter run, knowing that no American has ever won that race. Mills ran the 10,000 meter, won the Gold, and stands today as the only Native American to do so. The 1984 movie *Running Brave* is based on this victory.

November 4

All life is Wakan. So also is everything which exhibits power, whether in action, as the winds and drifting clouds, or in passive endurance, as the boulder by the wayside. For even the commonest sticks and stones have a spiritual essence which must be revered as a manifestation of the all-pervading mysterious power that fills the universe.

—FRANCIS LAFLESCHE,
OSAGE

On This Date in
Native American History

November 4, 1879: William Penn Adair Rogers, Cherokee Indian, known to the world as Will Rogers, was born in Indian Territory (present-day Oklahoma).

November 5

We shall not fail . . . to nourish your hearts . . . about the renewal of our amity and the brightening of the Chain of Friendship . . .

—CANASSATEGO,
ONONDAGA, 1742

On This Date in Native American History

November 5, 2000: Ralph Nader and Winona LaDuke continued their campaign to secure the positions of president and vice-president of the United States of America under the Green Party ticket. LaDuke, a member of the Mississippi Band of Anishinaabe (Ojibway) from the White Earth Reservation in Minnesota, received her B.A. from Harvard, serves as the director of the White Earth Land Recovery Project, is a board member of Greenpeace Action, and received the Reebok Human Rights Award in 1988.

November 6

There needs to be room in a political party for all of us, because if we actually want to get things done we've got to make room for the diversity of people.

—WINONA LaDUKE, OJIBWAY, GREEN PARTY VICE-PRESIDENTIAL CANDIDATE

On This Date in Native American History

November 6, 1986: Ben Nighthorse Campbell was elected to the U.S. House of Representatives (Colorado). Campbell, a Northern Cheyenne Indian from Montana, is the second Native American elected to such a position.

November 7

Never be elevated above measure by success . . . nor delighted with the sweets of peace to suffer insults.

—PUSHMATAHA,
CHOCTAW TRIBAL LEADER, 1764–1824

On This Date in Native American History

November 7, 1811: Shawnee chief, Tecumsch, and others were traveling through southern American Indian communities seeking an alliance of nations for his confederacy against the white takeover within their homelands. In his absence, his brother, Tenskwatawa was to care for the Shawnee people and was ordered by Tecumseh not to engage in battles with the whites. Knowing of Tecumseh's absence, William Henry Harrison and more than 1,000 of his men invade the village and force Tenskwatawa into battle that devastates the Shawnee. Today this fight is called "The Battle of Tippecanoe."

November 8

We first knew you a feeble plant which wanted a little earth whereon to grow. We gave it to you; and afterward, when we could have trod you under our feet, we watered and protected you; and now you have grown to be a mighty tree, whose top reaches the clouds, and whose branches overspread the whole land, whilst we, who were the tall pines of the forest, have become a feeble plant and need your protection.

—RED JACKET (SAGOYEWATHA),
SENECA, C. 1752–1830

November 9

Those who know how to play can easily leap over the adversities of life. And one who knows how to sing and laugh never brews mischief.

—IGLULIK PROVERB

On This Date in
Native American History

November 9, 1969: The occupation of Alcatraz, a defining moment in modern Native American history. In 1969, Indian activists, following the lead of the black civil rights movement, staged several protests. One of the most newsworthy was the occupation of Alcatraz Island, once the country's most notorious prison. The occupation, which helped American Indians achieve a visibility long denied them, was solidly based on treaty rights, and helped build a movement that continues to support members of the community to this day.

November 10

The Creator made it to be this way. An old woman shall be as a child again and her grandchildren shall care for her. For only because she is, they are.

—HANDSOME LAKE,
SENECA, C. 1735–1815

Did You Know?

"Missouri" is an Algonquin word meaning "river of big canoes."

November 11

Try to do something that is brave. That man is most successful who is foremost.

—JUMPING BULL,
HUNKPAPA SIOUX

A Native to Know

In early 1800, Sacagawea was kidnapped from her tribe, the Shoshone, by Crow Indians and sold to Mandans. She married a French fur trapper, and by the time she was 18, she had his child. She remained a captive until the fur trapper made a deal with Lewis and Clark that allowed Sacagawea to be the interpreter and guide they needed to lead them through the wild terrain. Sacagawea and her child made history when they embarked on the lengthy journey. She was eventually reunited with her Shoshone people.

November 12

Brother, listen to us, your younger brothers. As we see something in your eyes that looks dissatisfaction, we now clear them. You have credited bad stories against us. We clean your ears, that you may hear better hereafter. We wish to remove every thing bad from your heart, that you may be as good as your ancestors. We saw you coming with an uplifted tomahawk in your hand. We now take it from you, and throw it up to God. Brother, as you are a warrior, take hold of this chain of friendship, and let us think no more of war, in pity of our old men, women, and children. We, too, are warriors.

—RED HAWK, SHAWNEE,
ADDRESSING BRITISH COLONEL HENRY BOUQUET,
NOVEMBER 12, 1764

November 13

That people will continue longest in the enjoyment of peace who timely prepare to vindicate themselves and manifest a determination to protect themselves whenever they are wronged.

—TECUMSEH,
SHAWNEE, 1768–1813

November 14

Be happy in order to live long.
Worry makes you sick.

—HOPI TEACHING

Did You Know?

Buffalo skulls were used as a sacred decoration by many Plains tribes during celebrations and ceremonies such as the Sun Dance.

Red Road Lesson 11
Children Are the Future

Children are gifts of the Creator and of ourselves. By raising them to the best of our ability, we are reciprocating that gift and showing our thankfulness for life and for the blessings of the Great Spirit. This requires much time, love, forgiveness, and understanding on the part of the parents and grandparents—but the rewards for the child (and for the community as a whole) are immeasurable.

Also, it is not enough to raise your own children and grandchildren. You should bestow what you can to *all* children of the Earth.

It is strictly believed and understood by the Sioux that a child is the greatest gift from Wakan Tanka in response to many devout prayers, sacrifices, and promises. Therefore the child is considered "sent by Wakan Tanka" through some element—namely the element of human nature.

—ROBERT HIGHEAGLE,
TETON SIOUX, EARLY 20TH CENTURY

November 15

Hold on to what is good, even if it is a handful of dirt. Hold on to what you believe, even if it is a tree that stands by itself. Hold on to what you must do, even if it is a long way from here. Hold on to life, even if it is easier to let go. Hold on to my hand, even if I have gone away from you.

—Pueblo blessing

A Native to Know

Clyde Bellecourt, Ojibway, was born on the White Earth Reservation in Minnesota in 1939. He is one of the founders of the American Indian Movement and is instrumental in many Native activist projects to this day.

November 16

As there is no alternative between a falsehood and a lie, they (the American Indian) usually tell any person, you "lie," as a friendly negative to a reputed truth.

—ADAIR

On This Date in Native American History

November 16, 1990: Congress passed the Native American Graves Protection and Repatriation Act.

November 17

When we go hunting, it is not our arrow that kills the moose, however powerful the bow; it is nature that kills him.

—BEDAGI (BIG THUNDER), WABANAKÍ ALGONQUIN, LATE 19TH CENTURY

On This Date in Native American History

November 17, 1945: Tlingit filmmaker Carol Geddes was born.

November 18

It is our desire that we and you should be as one heart, one mind, and one body, thus becoming one people, entertaining a mutual love and regard for each other, to be preserved firm and entire, not only between you and us, but between your children and our children, to all succeeding generations.

—KANICKHUNGO,
IROQUOIS

November 19

You have spoken words of comfort . . . as though the Great Spirit was speaking through you.

—Little Beaver

On This Date in Native American History

November 19, 1986: The American Indian Vietnam Plaque, commemorating the diligent service of nearly 43,000 Native American Indians who served in the Vietnam war, was dedicated at Arlington National Cemetery.

November 20

On This Date in
Native American History

November 20, 1890: The stronghold plateau was on the Pine Ridge Reservation. Wovoka had his Ghost Dance vision in 1889, and the prophecy soon caught on and swept across the West. The dance was soon outlawed by the United States government, because they thought the dance would inspire the Sioux to rise up and fight. The people started a journey to Pine Ridge to learn the prophecy and learn the dance throughout early and mid 1890. By November 20, over 3,000 people had made the pilgrimage.

November 21

We bury them from sight forever and plant again the tree.

—DEKANAWIDAH,
IROQUOIS, C. 1300

A Native to Know

Dekanawidah, a peaceful prophet, is best known as the author of the Great Law of the Iroquois Confederacy, one of the earliest constitutions in the country, which established a system of justice and law administered by chiefs of various nations. Known for his charisma, intelligence, and honesty, Dekanawidah brought unity and brotherhood to many of his neighboring nations.

November 22

If the Indian loves,
he speaks the truth;
but if he does not,
he is silent.

—Tecumseh,
Shawnee, 1808

Did You Know?

Just as little girls today play with miniature doll houses, little girls of the Plains tribes often played with miniature versions of tipis.

November 23

A Native to Know

Lucy Lewis, Hopi-Tewa, born in 1895, is ranked as one of the best Pueblo potters of the 20th century. She won numerous awards and honors in many of the exhibitions she entered after learning pottery making from her aunt. Since her death in 1992, her work has been carried on by her daughters and granddaughters.

November 24

Let me do the right things for my people. Not for the sake of merit, but because of the sacrifice of my people in this land which belongs to them.

In Remembrance

Of Mohawk Indian Joseph Brant (also referred to as Captain Brant or Brandt), who crossed over on November 24, 1807.

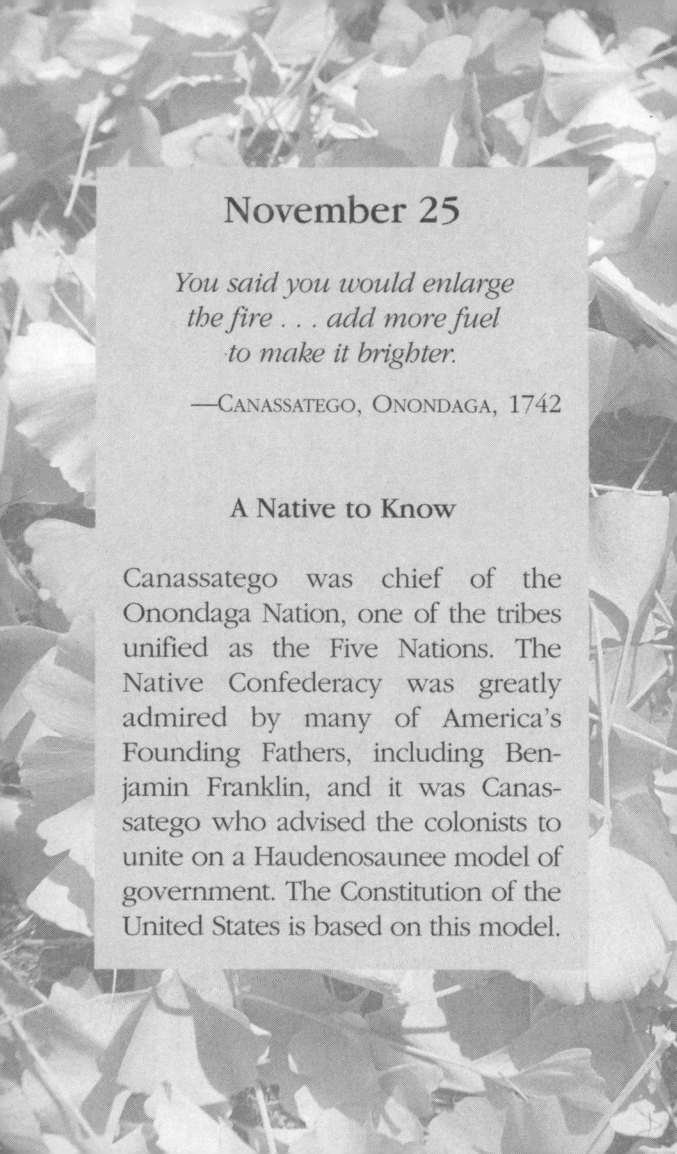

November 25

You said you would enlarge the fire . . . add more fuel to make it brighter.

—Canassatego, Onondaga, 1742

A Native to Know

Canassatego was chief of the Onondaga Nation, one of the tribes unified as the Five Nations. The Native Confederacy was greatly admired by many of America's Founding Fathers, including Benjamin Franklin, and it was Canassatego who advised the colonists to unite on a Haudenosaunee model of government. The Constitution of the United States is based on this model.

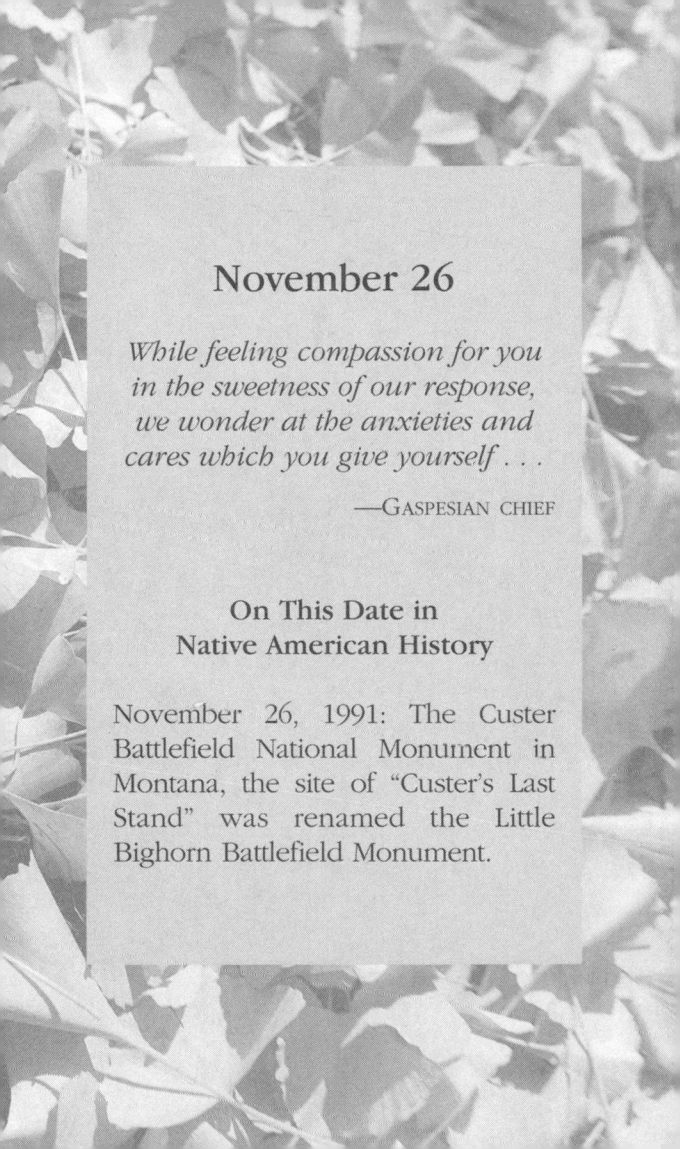

November 26

While feeling compassion for you in the sweetness of our response, we wonder at the anxieties and cares which you give yourself . . .

—GASPESIAN CHIEF

On This Date in Native American History

November 26, 1991: The Custer Battlefield National Monument in Montana, the site of "Custer's Last Stand" was renamed the Little Bighorn Battlefield Monument.

November 27

*The Great Spirit knows that
I have spoken the truth.*

—STRUCK BY THE REE,
YANKTON SIOUX, 1865

A Native to Know

Hiawatha helped to organize five separate Iroquoian tribes into one confederacy known as the Five Nations. His courageous work is legendary, and to some, has even reached mythological proportions. Hiawatha is known today as an intelligent, innovative leader who succeeded in uniting nations that otherwise would have been at war.

November 28

*You can't wake a person
who is pretending to be asleep.*

—NAVAJO PROVERB

On This Date in
Native American History

November 28, 1989: The Native American Grave Protection and Repatriation Act was signed into law by President George Bush. Hundreds of thousands of pieces of Native American human remains, cultural pieces, and funeral objects are held by museums and universities across the country, and this act requires the return of those remains and items that are attached to a particular tribe.

November 29

No person among us desires any other reward for performing a brave and worthy action, but the consciousness of having served his nation!

—THAYENDANEGEA,
(JOSEPH BRANT), MOHAWK, 1741–1807

In Remembrance

On the morning of November 29, 1864, Colonel John Chivington led a regiment of 700 volunteer militiamen into a sleeping Cheyenne and Arapaho village at Sand Creek, Colorado. Though their leader, Black Kettle, flew the American flag above his teepee, symbolizing passiveness and peace and he raised the white flag of surrender and instructed his people to stand under the post to prove to the soldiers that they were unarmed and not hostile, Chivington and his men viciously murdered 200 to 600 people—mostly women, children, and the elderly—and only a handful of men who were not participating in the hunting expedition escaped.

November 30

"To hi ge se s di"
means "peace on earth."

—CHEROKEE

Did You Know?

In many tribal communities it was the grandparents who instructed the child, and the parents who worked and hunted for the family. The grandparents taught tribal laws, creation stories, histories, and wisdom through stories.

Red Road Ethic 12
Take What You Need, Leave the Rest Be

There is nothing placed upon this Earth that deserves to be destroyed or wasted for the purpose of human convenience. To destroy trees and leave them unused simply because they blocked the view of the garden, or to kill animals only for their fur, is not a rightful way to share the world with another. To waste and discard something due to your own selfishness is an act that goes against the Creator, and strays you from the Red Road.

Now tell me this one little thing, if thou hast any sense: Which of these two is the wisest and happiest—he who labours without ceasing and only obtains, and that with great trouble, enough to live on, or he who rests in comfort and finds all that he needs in the pleasure of hunting and fishing?

—GASPESIAN CHIEF

December

December Anishinaabe Moon:
Small Spirits Moon

*Winter—known as Wicta in Yuchi—
is upon us.*

December 1

A long time ago the Creator came to Turtle Island and said to the Red People, You will be the keepers of the Mother Earth. Among you I will give the wisdom about Nature, about the interconnectedness of all things, about balance and about living in harmony. You Red People will see the secrets of Nature. You will live in hardship and the blessing of this is you will stay close to the Creator. The day will come when you will need to share the secrets with other people of the earth because they will stray from their Spiritual ways. The time to start sharing is today.

—DON COYHIS,
MOHICAN

December 2

Some of you think an Indian is like a wild animal. This is a great mistake.

—CHIEF JOSEPH
(HIN-MAH-TOO-YAH-LAT-KEKT), NEZ PERCE, 1879,
ADDRESSING POLITICIANS IN WASHINGTON, D.C.

On This Date in
Native American History

December 2, 1987: The U.S. House of Representatives passed legislation to commemorate the centennial anniversary of the forced removal of the Cherokees from their eastern homelands—an event that cost the lives of approximately 4,000 people and is known as the Trail of Tears.

December 3

Face the rising sun with a cheerful spirit, as did our ancestors in the days of plenty. Their rain fell on all the land. But in these evil days it falls only on the fields of the faithful.

—WHITE BUFFALO CALF WOMAN, TETON SIOUX

December 4

We humans must come again to a moral comprehension of the earth and air. We must live according to the principle of a land ethic. The alternative is that we shall not live at all.

—N. Scott Momaday,
Kiowa, 1970

A Native to Know

John Trudell, Santee Sioux, is a passionate activist for his people. He participated in the occupation of Alcatraz Island, joined the American Indian Movement in 1970, and participated in the 1972 Trail of Broken Treaties. He's served as consultant and actor in Native American film, and in 1992 released a record album, *AKA Graffiti Man*.

December 5

Great Spirit . . . To the center of the world you have taken me and showed me the goodness and the beauty and the strangeness of the greening earth . . . you have shown me, and I have seen.

—BLACK ELK,
OGLALA SIOUX, 1863–1950

December 6

Rise to the dignity and grandeur of your honored position . . . shake off the base fetters of the bad spirit . . .

—Keokuk

Did You Know?

"Kansas" is the Sioux word for "south wind people."

December 7

How inhuman it was in those wretches to come into a country where nature shone in beauty, spreading her wings over the vast continent, sheltering beneath her shades these natural sons of an Almighty Being, that shone in grandeur and lustre like stars of the first magnitude in the heavenly world; whose virtues far surpassed their more enlightened foes, notwithstanding their pretended zeal for religion and virtues.

—WILLIAM APESS,
PEQUOT, JANUARY 6, 1836

December 8

When I caught any kind of bird, when I killed I saw that life went out with its blood. This taught me for what purpose I am here. I came into this world to die. My body is only to hold a spirit life. Should my blood be sprinkled I want no wounds from behind. Death should come fronting me.

—TOOHOOLHOOLZOTE,
NEZ PERCE CHIEF, MID-19TH CENTURY

December 9

The Indian was a religious man from his mother's womb. From the moment of her recognition of the fact of conception to the end of the second year of life, which was the ordinary duration of lactation, the mother's spiritual influence counted for most. Her attitude and secret meditations must be such as to instill into the receptive soul of the unborn child the love of the "Great Mystery" and a sense of brotherhood with all creation.

—OHIYESA (CHARLES EASTMAN), SANTEE SIOUX, 1858–1939

On This Date in Native American History

December 9, 1993: Sisters Marie and Carrie Dann, from the Western Shoshone nation were awarded the 1993 Right Livelihood Award (sometimes called "the other Nobel Peace Prize") and a monetary prize for their "courage and perseverance in asserting the rights of indigenous people to their land."

December 10

The trees, the animals, are all where He has stopped, and the Indian thinks of these places and sends his prayers there to reach the place where God has stopped and win help and a blessing.

—OLD DAKOTA WISEMAN

On This Date in
Native American History

December 10, 1992: For the first time in United Nations history, indigenous people were invited to participate in the UN General Assembly. Over 200 tribal representatives gathered in New York City. Arvol Looking Horse, keeper of the Lakota sacred pipe, initiated the event with a prayer.

December 11

The Indian loved to worship. From birth to death he revered his surroundings. He considered himself born in the luxurious lap of Mother Earth, and no place to him was humble.

—LUTHER STANDING BEAR, OGLALA SIOUX, 1868–1937

On This Date in Native American History

December 11, 2000: Various Native American Indians, including the same Sioux tribe once led by the legendary leader Crazy Horse, continued their demonstrations and protests at Liz Claiborne headquarters to block the company from using the Crazy Horse name on its product line. The Native people claim Liz Claiborne exploits the name, legend, and image of their heroic ancestor, and they do not give their permission to use his name or likeness to sell products.

December 12

Your words circle like soaring birds which never land. I will try to catch them and take them back for my people to hear.

—BLUE JACKET (WEYAPIERSENWAH), SHAWNEE, 1791

Did You Know?

Ed Morrissette (Ojibway) was the first Native American inducted into the Softball Hall of Fame.

December 13

In my early days I was eager to learn and to do things, and therefore I learned quickly.

—HUNKESNI (SITTING BULL),
HUNKPAPA SIOUX, 1831–1890

Did You Know?

A wampum was an important piece of Native culture. Made from polished shell or glass and then bound together to form a belt or strands, the wampum was a historical archive, a trading item, and a method of communication. If a red belt was given at a peace conference between two nations, it meant war. White meant peace.

December 14

This brings rest to my heart.
I feel like a leaf after a storm,
when the wind is still.

—PETALASHARO,
PAWNEE

On This Date in
Native American History

December 14, 1985: Wilma Mankiller was sworn into the Oklahoma Cherokee Nation Council as principal chief, becoming the first woman in modern history to lead a large tribe, and the very first to head the Cherokee Nation.

Red Road Lesson 12
The Importance of Dance

For generations upon generations, dance has played a significant role in the spiritual and cultural life of Native peoples from all over the American continent. It may represent an event such as the end of a harvest, or it may symbolize a spiritual legend or teaching.

Dancers are taught not only the meaning of the dance, but the meaning of every element within the dance—such as the custom, the steps, the cultural history, and the decoration of the community event. Examples of such events include the Corn Dance, the Butterfly Dance, the Hoop Dance, and the Sunrise Dance.

It is a strict law that bids us dance. It is a strict law that bids us distribute our property among our friends and neighbors.

—Anonymous Kwakiutl, c. 1886

December 15

We sang songs that carried in their melodies all the sounds of nature . . .

—ANONYMOUS AMERICAN INDIAN

On This Date in
Native American History

December 15, 1970: Blue Lake was returned to the Taos people many years after the U.S. government seized it from them. Blue Lake was part of the Taos culture for more than 700 years and is considered sacred land.

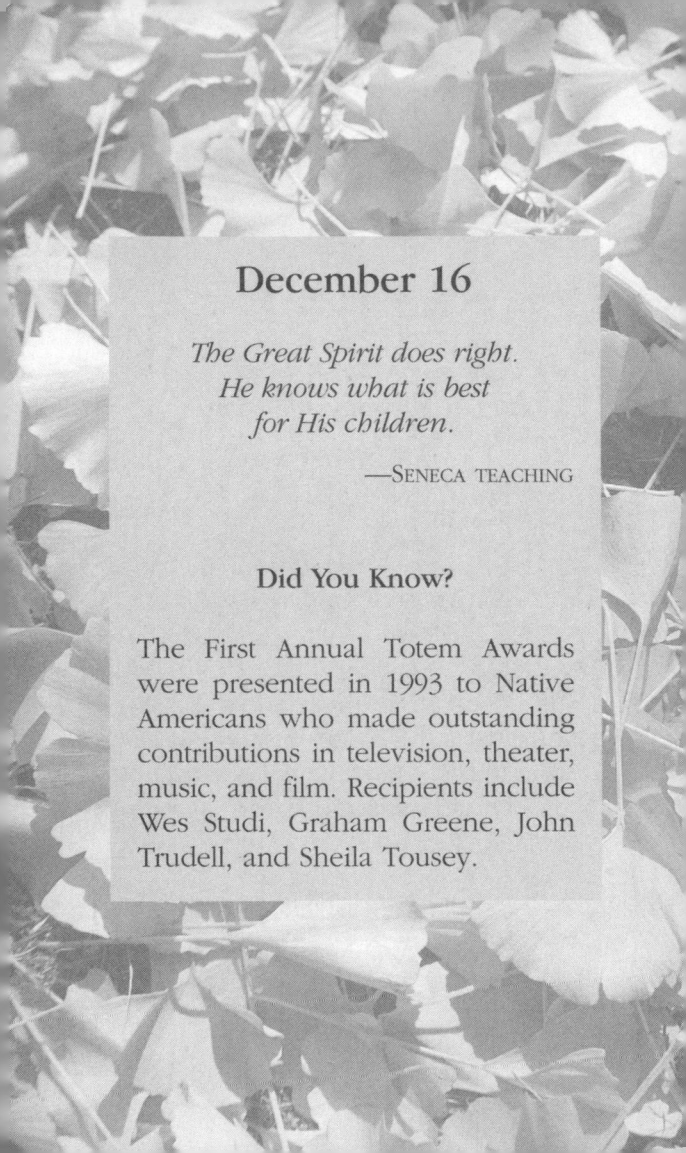

December 16

The Great Spirit does right.
He knows what is best
for His children.

—SENECA TEACHING

Did You Know?

The First Annual Totem Awards were presented in 1993 to Native Americans who made outstanding contributions in television, theater, music, and film. Recipients include Wes Studi, Graham Greene, John Trudell, and Sheila Tousey.

December 17

*One never forgets to acknowledge
a favor, no matter how small.*

—MORAL TEACHING OF THE OMAHA

Did You Know?

Some tribes did not cut their hair
unless they were in mourning.

December 18

Day and night cannot dwell together. Your religion was written on tables of stone, ours was written on our hearts.

—Chief Seattle (Seathl), Duwamish-Suquamish, 1785–1866

A Native to Know

Gertrude Simmons Bonnin, Sioux (Red Bird or Zitkala-Sa), was born in 1876 (died 1938) at the Yankton Sioux Agency. She attended Earlham College, taught school, and in 1916 was elected secretary of the Society of American Indians. She relocated to Washington, D.C., lectured, edited a periodical, and co-wrote the Indian opera *Sun Dance*.

December 19

The wildwood birds . . . sang in concert, without pride, without envy, without jealousy . . .

—SIMON POKAGON,
POTAWATOMI, 1830–1899

On This Date in
Native American History

December 19, 2000: The Navajo Code Talkers were recognized for their service in World War II.

December 20

Can things go well in a land where freedom of worship is a lie, a hollow boast?

To each nation is given the light by which it knows God, and each finds its own way to express the longing to serve Him . . . If a nation does not do what is right according to its own understanding, its power is worthless.

—THUNDERCHILD,
PLAINS CREE, 1849–1927

December 21

*May the warm winds of heaven
blow softly upon your house.
May the Great Spirit bless all
who enter there.
May your moccasins make
happy tracks in many snows,
And may the rainbow always
touch your shoulder*

—CHEROKEE BLESSING

December 22

Youth is impulsive. When our young men grow angry at some real or imaginary wrong, and disfigure their faces with black paint, it denotes that their hearts are black, and that they are often cruel and relentless, and our old men and old women are unable to restrain them . . . Revenge by young men is considered gain, even at the cost of their own lives, but old men who stay at home in times of war, and mothers who have sons to lose, know better.

—CHIEF SEATTLE (SEATHL),
DUWAMISH-SUQUAMISH, 1785–1866

December 23

A Native to Know

Maria Tallchief, Osage, was born Betty Marie Tall Chief on the Indian lands of Oklahoma in 1925. At an early age she set her sights on being a star and became America's pre-eminent "prima ballerina." In 1953, President Dwight D. Eisenhower declared her "Woman of the Year." She later taught at the School for American Ballet in New York City, and in 1981 she cofounded the Chicago City Ballet. At present, Maria Tallchief is a member of the Lyric Opera of Chicago's Women's Board and she is the opera company's director of ballet. She also works with young singers in the Lyric Opera Center for American Artists.

December 24

Treat the earth well: it was not given to you by your parents, it was loaned to you by your children. We do not inherit the Earth from our Ancestors, we borrow it from our Children.

—Ancient Indian proverb

Did You Know?

"Ohio" is the Iroquois word for "fine (or good) river."

December 25

We also have a religion which was given to our forefathers, and has been handed down to us, their children. It teaches us to be thankful, to be united, and to love one another! We never quarrel about religion.

—RED JACKET (SAGOYEWATHA), SENECA, C. 1752–1830

Did You Know?

A Croatan (or a Cro) is a person of mixed Indian, white, and black ancestry.

December 26

Develop your body, but do not neglect your mind. It is the mind that leads a man to power, not strength of body.

—CROW TEACHING

In Remembrance

The largest public execution was held in 1862 on this day in Mankato, Minnesota, where 38 Santee Sioux were hanged simultaneously for their alleged involvement in crimes committed during the Sioux Uprising. Originally, more than 300 men were condemned to death, but President Abraham Lincoln investigated the charges and allowed 38 of the sentences to stand.

December 27

*First you are to think always of God,
of Wankan-Tanka. Second, you are to
use all your powers to care for your
people and especially for the poor.*

—BLACK MOON,
HUNKPAPA SIOUX

Did You Know?

In traditional Cherokee culture, according to the book *Voices of Our Ancestors* by Dhyani Ywahoo (Cherokee), a person does not reach adulthood until age 51.

December 28

*A chief must not seek
profit for himself.*

—SWEET MEDICINE,
CHEYENNE

In Remembrance

Of the more than 300 Sioux
Indians who crossed over on
December 28, 1890, during the
massacre at Wounded Knee.

December 29

It is the office of man to kindle the fire, but the part of the woman to keep it burning.

—PIMA ETHIC

Did You Know?

Montezuma lived in an elegant palace with buildings, an aviary, lush gardens, and even a private zoo.

December 30

It is always good to do good, it is said.

—SAM BLOWSNAKE, WINNEBAGO

Did You Know?

There are many stereotypes of American Indians that must be avoided. The truth is as follows:

- Indians do not all look alike.
- Not all Indians know Native history and culture, especially that which is not their own.
- Indians observe the religion of their choice.
- Not all Indians are alcoholics.
- "Indian-ness" is not decided by the percentage of Indian blood in your body.
- Indians do not always have an Indian name.
- Indians were not uncivilized before the white man came to the Western Hemisphere.
- Indians were not conquered.
- There are many American Indian heroes.

December 31

On This Date in
Native American History

December 31, 1910: The film *The Yaqui Girl*, a love story about an Indian woman and a Mexican man, was produced. James Young Deer, Winnebago, became the head of studio production soon after this film.

Web Sites

www.angelfire.com/mo/nativeamericanjrnl/page6.html

http://www.carnegiemuseums.org/cmnh/exhibits/north-south-east-west/iroquois/handsome_lake.html

http://cherokee-indians-of-ga-inc.0pi.com/custom2.html (Cherokee Cultural Page)

http://www.countryroadchronicles.com/

http://www.emily.net/~schiller/whitston.html

www.falcon.jmu.edu/~ramseyil/natauth.htm

http://www.fallenmartyrs.com (Tribute To Fallen Martyrs)

www.fortunecity.com/tinpan/oldsquire/285/quotes.html

http://www.hallman.org/indian/scotseye.html

www.ilhawaii.net/~stony/quotes.html

http://www.ohiokids.org/ohc/history/h_indian/events/gnadenhu.html

http://www.pbs.org/wgbh/aia/part4/4h3083.html (Cherokee letter protesting the Treaty of New Etocha)

www.unity.edu/sari/2000/acoache/Native%20Links.html

http://www.wovoca.com/native-american-quote.htm

http://www.yale.edu/lawweb/avalon/ntreaty/ncase001.btm

BMW Art Guide by Independent Collectors. The global guide to private yet publicly accessible collections of contemporary art.

Revised edition with 32 additional collections

HATJE
CANTZ

A Unique Compendium for Art Lovers

On collectors' homes and the sharing of passion

——

Welcome to the third edition of the *BMW Art Guide by Independent Collectors.*
Once again, our dedicated team has scoured the globe to add a host of new
locations at which to enjoy art presented in the most fascinating settings.
They have also updated the entries from the past two editions of this guide.
The 236 collections featured throughout these pages are comprised solely
of sites where privately owned art, normally hidden behind closed doors,
has been made accessible to the public. Some, we should add, are listed
exclusively in this guide and can be visited by readers upon personal request.
Since the beginning of this project it has been important to us that this
book not be conceived of as a conventional travel guide, but rather as a
unique compendium to be enjoyed by likeminded art lovers. Now in its
third edition, it has once again expanded the diversity of its offerings,
exemplified by several cities represented here for the first time: Hong Kong,
Cape Town, Marseille, and Siena, among others. From cosmopolitan Beijing
to the small German town of Überlingen, this volume offers readers a full
spectrum of the contemporary art world—from its bustling metropolises to
its tranquil provinces. These diverse locations are connected by a powerful
common thread: they are all home to collectors who have shared with us
their immense passion for contemporary art. All of them deserve our sincere
gratitude. This goes as well for the many contributors who made this book
possible, working many months on its new edition and enriching our blog
with articles and interviews on a regular basis, tracing out the many facets
of art and collecting. You can find it all at www.bmw-art-guide.com.
Let your travels begin!

Dr. Steven Althaus
Senior Vice President
Brand Management BMW,
Marketing Services BMW Group

Karoline Pfeiffer
Director,
Independent Collectors

A ——
B
C
D
E
F
G
H
I
J
K
L
M
N
O
P
Q
R
S
T
U
V
W
X
Y
Z

1 Colección de Arte
Amalia Lacroze de Fortabat
*Argentina's richest woman presents six decades
of art-treasure collecting*

Collector:
Amalia Lacroze de Fortabat

Address:
Olga Cossettini 141
Puerto Madero Este
C1107CCC Buenos Aires
Argentina
Tel +54 11 43106600
info@coleccionfortabat.org.ar
www.coleccionfortabat.org.ar

Opening Hours:
Tues–Sun: 12–8pm

The Colección de Arte Amalia Lacroze de Fortabat lies
in the middle of Puerto Madero, the newly trendy quarter
of the Argentine capital. Until the end of the 1990s, this
neighborhood was still a no-go area of rundown houses
ringing the harbor. It's been heavily restored and added
to over the past few years by world-class architects like Sir
Norman Foster, Philippe Starck, and Santiago Calatrava.
The architect of the Colección Fortabat, which opened in
fall 2008, is the Uruguay-born New Yorker Rafael Viñoly.
He built a modern, light-filled house for the art collection
of Argentina's richest woman: 1 000 works ranging from
Pieter Bruegel to Andy Warhol, who made a portrait of
her in 1980. The socially critical artist Antonio Berni has
a gallery all to himself.

A   *2*   Fundación Federico Jorge Klemm
The idiosyncratic collection of an artistic multi-talent
with opulent leanings

Opera singer, organizer of happenings and performances, painter, photographer, author of a television series about artists from Rembrandt to Jean-Michel Basquiat, gallerist, collector, and patron. Frederico Jorge Klemm (1942–2002), a flashy Argentine with German-Czech roots, was all of these things—at night. During the day, he lorded over a chemical company founded by his father. The part-time eccentric with platinum blonde hair was a wild mixture of Gianni Versace, Andy Warhol, and Liberace. His art collection reflects his unconventional style: blasphemous works of photography by Andres Serrano meet knick-knack sculptures by Jeff Koons and naked men by Robert Mapplethorpe. Additionally: Argentine artists emerging onto the international scene, like Guillermo Kuitca or Nicola Costantino. In 1995 Klemm started a foundation dedicated to supporting, above all, young Argentine art.

Collector:
Federico Jorge Klemm

Address:
Marcelo T. de Alvear 626
C1058AAH Buenos Aires
Argentina
Tel +54 11 43123334
admin@fundacionfjklemm.org
www.fundacionfjklemm.org

Opening Hours:
Mon–Fri: 11am–8pm

There is no shortage of museums, galleries, and other art venues in

Buenos Aires, the bustling metropolis on the Río de
la Plata. Too bad, then, that they are spread across so many different quarters, with melodious names like Recoleta, Retiro, Palermo, and Belgrano. Carefully planning your art sojourn, therefore, is crucial. The comparatively cheap black-and-yellow taxis and their friendly drivers will do the rest. Aside from the private museums presented in this guide, one should definitely visit the Museo Nacional de Bellas Artes (MNBA), with its extensive collections of European and Argentine art from the Middle Ages to the twentieth century. International art discourse continues at the private Fundación Proa, in the colorful harbor district of La Boca. Whether Ron Mueck, Louise Bourgeois, or the young Argentine rising star Eduardo Basualdo—all have had a big show in this gleaming white building. You can find a fine selection of Argentine and international art books and magazines in the well-stocked Librería Purr, on the grand boulevard Avenida Santa Fe. Located in the bourgeois district of Retiro, the galleries Ruth Benzacar and Jorge Mara–La Ruche, both regular exhibitors at Art Basel Miami Beach, offer Argentine avant garde at the highest level. Whoever wishes to discover both the younger Argentine and international scene is in good hands at Miau Miau, in Palermo. Each year, in late May, right in Argentina's autumn, the art fair ArteBA takes place. Also Located in Palermo, the fair initially specialized in Latin American art but has become increasingly international. Friends of photography will find fine works at the photography fair Buenos Aires Photo, at the end of October. It's located in the communal Centro Cultural Recoleta, which exhibits the work of international greats like August Sander or Roger Ballen, in addition to Argentine artists. There are also off-spaces, but here they have a rather nomadic character and are often open for just a single show. It's best to pay attention to local flyers to discover what's going on.

Nicole Büsing & Heiko Klaas

3   MACBA—Museum Art Center   **A**
Buenos Aires
*An art center with a focus on international
geometric art*

Collector:
Aldo Rubino

Address:
Avenida San Juan 328
C1147AAO Buenos Aires
Argentina
info@macba.com.ar
www.macba.com.ar

Please check the website
for most current information
on opening hours.

MAMBA, MALBA, MACBA. Anyone flaneuring through Buenos Aires on a museum tour could get them mixed up. While the first two have been around for a long time, the MACBA arrived on the scene in 2012. The Museum Art Center Buenos Aires was founded by native Aldo Rubino, who now lives in Miami and is a frequent guest on the collectors' panel at Art Basel Miami Beach. Rubino's private collection concentrates on geometric abstraction: Op Art, Hard Edge, and Neo-Geo, from Manuel Álvarez Bravo and Victor Vasarely, all the way to the American Sarah Morris. Special exhibitions feature all varieties of current art. Shows take place in the 2 400-square-meter translucent building brought to life by local architect duo Vila/Sebastián. The location is great: the MACBA, which sits adjacent to the MAMBA, is in the lively flea-market quarter of San Telmo.

4   Fundación Costantini/MALBA—
Museo de Arte Latinoamericano
de Buenos Aires
*A grandiose overview of a century
of Latin American art*

Collector:
Eduardo F. Costantini

Address:
Avenida Figueroa Alcorta 3415
C1425CLA Buenos Aires
Argentina
Tel +54 11 48086500
info@malba.org.ar
www.malba.org.ar

Opening Hours:
Thurs–Mon: 12–8pm
Fri: 12–9pm

Unaware "gringos" come across places in South America that they couldn't have imagined in their wildest dreams. The Museo de Arte Latinoamericano de Buenos Aires (MALBA) is one such place. The museum of art features work from the Caribbean to Tierra del Fuego and is located in the posh district of Palermo Chico. It looks like an outpost of New York's Museum of Modern Art. Here, too, people know how to erect elegant structures; here modernism is self-consciously defined—naturally, from a Latin-American perspective. Nearly 300 key works from businessman Eduardo F. Costantini's collection are on permanent display: politically charged Conceptual Art by Léon Ferrari; the Chilean surrealist Roberto Matta is also well represented, as is the Brazilian Lygia Clark, whose fragile metal objects have leapt to premium prices internationally.

A

5 Museo James Turrell—
The Hess Art Collection, Colomé
*Turrell's largest Skyspace and additional light rooms
in breathtaking surroundings*

Far away from all the art metropolises, in a majestic location underneath the bright blue sky of the Argentine Andes, lies the world's first James Turrell Museum, opened in 2009. Here the light-and-land artist from Arizona completed the biggest *Skyspace* at his collector and friend Donald M. Hess's vineyard, Colomé: 2 300 meters up a mountainside sits a Turrell observatory with an open roof, joined by an orchestration of subtle light. Eight more light rooms, works acquired by Hess over the past forty years, are grouped around the spectacular centerpiece. Here you experience pure meditative inwardness. The Museo James Turrell, which Hess maintains along with his collections in South Africa and North America, is a truly magical space in a fascinating location.

Collector:
Donald M. Hess

Address:
Ruta Provincial 53
km 20 Molinos 4419
Salta
Argentina
Tel +54 3868 494200
museo@bodegacolome.com
www.bodegacolome.com

Opening Hours:
Tues–Sun: 2–6pm
And by appointment.
Reservations encouraged.

Additional exhibition locations:
Klapmuts, South Africa, p. 164
Napa, United States of America,
p. 203

— **A**

Collector:
David Walsh

Address:
655 Main Road
Berriedale TAS 7011
Hobart
Australia
Tel +61 3 62779900
info@mona.net.au
www.mona.net.au

Opening Hours:
May–September
Wed–Mon: 10am–5pm
October–April
Wed–Mon: 10am–6pm

6   Museum of Old and New Art (MONA)
*A collection that puts personal predilection
over speculative intention*

Small gestures are not his thing: Australian millionaire
David Walsh owns one of the largest museums in the
southern hemisphere. This building without daylight is
burrowed deep into the Tasmanian bedrock. Aside from
contemporary art, the museum also houses Egyptian
mummies and Greek coins. Walsh, who made his fortune
developing complex winning-systems for gambling, combines antique treasures with Australian contemporary art,
as well as works by internationally renowned artists like
Jannis Kounellis, Hans Bellmer, Anselm Kiefer, the Viennese group Gelitin, or Wim Delvoye's excrement machine,
Cloaca. Walsh prefers works that confront viewers immediately with subjects like sex and death. He conceives his
Museum of Old and New Art (MONA), opened in 2011, as
a kind of secular temple in which one is snapped back into
humanity's existential conditions.

A   7   Lyon Housemuseum
*The private house as museum: living with art and
showing it to strangers*

If you want to visit Corbett and Yueji Lyon, you first have to make an appointment. For good reason: the architect built a house for his family that also functions as a museum. In the cavernous rooms the artworks are arranged biannually anew. Lyon draws upon a long tradition, such as Peggy Guggenheim's Venetian home, where she showed her private collection. The Australian pair has specialized in the artists of their own country, collecting paintings from the likes of Tim Maguire, sculptures by Peter Hennessey, or large C-print photographs by Anne Zahalka. Two decades ago the Lyons decided to collect the work of a new generation, such as that by Peter Atkins, Callum Morton, and Patricia Piccinini, who have since become established internationally. The couple has remained true to their pioneering spirit.

Collectors:
Corbett & Yueji Lyon

Address:
219 Cotham Road
Kew VIC 3101
Melbourne
Australia
Tel +61 3 98172300
museum@lyonhousemuseum.com.au
www.lyonhousemuseum.com.au

By appointment only. To arrange an appointment, send an e-mail, or call on Mondays or Tuesdays between 9:30–11:30am.

8   White Rabbit—
Contemporary Chinese Art Collection
*One of the largest collections for Chinese art since
the beginning of the millennium*

Judith and Kerr Neilson have chosen to limit themselves: they only collect Chinese art, and of that, art only created after the year 2000. When Judith Neilson travelled to Beijing in 2001 she realized that her understanding of Chinese art was based on an outdated cliché. When she returned, she restructured their existing collection and, together with her husband, she bought an old factory in Sydney's industrial district. There she began to systematically acquire contemporary work by artists like Ai Weiwei, Huang Zhen, Qi Zhilong, or Huang Yan. Each artist's age did not matter; it was rather "creativity and quality" Neilson was after. Instead of buying at art auctions, the couple buys directly in China from gallerists and artists' studios. Their collection, which held just a handful of Chinese works in 2000, now counts as one of the most important and focused in the world.

Collectors:
Judith & Kerr Neilson

Address:
30 Balfour Street
Chippendale NSW 2008
Sydney
Australia
Tel +61 2 83992867
info@whiterabbitcollection.org
www.whiterabbitcollection.org

Opening Hours:
Thurs–Sun: 10am–5pm

Collectors:
Gertraud & Dieter Bogner

Address:
Buchberg am Kamp 1
3571 Gars am Kamp
Austria
Tel +43 1 5128577
office@bogner-cc.at
www.bogner-cc.at/projekte/
kunstraum

By appointment only.

9   Kunstraum Buchberg
*Permanent contemporary installations
and projects in the park*

Gertraud and Dieter Bogner are museum experts. The couple runs an international agency for museum planning in Vienna. Some of their prestige projects of the last years include the New Museum in New York City and the new Folkwang Museum, in Essen. Of course, if you have such a background, you also want to surround yourself with art projects privately. The Bogners do this—but far away from Vienna, in their twelfth-century castle, Buchberg, located in lower Austria, where since 1979 they have invited artists to modify its rooms. Thus far there have been twenty-two permanent room-alterations: color interventions, wall works, and sculptures. And in the green environs surrounding the castle, stars like Dan Graham or Heimo Zobernig have executed distinctive works relating to the architecture.

A   *10*   Essl Museum—Kunst der Gegenwart
                 Museum-level international art since 1945

The entrance into the world of contemporary art could not
have been more perfect: the collector couple Essl met by
chance in New York City at the end of the 1950s. Agnes Essl
worked at the renowned Zabriskie Gallery, and Karlheinz
Essl, who would later establish a chain of building-supply
stores, was there to study the phenomenon of supermarkets.
Museum visits and encounters with artists and gallerists
were the basis of their enthusiasm for art. In order to save
their company, in 2014, the collectors were forced to auction off forty-four key artworks. At the same time, the industrialist Hans Peter Haselsteiner took over sixty percent
of the collection, which includes more than 5 000 works and
is still housed at the Essl Museum, in Klosterneuburg, near
Vienna. Five to ten exhibitions each year present works by
such diverse artists as Jonathan Meese, Cecily Brown, or
Valie Export.

Collectors:
Agnes & Karlheinz Essl

Address:
An der Donau-Au 1
3400 Klosterneuburg
Austria
Tel +43 2243 37050150
info@essl.museum
www.essl.museum

Opening Hours:
Tues: 10am–6pm
Wed: 10am–9pm
Thurs–Sun: 10am–6pm

11   Schlosspark Eybesfeld
       *Carefully executed art projects in a
       palace garden setting*

A palace, a garden, and an enthusiastic couple. Christine
and Bertrand Conrad-Eybesfeld do not buy their art off
the rack. It originates on site, sometimes in a few weeks,
sometimes over a period of years. The owners of a culture-
management agency do not consider themselves collectors
or patrons, but rather artists' partners for these outdoor
projects. Indeed, the couple has enough space: the castle
is located in the sparsely populated state of Styria, in
southeastern Austria. It all started with the artist Heimo
Zobernig, who in 1989 made his mark on the castle's former tennis court with a fifteen-centimeter-thick concrete
plate. Sol LeWitt executed a large-scale work shortly before
his death, in 2007. For the Conrad-Eybesfelds, at least as
important as the end result is getting people involved in
the whole process, including the local community.

Collectors:
Christine & Bertrand
Conrad-Eybesfeld

Address:
Jöss 1
8403 Lebring
Austria
Tel +43 3182 240812
Tel +43 3182 240818
cce@eybesfeld.at
bce@eybesfeld.at
www.eybesfeld.at

Only guided tours by appointment.

12   Museum Liaunig   **A**
*Austrian art after 1950 and prominent works
by international artists*

Collector:
Herbert W. Liaunig

Address:
Neuhaus 41
9155 Neuhaus
Austria
Tel +43 4356 21115
office@museumliaunig.at
www.museumliaunig.at

Opening Hours:
Wed–Sun: 10am–6pm
Only guided tours by appointment.

With its slim, slightly rounded form, the Museum Liaunig
resembles a gigantic USB-stick plugged into green hills.
Outside the metropolises, the Carinthian businessman
Herbert W. Liaunig opened this radically modern looking
museum in the summer of 2008, and had it greatly expanded in 2014 and 2015. The building was masterminded by
the Viennese architects Querkraft, who lean toward understatement: ninety percent of the rooms are located underground. Liaunig collected "what resulted from personal
encounters and predilections." The roughly 3 000 works
include key pieces of Austrian postwar art by figures like
Arnulf Rainer or Maria Lassnig, but also undiscovered or
overlooked work, as well as young positions. Since the museum was founded, Liaunig has collected with more focus
and closed some previous gaps, such as his acquisition of
some Viennese Actionists. His goal is to bring Austrian art
since 1950 alive for the visitor.

A

13   Museum Angerlehner

*The unique collection of an entrepreneur fascinated
by art and artists*

The Upper Austrian entrepreneur Heinz J. Angerlehner describes himself as "a collector with heart and soul." Within thirty years he acquired over 2 500 works of art. They have either attracted him emotionally or spontaneously— without regard for any art-historical classification, but with a high regard for quality. This is how his collection grew over the years to include many famous names from his homeland, such as Arnulf Rainer, Gunter Damisch, Hubert Schmalix, or Andreas Leikauf. In September 2013 the Museum Angerlehner opened in Thalheim, near Wels. It is housed in a former assembly hall covered with iridescent black metal panels, which in addition to showing the collection also hosts temporary exhibitions in its roughly 2 000-square-meter space. An added highlight is the fifty-meter-long display storeroom with retractable walls.

Collector:
Heinz J. Angerlehner

Address:
Ascheter Strasse 54
4600 Thalheim/Wels
Austria
Tel +43 7242 2244220
office@museum-angerlehner.at
www.museum-angerlehner.at

Opening Hours:
Thurs: 1–9pm
Fri–Sun: 10am–6pm

14   TBA21—Augarten

*Worldwide support of art projects, local cooperation
with Vienna's Belvedere*

For seven years, the private foundation Thyssen-Bornemisza Art Contemporary presented exhibitions in a historic apartment in the heart of Vienna. Since the summer of 2012, the foundation's art space has been located in the Atelier Augarten, working in conjunction with the state-run museum Belvedere ever since. Three exclusive projects take place at TBA21–Augarten each year, projects that often blossom at the interstice between exhibition and performance. But that's not all they do: here, at the nerve center of a worldwide foundation, the mission is to work closely with international artists, from Vienna to Reykjavík to New Delhi. Chairwoman Francesca von Habsburg, daughter of the super-collector Baron Hans Heinrich Thyssen-Bornemisza, grew up with art. And now the former "it girl" of London society has become one of the most experiment-friendly patrons of contemporary art since the foundation opened, in 2002.

Collector:
Francesca von Habsburg

Address:
Scherzergasse 1A
1020 Vienna
Austria
Tel +43 1 51398560
exhibitions@tba21.org
www.tba21.org

Opening Hours:
Wed–Thurs: 12–5pm
Fri–Sun: 12–7pm

Bangladesh

15

Collectors:
Nadia & Rajeeb Samdani

Address:
Level 5, Suite 501 & 502
Shanta Western Tower
186 Gulshan—Tejgaon Link Road
Tejgaon I/A, Dhaka-1208
Bangladesh
Tel +8802 8878784-7
info@samdani.com.bd
www.samdani.com.bd

E-mail appointment only.

15   Samdani Art Foundation
*A discovery of modern and contemporary art
from Bangladesh*

Globalization has put previously ignored countries on
the art map—Bangladesh, for example. Bangladeshi industrialist Rajeeb Samdani and his wife, Nadia, are well
aware of this, so their aim is to acquaint an international
audience with art from their country. In April 2011 they
opened a foundation to promote local art via exhibitions,
film screenings, and events like the Dhaka Art Summit.
Their collection, spread over three floors of their private
home, includes local artists such as Shumon Ahmed,
Tayeba Begum Lipi, and Mahbubur Rahman, alongside
international artists such as Ai Weiwei, Tracey Emin, Anish Kapoor, and Prabhavati Meppayil. Samdani, who is
also a founding member of the South Asian Acquisitions
Committee of the London Tate, has an additional project:
a sprawling sculpture park in the country's northeast.

B

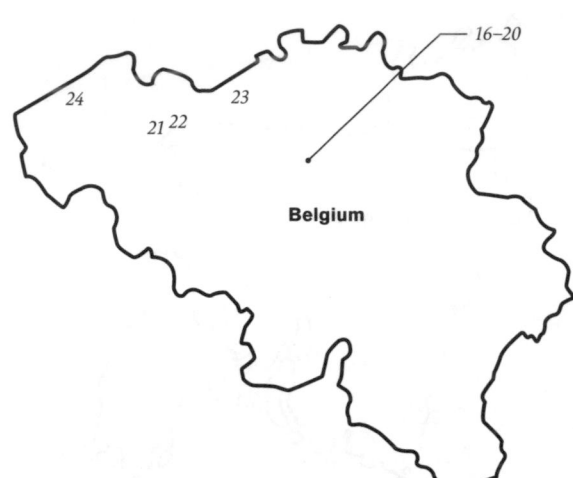

16–20

24

21 22

23

Belgium

16   Frédéric de Goldschmidt Collection
Reduced aesthetics and humble materials in
three locations in the center of Brussels

He had purchased art before, but only since 2009 has
Frenchman Frédéric de Goldschmidt considered himself
a collector. That's when he first acquired works that blew
the dimensions of his loft apartment, located in a seventeenth-century building in central Brussels. Today he owns
two additional showrooms: one of seventy square meters
and the other 160. The conceptual core of his collection is
the group Zero and their associates, with works by Günther
Uecker, Heinz Mack, or Piero Manzoni. In the meantime,
de Goldschmidt, who works as a film producer, has begun
collecting mostly younger artists, such as the Berliner Stef
Heidhues, or Joel Andrianomearisoa, from Madagascar. The
collection's common thread is a reduced aesthetic and great
sensitivity to rather humble materials. De Goldschmidt
rearranges his collection each year in time for Art Brussels.

Collector:
Frédéric de Goldschmidt

Address:
Brussels, Belgium
frederic@frederic.net

Visitation permitted only
occasionally. Please inquire
by e-mail.

17   Maison Particulière

Exhibitions in a private home curated by collectors,
artists, and men of letters

B

Collectors:
Amaury & Myriam de Solages

Address:
Rue du Châtelain 49
1050 Brussels
Belgium
Tel +32 2 6498178
info@maisonparticuliere.be
www.maisonparticuliere.be

Opening Hours:
Tues–Wed: 11am–6pm
Fri–Sun: 11am–6pm

It would be hard to be more innovative. The Brussels-based French couple Amaury and Myriam de Solages assigns a thrice-yearly team of four collectors and one artist to curate an exhibition based on a predetermined theme. A sixth person, an *Homme des Lettres,* chooses related texts. The location is as unique as the idea: an uninhabited aristocratic domicile in the lively district of Châtelain. Three storeys, dark hardwood floors, high ceilings, lots of light, and chock-full of premium furniture by Ludwig Mies van der Rohe, Arne Jacobsen, and young designers. The whole project has been applaudingly received in Brussels: since its opening, in April 2011, the Maison Particulière has become an absolute hotspot of the city. Works as varied as those by Cindy Sherman, Kiki Smith, and Hans Bellmer can be seen alongside young Belgian artists, African sculptures, and porcelain objects. Eclecticism with style.

B

18   Charles Riva Collection
*Charming presentation of contemporary art
in a private Brussels mansion*

The Frenchman Charles Riva is co-owner of galleries in
Brussels, Paris, and London. He sees his Charles Riva Collection, in Brussels, as a nonprofit space. Here he lives with
his collection in a centrally located luxurious nineteenth-
century townhouse. In the spring of 2009 Riva began to
organize twice-yearly or quarterly exhibitions generated
from within the collection, including of Leipzig painter
and printmaker Christoph Ruckhäberle, as well as of Californian performance artist and pop-culture antagonist
Paul McCarthy, or of the fictional New York artist Reena
Spaulings, whose true identity remains a riddle. To go to
galleries is a serious thing, Riva says, kind of like going
to church. Whoever visits his collection should experience the novel ways in which art unfolds when viewed in
private rooms.

Collector:
Charles Riva

Address:
Rue de la Concorde 21
1050 Brussels
Belgium
Tel +32 2 5030498
info@charlesrivacollection.com
www.charlesrivacollection.com

Opening Hours:
Wed–Sat: 12–6:30pm
And by appointment.

"Brussels is booming, when it comes to culture and the arts," says Katerina Gregos, the artistic director of Art Brussels. "The art scene here is very strong and varied." Each April, when Art Brussels opens its doors, in the exposition halls of the 1958 World Fair, in the shadow of the Atomium, all of **Brussels** lights up: parties, gallery nights, and open houses hosted by scores of private collectors determine the program. For young artists and international art collectors, this European capital—with both its charm and rough edges—is the new Mecca: studios, galleries, private collections, and institutions are here en masse. The Palais des Beaux-Arts (for short: Bozar) lures visitors with exhibitions by Jeff Wall to Michaël Borremans. Art-goers interested in younger positions are in good hands at the Wiels–Centre d'Art Contemporain, in the multicultural neighborhood of Forest. Nine artists' studios for international newcomers are available for residencies in this art center, which opened in 2007, in an old brewery. If you want to explore Brussels versatile gallery scene, it's best to take a tour of the Ixelles district, around Avenue Louise, or the Lower Town, called Downtown. Situated here are the spaces of the avant-garde gallerist Jan Mot, the long-established Greta Meert, and the gallery Dépendance, led by a German, Michael Callies. On the walk towards Ixelles you'll also pass the Brussels branch of the New York blue-chip gallery Barbara Gladstone, located in a renovated Art Nouveau building. Among the galleries in elegant Ixelles itself are Almine Rech, Xavier Hufkens, and, the young Elaine Levy. Whoever wishes to stock up on art books in otherwise comic-enthusiast Belgium should head straight to the magnificent Galeries Royales Saint-Hubert Passage, near the Grand-Place. Here, the Librairie Saint-Hubert and the bookshop Tropismes provide an opportunity for endless hours of browsing.

Nicole Büsing & Heiko Klaas

19 Servais Family Collection
*Art that poses questions, in a converted factory loft
in the North of Brussels*

B

Collector:
Alain Servais

Address:
Brussels, Belgium
collection.servais@gmail.com

E-mail appointment only.

Alain Servais is omnipresent in the art world. Sometimes
he sits on the expert panel for the collection of new media at Art Basel. Sometimes he rushes during Berlin Art
Week on a rented Vespa from one gallery to another. He
is also an avid Twitter user. The extremely well-connected Frenchman, who lives in Brussels, is hungry for art.
In his opinion, good art should question certainties: "It
should teach me something that I don't know about myself or my environment." Servais converted an old factory
into a 900-square-meter loft in the multicultural district
of Schaerbeek. He lives here surrounded by his collection, which includes established names such as Gilbert &
George and Barbara Kruger as well as younger positions,
like the video works by Mexican artist Arturo Hernández
Alcázar. Once a year he rearranges eighty percent of his
collection's holdings.

20 Vanhaerents Art Collection
*Art and film since the 1970s: Warhol, Naumann,
and the consequences*

Collector:
Walter Vanhaerents

Address:
Rue Anneessens 29
1000 Brussels
Belgium
Tel +32 2 5115077
www.vanhaerentsartcollection.com

Online registration required.

Walter Vanhaerents's family has been in the construction
business for eighty years; naturally he went into the business, too. But as a young man he had studied film. He was
so impressed with Andy Warhol's five-hour-long *Sleep* that
he wanted to see other works by the Pop icon. No surprise,
then, that Warhol, along with Bruce Naumann, is one of
the anchors of the Vanhaerents Art Collection. How did
younger artists react to the impulses unleashed by these
giants? They were further investigated by Cindy Sherman,
Matthew Barney, and Ugo Rondinone, all up to the provocative neo Pop-Art businessman Takashi Murakami.
The collection is housed in a charmingly remodeled 1926
industrial building on the outskirts of the hip fashion
and gallery district Dansaert. Starting in 2007, new exhibitions have been shown biannually on three floors.

B

21   Museum Dhondt-Dhaenens
*In the middle of Flanders, international art stars shown
in quick succession*

The Flanders industrialist couple Jules and Irma Dhondt-Dhaenens began collecting art in the 1920s. Belgium was just as divided then as it is today, which is why the couple focused almost exclusively on Flemish artists from 1880 to 1950, including James Ensor and Frits Van den Berghe. Toward the end of their lives, the collector couple decided to have a museum built to house their collection. Not in Brussels or Ghent, but in the countryside at Deurle, a beautifully located village on the river Leie and close to the artist colony Sint-Martens-Latem. The bright white, flat-roofed modernistic structure was opened in 1968. Today the museum continues to sharpen its contemporary profile with around eight annual exhibitions devoted to such international artists as Thomas Hirschhorn, Wade Guyton, and Monika Sosnowska.

Collectors:
Jules & Irma Dhondt-Dhaenens

Address:
Museumlaan 14
9831 Deurle
Belgium
Tel +32 9 2825123
info@museumdd.be
www.museumdd.be

Opening Hours:
Tues–Sun: 10am–5pm

22   Herbert Foundation
*A highly intellectual private collection in an industrial
complex in Ghent*

To utopia and back. The collection of the Ghent-based couple Annick and Anton Herbert focuses on art produced between 1968 and 1989. In a former steam-engine factory near the center of the Flemish city they present in temporary exhibitions works by concept and avant-garde artists such as Bruce Nauman, Marcel Broodthaers, Carl Andre, Robert Barry, and Lawrence Weiner as well as Martin Kippenberger, Franz West, and Thomas Schütte. What connects them all is their critical reflection upon social and artistic issues. What makes the collection so unique is its profound archive of artist books, letters, postcards, posters, invitations, and other documents, which show the friendly ties and decades of intellectual debate between the Herberts and "their" artists.

Collectors:
Anton & Annick Herbert

Address:
Coupure Links 627 A
9000 Ghent
Belgium
Tel +32 9 2690300
contact@herbertfoundation.org
www.herbertfoundation.org

Opening hours vary depending on exhibition. Please check the website for most current information.

Collectors:
Geert & Carla Verbeke-Lens

Address:
Westakker
9190 Kemzeke, Stekene
Belgium
Tel +32 3 7892207
info@verbekefoundation.com
www.verbekefoundation.com

Opening Hours:
Thurs–Sun: 11am–6pm

23   Verbeke Foundation
*An impressive terrain for hiking and discovering
unorthodox art*

B

Dynamic, not static. This is the motto of the Belgian collector
pair Geert and Carla Verbeke-Lens. "Our exhibition space
does not aim to be an oasis. Our presentation is unfin-
ished, in motion, unpolished, contradictory, untidy, complex, inharmonious, living, and unmonumental," says
Geert Verbeke. The former logistics businessman opened
a twelve-hectare art park in 2007 on his company's property. Storage buildings and greenhouses offer 20 000 square
meters of covered space for two enormous special exhibitions per year. The Verbekes started with collages and
assemblages, but now they prefer "Bio-Art"—art that includes living animals, plants, and even scents. Visitors unable to see the whole display in a single day can even spend
a night in a truly new environment: Joep van Lieshout's
eccentric polyester sculpture *CasAnus,* a gigantic recon-
struction of a human rectum.

Collector:
Mark Vanmoerkerke

Address:
Oud Vliegveld 10
8400 Ostend
Belgium
Tel +32 473 997745
info@artcollection.be
www.artcollection.be

E-mail appointment only.

24   Collection Vanmoerkerke
Highlights of European and American Post-Conceptual art

He is a manic collector, admits businessman Mark Vanmoerkerke, from the seaside resort town of Ostend, in
Belgium. He has managed to group together over 1 000
works in just fifteen years, mainly European and American Post-Conceptual art. What is that? Works by artists
like Francis Alÿs, Sophie Calle, or Andreas Slominski, all
of which contain degrees of humor and irony. Following
the carte blanche principle, every year one internationally
established curator is allowed to come up with a new way
to present the collection. Vanmoerkerke refrains from
interfering. Moreover, the acting curator decides which
curator will be next—a surprise not just for the collector,
but also for visitors. The cult curator Jan Hoet was one of
the first figures allowed to mix it up in the former airplane
hangar that houses the collection.

B

25   Inhotim—Instituto de Arte
      Contemporânea & Jardim Botânico
*The harmony of art and nature at one of the world's
most sensual locations*

Admittedly, it's hard to get here—but it's worth it. Inhotim completely redefines the production, exhibition, and experience of major outdoor-art projects. The collector, commodities magnate and philanthropist Bernardo Paz, invites well-known artists to his 600-hectare tropical expanse to unleash their most extravagant ideas. A team of four curators, which includes a German, Jochen Volz, supports the artists however it can. Cildo Meireles, Matthew Barney, Olafur Eliasson, Yayoi Kusama, and Chris Burden have all left their traces. Getting to Doug Aitken's *Sonic Pavilion,* which funnels the sounds of inner earth to the surface, or to Hélio Oiticica's color-orgy *Magic Square #5,* might take a while. Best is to take one of the many golf carts available, but if you decide to walk, there are plenty of benches along the way to let your dreams fly.

Collector:
Bernardo Paz

Address:
Rua B 20
Brumadinho, MG
35460-000
Brazil
Tel +55 31 32270001
malu.goncalves@inhotim.org.br
www.inhotim.org.br

Opening Hours:
Tues–Fri: 9:30am–4:30pm
Sat–Sun: 9:30am–5:30pm

26   Casa Daros—
Daros Latinamerica Collection   **B**
Contemporary art from Latin America at
Sugarloaf Mountain

Collector:
Ruth Schmidheiny

Address:
Rua General Severiano 159
Botafogo, Rio de Janeiro RJ
22290 040
Brazil
Tel +55 21 2275-0246
rio@casadaros.net
www.casadaros.net

Opening Hours:
Wed–Sat: 11am–7pm
Sundays and public holidays:
11am–6pm
And by appointment.

In March 2013, the Casa Daros opened at the Botafogo district in Rio de Janeiro. It shows Latin American art on 12 000 square meters in a converted neoclassical orphanage from the nineteenth century. With 1 200 works by 120 artists, the Daros Latinamerica Collection is the largest collection of contemporary Latin American art held by European collectors. It was founded in 2000 by the Zurich business couple Ruth and Stephan Schmidheiny. Since 2003, Ruth Schmidheiny has run the collection without her husband, supported by the South America expert Hans-Michael Herzog as artistic director and curator. The Casa Daros is an open place with education programs, artist talks, and discussions. Two annual exhibitions with art from across Latin America enrich the artistic offerings of the Copacabana.

C

Canada

28

27 —

27   Scrap Metal Gallery
Art focused on the relationship between word and
image in an industrial hall

The name of the collection is doubly misleading: investor
Joe Shlesinger and his wife, Samara Walbohm, did not, in
2011, open a "gallery" for their collection, but rather a private showroom, where they put on three to four exhibitions
a year. Secondly, while much is presented here, none of it is
"scrap metal," as the space's name advertises, with a wink.
The focus is rather on Canadian and international artists
whose work is similarly humorous, subtle, and ambiguous.
This includes art by the collective General Idea, Bill Viola,
Jeff Wall, Camille Henrot, or other global players. The
names Dave Dyment, Micah Lexier, or Laurel Woodcock,
however, are not so well known. Their works all interrogate
the complex relationship of language, text, and image.

Collectors:
Samara Walbohm &
Joe Shlesinger

Address:
11 Dublin Street
Unit E, M6H 1J4 Toronto
Canada
Tel +1 416 5882442
info@scrapmetalgallery.com
www.scrapmetalgallery.com

Please check the website
for most current information
on opening hours.

28   Rennie Collection at Wing Sang
Continuity for over thirty years: from trailblazing giants to new talents

C

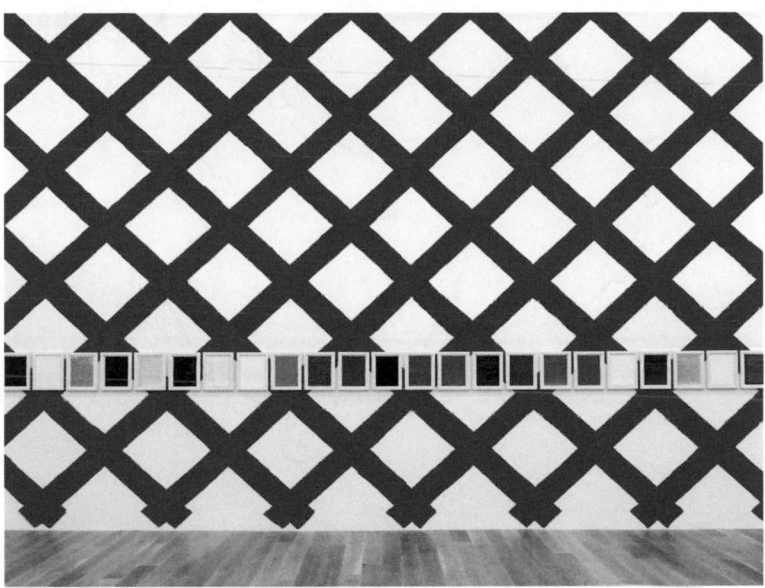

Collector:
Bob Rennie

Address:
51 East Pender Street
Vancouver BC V6A 1S9
Canada
www.renniecollection.org

Only guided tours with prior online registration.

A guided tour through Chinatown's Wing Sang Building, where collector Bob Rennie presents his works, takes exactly fifty minutes. This is not a lot of time for one of the largest collections in Canada. But Rennie focuses on central positions, like John Baldessari, Mike Kelley, Mona Hatoum, Rodney Graham, or the Belgian artist David Claerbout, who lengthens seconds-long film sequences from Hollywood classics to last an entire day. The works that the real-estate marketer owns are rearranged annually in two to three solo exhibitions. Rennie, who had the oldest building in the district lavishly renovated, has been collecting for over thirty years, assembling many pieces that came to be considered trailblazing. He now spends his time catching up with contemporary art by purchasing work by figures such as the Turner-prize-winning talents Martin Creed and Simon Starling.

C

China

29

31   — *32–34*

30

29   M Woods
*Contemporary art in a former factory
in the 798 Art Zone*

"Art has changed me very much—in the way I think and see the world. Art is magical." Even if Lin Han began collecting only in 2013, his words evidence the considerable impact art has already had upon his life. So far, the young industrial designer, who now runs a PR agency and works at his family's investment company, has acquired more than one hundred works by by renowned artists such as Tracey Emin, Zeng Fanzhi, Kader Attia, and Yoshitomo Nara. Since October 2014, Lin has presented his collection in spacious exhibition rooms in a former munitions factory built in the Bauhaus style in the bustling arts district 798 Art Zone. The name of the collection alludes to Lin's family: The "M" is the first letter of the name of his mother, who awakened his love for art. "Woods" is the English translation of his family name, "Lin."

Collector:
Lin Han

Address:
D-06, 798 Art Zone
No. 2, Jiuxianqiao Rd.
Chaoyang District
Beijing 100015
China
Tel +86 10 83123450
info@mwoods.org
www.mwoods.org

Only guided tours with prior online registration.

Since the opening of the Chinese economy in the 1980s, the Chinese art market has been rapidly expanding, later experiencing a boom and eventually making headlines around the world. Works by Chinese artists command record prices, and the local **Beijing** scene has grown like wildfire. But asking where the hotspot of Chinese contemporary art is centered yields no reliable answer; it's seemingly everywhere. New artist neighborhoods and complexes are constantly emerging, and the art scene is developing as quickly as the Chinese economy itself. And museums are multiplying so fast that one speaks of the phenomenon of "museumification" in China: in addition to traditional institutions, such as the National Art Museum of China (NAMOC), there is a new generation of collectors who are building their own private museums. Examples include the Beijing He Jing Yuan Art Museum and the Ullens Center for Contemporary Art (UCCA), which was founded by the Belgian collectors Guy and Myriam Ullens. Young art can also be discovered in exhibitions at the CAFA Art Museum of the Beijing Art Academy, or at the Art Beijing art fair, in April, as well as at the Beijing International Art Biennale (BIAB), from September to October. The most well known art address is 798 Art Zone, also called Dashanzi Art District, in the northeast part of the city. The former factory site has evolved since the mid-1990s as a magnet for galleries and creative people. Not far away are other artist quarters, like the Jiuchang Art Complex, the Caochangdi district, or the artist colony Songzhuang Art Community. Among the important galleries in Beijing are the Aye Gallery, the Long March Space, White Space Beijing, and, of course, the international galleries that have opened branches here, including Pace from New York, the Italian Galleria Continua, or the Swiss galleries Boers-Li Gallery and Galerie Urs Meile.

Silvia Anna Barrilà

30 Living Collection
*Contemporary art from Hong Kong in the loft
of a former industrial building*

Collectors:
William Lim

Address:
Hong Kong, China
info@CL3.com
www.livingcollection.hk

E-mail appointment only.

Since the founding of Art Basel Hong Kong, the former **C**
British colony has become a hotspot of the international art scene. But if you are particularly interested in its
local art, you should visit the imposing exhibition space
of the collector William Lim. In 2004, during his travels,
the architect began to acquire works by Chinese artists.
Two years later he decided to focus more strongly on artists from Hong Kong. Since then, he has been collecting,
among others, the works of Lee Kit, Nadim Abbas, or
Tsang Kin-Wah—young artists who deal with society and
their lives in Hong Kong. But you also find international
positions such as Lee Bul, Hernan Bas, or Callum Innes
in Lim's nearly 400-square-meter loft. That his studio is a
place of lively exchange is evidenced not least in the artists'
dinners that Lim hosts on a regular basis.

31 Sifang Art Museum
*Emerging and blue-chip artists in a building
by Steven Holl*

Collector:
Lu Xun

Address:
Sifang Art Museum
No. 9, Zhenqi Road
Pukou District
Nanjing 210031
China
Tel +86 25 58609999
contact@sifangartmuseum.org
www.sifangartmuseum.org

Opening Hours:
Wed–Sun: 10am–5pm

"The way art brings joy to the heart and challenges your
existing perceptions is fascinating," is how the Chinese
collector Lu Xun describes the motivation behind his collecting activity, which has become a great passion since
2009. The first works that Lu acquired were a sculpture by
Yayoi Kusama and a watercolor by Marlene Dumas. Since
then, he has collected about 200 artworks by Chinese
and international artists, such as Yang Fudong, Xu Zhen,
William Kentridge, and Luc Tuymans. But Lu is increasingly interested in emerging artists, particularly from
China. His collection is housed in a spectacular building,
designed by Steven Holl, in the middle of the Laoshan
National Park, on the outskirts of Nanjing. Opened in
November 2013, the museum is part of the Sifang Park-
land, a versatile area that includes a conference center, a
hotel, a recreation center, and artist residences—the ideal
space to find peace and harmony with nature and art.

32   Long Museum
*An overview of Chinese art history and
contemporary art*

C   The first collectors from Mainland China to make it onto
the 2012 *Artnews* list of the 200 top collectors were the investor Liu Yiqian and his wife, Wang Wei. In December of that
same year the billionaires made their collection of Chinese
art public, in the Long Museum, in Shanghai. Liu Yiqian's
story began in the late 1980s, with the opening of the Chinese market. First he turned his mother's small shop into
a thriving business. Then a friend familiarized him with
the newly created financial sector, where he augmented
his fortune. For the last twenty years the couple has bought
art from China, mainly at auctions. According to the BBC,
their collection is now worth more than one billion dollars.
It ranges from traditional art to Revolution-era works to
contemporary pieces by artists such as Zhou Chunya, Wang
Guangyi, Zhang Xiaogang, and Yue Minjun.

Collectors:
Liu Yiqian & Wang Wei

Address:
No. 210, Lane 2255
Luoshan Road
Shanghai
China
Tel +86 21 68778787
info@thelongmuseum.org
www.thelongmuseum.org

Opening Hours:
Mon–Sun: 9:30am–5pm

33   Qiao Zhibing Collection
*An idiosyncratic presentation of new Chinese artists
amid Shanghai's nightlife*

In a nightclub called Shanghai Night, in the southwestern part of the city, lives a modest but uniquely displayed
collection of Chinese and international art. The roughly
thirty works, in a variety of categories, spread over four
floors and 10 000 square meters, are supplied courtesy
of Qiao Zhibing, who's been collecting since 2006. The
glaring ambiance agrees with the artwork—and offers a
particularly interesting visual experience. The collection's
central concern is the new generation of Chinese artists,
including Qiu Xiaofei, Li Hui, Xu Zhen, or Gao Lei. An
additional focus is on Shanghai, with painters like Ding
Yi and Zhang Enli, next to internationally known artists
like Adel Abdessemed. Other works can be seen in Qiao's
neighboring restaurant. The opening of a third location
is planned for 2016: Qiao is converting several former oil
tanks in a disused industrial area at West Bund into an
art center.

Collector:
Qiao Zhibing

Address:
Shanghai Night
Caobao Road 400
Xuhui District
Shanghai
China
qiaozhibing@gmail.com

E-mail appointment only.

Hong Kong is without a doubt the center of the Asian

art market. Thanks to its buoyant economy, fiscal benefits, and freedom from Chinese censorship, the city has attracted the international auction houses Christie's and Sotheby's, as well as Western art galleries, including Gagosian, White Cube, Galerie Perrotin, Pace Gallery, Lehmann Maupin, and Simon Lee, which have opened branches in the skyscrapers of Central District, Hong Kong Island's buzzing financial hub. In 2011, Art Basel bought the local fair Art HK, completing another step on the way to Hong Kong's transformation into an art market giant. The next big event on the agenda is the planned 2017 opening of M+, a major museum for visual culture, designed by Herzog & de Meuron, which will host, among other treasures, the core of the collection of Uli Sigg, one of the most important collectors of Chinese contemporary art. The museum will be part of the West Kowloon Cultural District, a new, vibrant quarter located directly on the harbor's waterfront. This area already enjoys some important museums, including the Hong Kong Museum of Art, which holds an important collection of Chinese paintings and calligraphy. As for contemporary art, the Hong Kong Arts Centre, in Wanchai, is an active institution that includes theaters, a cinema, galleries, classrooms, studios, and office spaces. Other important institutions are Para Site, a nonprofit art space run by independent artists in the hip area of Sheung Wan, and the Asia Society Hong Kong Center, in the district of Admiralty. The trend towards contemporary art is positively expanding, seen in the rise of artistic hubs in Hong Kong's industrial areas, which are definitely worth a visit. Chai Wan, for example, is now home to galleries like Platform China and a branch of 10 Chancery Lane Gallery; and Wong Chuk Hang houses Spring, another nonprofit arts space, dedicated to an international cross-disciplinary program of artist and curatorial residencies and exhibitions.

Silvia Anna Barrilà

34   Yuz Museum
Asian and Western contemporary art of the
influential collector Budi Tek

C

Collector:
Budi Tek

Address:
No. 35 Feng Gu Road
Xuhui District
Shanghai
China
Tel +86 21 64261901
info@yuzmshanghai.org
www.yuzmshanghai.org

Opening Hours:
Tues–Sun: 10:30am–5:30pm
And by appointment.

For someone with a passion for large-scale installations,
there could be no better place for a private museum than an
aircraft hangar. For this purpose, the Sino-Indonesian entrepreneur Budi Tek chose the former hangar of Longhua
Airport, which he had modified by the Japanese architect
Sou Fujimoto. The 9 000-square-meter exhibition space
opened in May 2014. Tek had already initiated a museum
in Jakarta, which now serves as the headquarters of his
foundation. And although Tek began collecting as recently
as the beginning of the millennium, he has become one
of the most important collectors worldwide. While he initially focused on Chinese contemporary artists like Ai
Weiwei, Zhang Xiaogang, or Fang Lijun, he soon turned
towards Western artists: his favorites include Fred Sandback, Anselm Kiefer, and Adel Abdessemed.

D

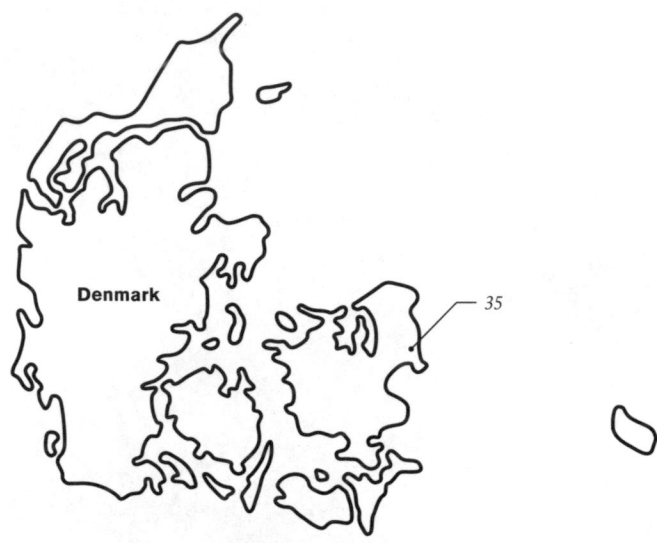

Denmark

35

35   Djurhuus Collection
*International contemporary art tending toward irony
and the grotesque*

If you have reservations, don't do it! This is the maxim of
the Copenhagen lawyer and art collector Leif Djurhuus,
who has been devoid of doubt roughly 2 000 times, the
number of works in his collection. He does not own a
private museum; they are stored in a warehouse. A selection of 200 works was exhibited from August 2011 to January 2012 at the Aros Aarhus Art Museum: works by the
1960s Danish avant garde, such as Poul Gernes or Sven
Dalsgaard. There are also international sky-rocketers like
Robert Kusmirowski or Kendell Geers, along with plenty
of young artists from all over the world. What interests
Djurhuus is "cutting edge," border-crossing, provocative young art. If you make an appointment with him,
Leif Djurhuus will show you his collection wherever it is
being exhibited.

Collector:
Leif Djurhuus

Address:
Copenhagen, Denmark
ldj@plesner.com
www.djurhuuscollection.com

Visitation permitted only
occasionally. Please inquire
by e-mail.

Finland

F

38

36, 37

0

Collectors:
Gunnar & Marie-Louise Didrichsen

Address:
Kuusilahdenkuja 1
00340 Helsinki
Finland
Tel +358 10 2193970
office@didrichsenmuseum.fi
www.didrichsenmuseum.fi

Opening Hours:
Tues–Sun: 11am–6pm

36   Didrichsen Art Museum
*International and Finnish art in a once
very modern Finnish home*

A house in the elegant International Style, flooded with
light, overlooking the ocean and a garden dotted with
sculptures by Henry Moore. This dreamy house is not located in the Pacific Palisades, California, but rather on a bay
near Helsinki. The modernist villa, built in 1958, belonged
to the collector pair Gunnar and Marie-Louise Didrichsen.
Its architect, Viljo Revell, once an assistant to Alvar Aalto,
later added a structure that in 1965 was opened as the
Didrichsen Art Museum. Gunnar Didrichsen, a Dane who
moved to Finland in 1928 and started a lucrative business,
began collecting with his wife, Marie-Louise, and he loved
progress as much as he liked art. The comprehensive collection includes classical modernist works alongside pre-
Columbian art and Chinese antiquities.

37 RKF Collection

Finland's finest assemblage of contemporary art stars

Located on the ground floor of the building that gallerist Kaj Forsblom and his wife, Rafaela Seppälä-Forsblom,
call home, the RKF Collection presents a superb selection
of international greats from the couple's approximately
1 500-work collection. The selection is striking in its depth,
especially considering that the couple has only been actively buying for around fifteen years—they were married
in 2000 and launched their efforts in earnest thereafter. A
particular focus has been placed on tracing painting in its
various forms from 1980, to the present, with artists such as
Jannis Kounellis, Donald Sultan, and Young British Artists
like Damien Hirst among their favorites. The by-appointment private museum features a permanent installation
by Scottish artist Charles Sandison—the full text of the
Encyclopedia Britannica is projected on a seventy-seven-year-
long loop in a mirrored room—but most other pieces are
swapped out a couple times each year.

F

Collectors:
Kaj Forsblom &
Rafaela Seppälä-Forsblom

Address:
Helsinki, Finland
info@galerieforsblom.com

Visitation permitted only
occasionally. Please inquire
by e-mail.

38 Sara Hildén Art Museum

One of the most important Finnish art hubs,
located on a beautiful lake

Typical Finland: the Sara Hildén Art Museum, in Tampere, is nestled harmoniously in an expansive sculpture
park backed up to a lakeshore. Sara Hildén (1905–1993)
was a successful entrepreneur in the fashion industry
who collected Finnish and international artists of her
time. In 1962 she established a foundation. The museum
was commissioned by the city of Tampere in 1979, and
was designed by the local architect Pekka Ilveskoski as a
two-storey, low-rise building with large windows. Over
1 500 square meters serve to showcase the collection's
works, some 5 000 objects. The focus remains on Finnish
art: from the "Finnish Frida Kahlo," Helene Schjerfbeck
(1862–1946), to very young artists. Wide-ranging special
exhibitions show internationally known artists like Alex
Katz, Subodh Gupta, or Wilhelm Sasnal.

Collector:
Sara Hildén Foundation

Address:
Laiturikatu 13, Särkänniemi
33230 Tampere
Finland
Tel +358 3 56543500
sara.hilden@tampere.fi
www.tampere.fi/english/sarahilden

Opening Hours:
Tues–Sun: 10am–6pm

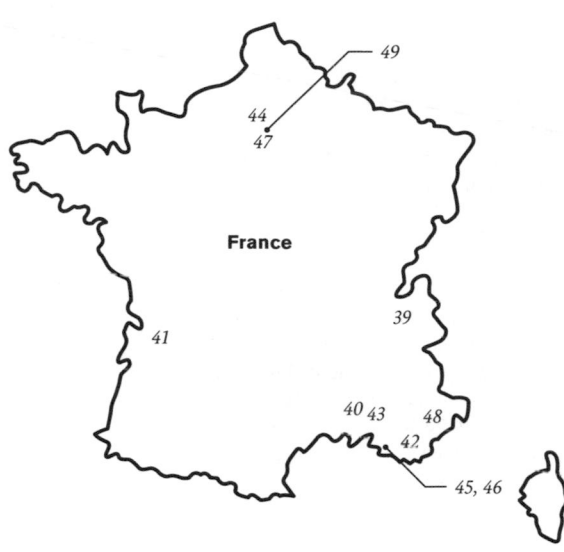

F

Collectors:
Claudine & Jean-Marc Salomon

Address:
191 Route du Château
74290 Alex
France
Tel +33 4 50028752
www.fondation-salomon.com

Please check the website
for most current information
on opening hours.

39   Fondation pour l'Art Contemporain—
Claudine & Jean-Marc Salomon
*Contemporary art in a castle, and sculpture
in the garden amidst the Savoyard Alps*

Claudine and Jean-Marc Salomon chose a beautiful, secluded location for the presentation of their contemporary art collection: encircled by small streams and earthy ponds, the Château d'Arenthon looks out onto the 900-soul village Alex, in the Savoyard Alps. Winter-sports fans are familiar with the name Salomon, the company that invented the modern ski-binding. The company was sold to Adidas in 1997, and Jean-Marc Salomon is the grandson of the company's founder. The Fondation Salomon opened with a drum roll in 2001: forty works by the eccentric artist duo Gilbert & George caused quite a stir in the tranquil mountain valleys—and bestowed the collection with the added attention from which it profits today. The two annual exhibitions feature either a single artist or a part of the collection. The sculpture park with works by Jan Fabre and Antony Gormley is also worth seeing.

40 Collection Lambert
Museum-quality international contemporary art since 1960

The inventory list of the Collection Lambert reads like the Who's Who of recent art history: from Francis Alÿs to Lawrence Weiner, and a slew of top names in between that would make any museum director jealous: Louise Bourgeois, Cy Twombly, and Jenny Holzer, to name just three. Yvon Lambert was one of the most trendsetting gallerists in all of France. In 2014 he gave up this gallery, founded in 1966, in order to devote himself more to his own collection and to publishing. With the Collection Lambert, opened in 2000, in Avignon, he has fulfilled the dream of bringing his collection to his hometown in southern France. Here 350 works from Lambert's 1 200 are housed in the Hôtel de Caumont, an eighteenth-century palace. As of July 2015 the exhibition space will be doubled, making additional use of the neighboring Hôtel de Montfaucon.

F

Collector:
Yvon Lambert

Address:
5 Rue Violette
84000 Avignon
France
administration@collectionlambert.com
www.collectionlambert.com

Opening Hours:
Tues–Sun: 11am–6pm

41 L'Institut Culturel Bernard Magrez
French lifestyle and art in the heart of Bordeaux

Bernard Magrez may be known for his wine, which is how he made his fortune. At his Institut Culturel, in Bordeaux, he offers a broad audience access to his artistic interests. The elegant eighteenth-century townhouse Château Labottière presents parts of his collection of modern and contemporary art in temporary thematic exhibitions. Magrez deliberately avoids the expertise of professional art consultants, instead letting his personal response to art guide his acquisitions. His eclectic taste is mirrored in a wide range of artists, from Lucio Fontana and Peter Doig to Wim Delvoye, Sam Taylor-Wood, Takashi Murakami, and Joana Vasconcelos. The patron also maintains three additional castles in the region, each dedicated to literary or musical events and to intellectual exchange.

Collector:
Bernard Magrez

Address:
16 Rue de Tivoli
33000 Bordeaux
France
Tel +33 5 56817277
contact@institut-bernard-magrez.com
www.institut-bernard-magrez.com

Opening Hours:
Thurs–Sun: 2–7pm

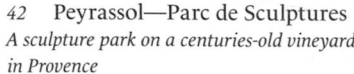

42   Peyrassol—Parc de Sculptures
*A sculpture park on a centuries-old vineyard
in Provence*

Collectors:
Valérie Bach & Philippe Austruy

Address:
Commanderie de Peyrassol RN 7
83340 Flassans-sur-Issole
France
Tel +33 4 94697102
contact@peyrassol.com
www.peyrassol.com

Opening Hours:
Early May–mid-September
Mon–Fri: 9am–7pm
Sat–Sun: 10am–7pm
Mid-September–end of April
Mon–Sat: 10am–6pm

Located on the historic vineyard estate Peyrassol, northwest
of Saint-Tropez, in the Var Département of the Provence
region, is one of France's youngest private sculpture parks.
In 2001 the Brussels entrepreneur Philippe Austruy and
his wife, gallery owner Valérie Bach, acquired the vineyard,
which dates back to the year 1256. For the Franco-Belgian
couple, wine, food, and hospitality are equally as important as contemporary art. Nestled on the wooded grounds
are over twenty sculptures by Jean Dubuffet, Cesar, Jean
Tinguely, and Jaume Plensa, among others—and the collection is being constantly expanded. In recent years, works
by French artists like Jeanne Susplugas or Fabrice Langlade
have been added. The perfect blend of art, Provençal flavors,
and warm Mediterranean sun comprise the charm of this
special place.

F

43   Château La Coste
*Exceptional art projects on a slightly different kind
of Provençal vineyard*

Collectors:
McKillen Family

Address:
2750 Route de la Cride
13610 Le Puy-Sainte-Réparade
France
Tel +33 4 42619292
reservations@chateau-la-coste.com
www.chateau-la-coste.com

Opening Hours:
Mon–Sun: 10am–7pm

Here is where art, architecture, nature, and wine enter into
an excellent liaison. When the Irish businessman Paddy
McKillen acquired the idyllic winery Château La Coste,
some fifteen years ago, the idea arose to forge a creative
space that would join artists and architects in the scenic
surroundings of Luberon. Since 2011 the 125-hectare site
has been open to art lovers, who should budget at least
two hours for a walking tour of the property's vineyards,
olive groves, and woods. Japanese architect Tadao Ando
designed the visitor center at the entrance, guarded by
a large Louise Bourgeois bronze spider standing in water.
Other highlights are site-specific works by Tracey Emin,
Liam Gillick, Richard Serra, and Franz West. New projects
by Carsten Höller, Renzo Piano, and Frank O. Gehry are
in development.

44 Le Silo
*Minimalism, Conceptual Art, and geometric abstraction
arranged perfectly in a former grain silo*

They don't consider themselves pure collectors; they're more artists' companions and contemporaries. For over thirty years the Parisian business couple Jean-Philippe and Françoise Billarant have been intensely engaged with Minimalism, Conceptual Art, and geometric abstraction. Their friendships with artists have played a central role: Carl Andre, Robert Barry, François Morellet, and Michel Verjux are all pals. In Marines, northwest of Paris, the couple had a 1948 grain silo transformed into exhibition spaces by the young architect Xavier Prédine-Hug, a former employee of Philippe Starck, who remodeled the simple structure into a reductive cathedral. And the artists? They thanked the collectors for their decades-long loyalty with perfect site-specific installations.

F

Collectors:
Jean-Philippe & Françoise Billarant

Address:
Route de Bréançon
95640 Marines
France
lesilo@billarant.com

By appointment only.

45 La Fabrique—Collection Gensollen
*A psychiatrist couple collects Conceptual Art
as intellectual challenge*

"We do not just want to show art; we insist upon having a dialogue with others about it," say Marc and Josée Gensollen, who have built up an impressive collection, with a focus on Minimal and Conceptual Art since the early 1970s. The psychoanalytically trained couple from Marseille presents their collection of more than 500 key works in a stylishly converted former mill. In La Fabrique, light-filled living and exhibition rooms merge on several floors into one another. A remarkable library and an archive convey the impression of a great proximity to artists such as Lawrence Weiner, Gianni Motti, Pierre Huyghe, Dan Graham, and Jonathan Monk. Art as an intellectual challenge: the eloquent pair relishes being inspired by their collection to complex reflections about the present.

Collectors:
Marc & Josée Gensollen

Address:
11–13 Rue du Commandant Rolland
13008 Marseille
France
gensollen.la.fabrique@hotmail.fr

E-mail appointment only.

46   Fonds M-ArCo—Le Box
Cutting-edge art on the grounds of a former
slaughterhouse in Marseille

F

Collectors:
Marc & Marie-Hélène Féraud

Address:
Anse de Saumaty
Chemin du Littoral
13016 Marseille
France
Tel +33 4 91969002
contact@marco.org
www.m-arco.org

E-mail appointment only.

One of Marseille's former *abattoirs* is located on a remote
harbor just outside the city limits. Here is where Marc
Féraud, a successful ship-outfitter, established both his
company and—behind a shiny silver aluminum façade—
his private exhibition space, Le Box. Across 1 000 square
meters he shows parts of his contemporary art collection,
from François Morellet and Wade Guyton to Sergej Jensen,
in one or two temporary exhibits a year. Together with his
wife, Marie-Hélène, Féraud has been committed to young
art since the late 1990s. In 2009 they founded the Fonds
M-ArCo (Marseille-Art Contemporain). Le Box opened in
September 2011 with an exhibition of Gérard Traquandi
and Alan Charlton. In addition to their own program, the
Férauds work closely with the public museum collections
of Marseilles.

47   La Maison Rouge
*Attractive guest collections in Paris and
exciting artist projects*

F

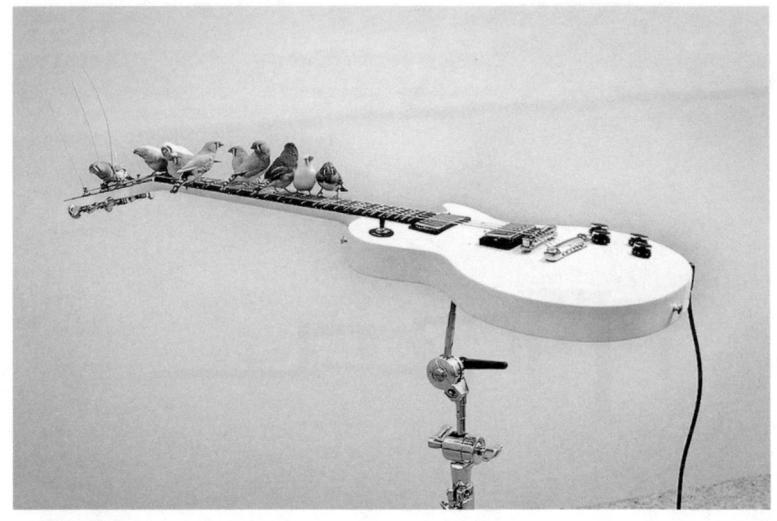

If you stroll along Boulevard de la Bastille, you will not
come upon this "red house," as the name implies. The only
thing red is a neon sign designating the private museum,
which was opened in 2004 by the political scientist and
supermarket-dynasty heir Antoine de Galbert. Once inside
the 2 000-square-meter complex, however, you will find
that red house, after all: in the covered courtyard stands a
bright red structure—housing the café. De Galbert enjoys
enigmatic staging. He also plays this kind of hide-and-seek
game with his collection, which is not on permanent display, but rather rotates with those of his friends. Numerous
top collections, like those of Thomas Olbricht or Harald
Falckenberg, have made appearances at La Maison Rouge.
Thematic and monographic exhibitions also take place
here, as well as projects with artists ranging from Arnulf
Rainer to Gregor Schneider.

Collector:
Antoine de Galbert

Address:
10 Boulevard de la Bastille
75012 Paris
France
Tel +33 1 40010881
info@lamaisonrouge.org
www.lamaisonrouge.org

Opening Hours:
Wed: 11am–7pm
Thurs: 11am–9pm
Fri–Sun: 11am–7pm

"**Paris** is simply fantastic," says the young Parisian artist Jeanne Susplugas. "You fall in love again and again with this city. The cultural scene is extraordinarily rich. From the museums to the opera, from the galleries and art centers to private art initiatives, like the Maison Rouge." One of the hotspots of the art scene is the Palais de Tokyo, that was reopened after an expansion in 2012: a 22 000-square-meter laboratory for young international contemporary art—perfect for night owls, as it's open until midnight. Major exhibitions of modern and contemporary art are on show at the Centre Pompidou, the Jeu de Paume, and the Musée d'Art Moderne de la Ville de Paris, all in the city center, as well as the Fondation Cartier, which lies a bit further south, in the 14th Arrondissement. Due to cuts in the cultural budget the extensive summer exhibition *Monumenta,* at the Grand Palais, now only takes place every two years. In 2016 the Chinese artist Huang Yong Ping will follow in the footsteps of stars like Daniel Buren and Anish Kapoor. The Grand Palais is also the venue of two high-profile autumn fairs: the FIAC art fair and Paris Photo. The biannual Mois de la Photo (Month of Photography) draws photo enthusiasts from all over the world to Paris with dozens of photo exhibitions in museums and galleries. If you want to visit commercial galleries, head to the Marais district. Here, for example, you'll find the representative spaces of the *grandes dames* of the Paris gallery scene Chantal Crousel, or Nathalie Obadia. In recent years, a hip new gallery district has also popped up in the dynamic neighborhood of Belleville. And uncompromisingly contemporary galleries like Bugada & Cargnel or Balice Hertling are always worth a visit. Even among art collectors word has spread that you won't just make discoveries inside this neighborhood's trendy galleries and cool off-spaces but also in the scenester restaurants and unconventional shops that lend this district its special flair.

Nicole Büsing & Heiko Klaas

48   Fondation Maeght

Key figures of the twentieth-century avant garde and a grandiose sculpture park

Collectors:
Aimé & Marguerite Maeght

Address:
623 Chemin des Gardettes
06570 Saint-Paul-de-Vence
France
Tel +33 4 93328163
accueil@fondation-maeght.com
www.fondation-maeght.com

Opening Hours:
October–June
Mon–Sun: 10am–6pm
July–September
Mon–Sun: 10am–7pm

It all started in the 1920s. Aimé Maeght, a lithographer, moved from the outskirts of Lille to Cannes and opened a small printing company with his wife, Marguerite, where they also sold radios and furniture. The then-unknown painter Pierre Bonnard asked them to take a few of his paintings on commission. They sold out in an instant, leading to one of the biggest success stories of twentieth-century art dealing. In 1946 the couple opened their legendary gallery in Paris and organized shows with Henri Matisse, Marc Chagall, and Wassily Kandinsky, and with Americans like Alexander Calder. The Fondation Maeght, founded in 1964, centers on works by all these artists and acts as a gift to posterity. With aesthetic assistance from the likes of Marc Chagall, Joan Miró, and Georges Braque, Spanish architect Lluís Sert constructed a museum of Mediterranean light that attracts roughly 200 000 visitors a year.

F

49   Fondation Francès

Contemporary photography in the service of discussion

Collectors:
Estelle & Hervé Francès

Address:
27 Rue Saint-Pierre
60300 Senlis
France
www.fondationfrances.com

Opening Hours:
Wed–Sat: 11am–1pm, 2–7pm

For Estelle and Hervé Francès, the collector's mission is not just to pile up works of art, but rather to be creative in bringing diverse art positions together in order to foster dialogue. In 2009 the head of a cultural communication office and her husband, an ad agency boss, opened their collection in Senlis, a small city outside of Paris. The 300-square-meter space in an eighteenth-century building offers enough room for thematic exhibitions every half year. There are also guest studios, where artists can spend a summer. The Francès' collection aims to provoke viewers into discussion, to foster new interactions, and to unsettle the emotions. Exhibiting photographs of vulnerable or sexually charged human bodies—works by Andres Serrano, Vanessa Beecroft, Dash Snow, or Larry Clark—often does the trick.

G

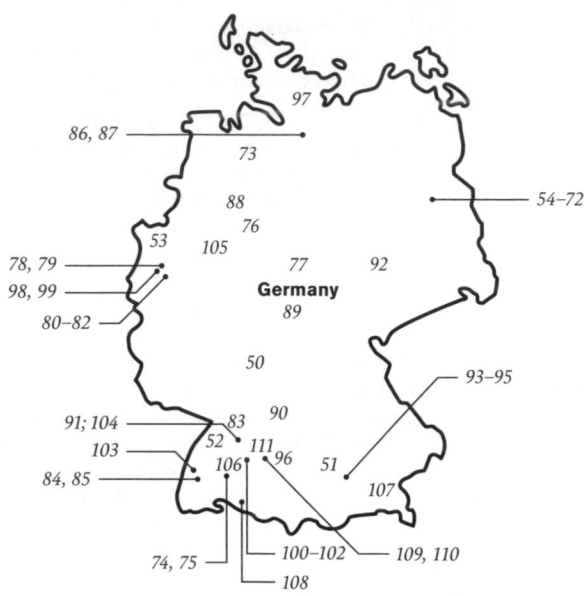

97

86, 87

73

88

76

53

105

78, 79

98, 99

80–82

77   92

Germany

89

54–72

50

91; 104

103

84, 85

83   90

52   111

106   96   51

93–95

107

74, 75

100–102

108

109, 110

50 Sammlung Fiede
Young contemporary art in very different locations

When Friedrich Gräfling was fifteen years old, he was faced with the decision to buy a PlayStation or the work of a graffiti artist. He opted for the latter, and thereby laid the foundation for this impressive collection of contemporary art. The architect shows his art today in his hometown of Aschaffenburg, where he converted a former slaughterhouse into an unconventional 600-square-meter venue, featuring one new exhibition annually. Additionally, Gräfling initiated an independent exhibition space, called Salon Kennedy, in a prestigious historic apartment in Frankfurt. "I am interested in the idea of sharing works with people who otherwise might not have the opportunity to see artists from abroad or even this kind of art," says the collector, who proved early on to possess a good sense for quality, acquiring works by Analia Saban, Gregor Hildebrandt, and Alicja Kwade.

Collector:
Friedrich Gräfling

Address:
Frohsinnstrasse 21 (rear building)
63739 Aschaffenburg
Germany
fiede@culturalavenue.org
www.sammlung-fiede.de

Only guided tours with prior registration.

51   Kunstmuseum Walter
*Former East meets West in a remodeled
industrial monument*

Collector:
Ignaz Walter

Address:
Beim Glaspalast 1
86153 Augsburg
Germany
Tel +49 821 8151163
office@kunstmuseumwalter.com
www.kunstmuseumwalter.com

Opening Hours:
Fri–Sat: 11am–8pm
Sundays and public holidays:
11am–6pm
And by appointment.

His motto: *Don't understand art the way others tell you to.*
The Augsburg developer Ignaz Walter has been collecting
modern and contemporary art since the early 1970s—mainly painting and sculpture, but also the less-than-popular
glass art. Big names of the early twentieth century like
Otto Dix, Lyonel Feininger, or August Macke find space in
Walter's collection, as does art from East and West Germany. Painters from the former East Germany—Bernhard **G**
Heisig, Wolfgang Mattheuer, or Werner Tübke—are represented as prominently as Georg Baselitz, Sigmar Polke, or
Gerhard Richter, who were all born in East Germany but
began their careers in the West. Walter exhibits his roughly
1 600 works in a 6 000-square-meter glass palace, a remodeled industrial landmark in Augsburg's garment district.

52   Museum Frieder Burda
*Classical modernism and luxury-class international
contemporary art*

Collector:
Frieder Burda

Address:
Lichtentaler Allee 8B
76530 Baden-Baden
Germany
Tel +49 7221 398980
office@museum-frieder-burda.de
www.museum-frieder-burda.de

Opening Hours:
Tues–Sun: 10am–6pm

For Frieder Burda, art is the elixir of life. The son of a pub-
lisher, Burda had proved to have good instincts already in
his early thirties: the first artwork he bought was by Lucio
Fontana. Now he owns about 1 000 works: classics of German Expressionism, as well as representatives of Abstract
Expressionism, like Jackson Pollock or Mark Rothko. His
Picasso collection ranks among the most important in Germany, as does his collection of German postwar art, with
numerous works by Georg Baselitz, Eugen Schönebeck, or
Gerhard Richter. Driven by his lust for painting, Burda
also buys current positions like Corinne Wasmuht or Karin
Kneffel. This extraordinary assembly of works demanded
a suitable home: in 2004 the collector opened his private
museum in the posh city of Baden-Baden—a snow-white
building designed by the American star architect Richard
Meier. It has already drawn over two million visitors.

53 Stiftung Museum Schloss Moyland
An extensive collection of Joseph Beuys's life and
work meets contemporaries

The art-enthusiast brothers Hans and Franz Joseph van der Grinten had a lifelong friendship with Joseph Beuys. This resulted in a vast collection of nearly 6 000 works and roughly 100 000 letters, photos, and notes by the action artist, as well as numerous works by other artists. The Schloss Moyland collection was made public in 1997, and under director Bettina Paust it has undertaken a new conceptual turn: international research on Beuys has taken center stage since 2009, and the number of exhibited works was reduced by ninety percent. Furthermore, the house has shined anew since a 2011 renovation. Special exhibits featuring young artists or Beuys's students, such as Katharina Sieverding, should certainly sustain visitors to this idyllic moated castle on the Lower Rhine.

G

Collectors:
Hans & Franz Joseph van der Grinten

Address:
Am Schloss 4
47551 Bedburg-Hau
Germany
Tel +49 2824 951060
info@moyland.de
www.moyland.de

Opening Hours:
April–September
Tues–Fri: 11am–6pm
Sat–Sun: 10am–6pm
October–March
Tues–Sun: 11am–5pm

54 Galerie Bastian
Hybrid use: private-collection showroom and/or
commercial gallery

The corner building across from the Neues Museum is a good address: Heiner Bastian bought the prime property at the Kupfergraben in 2000 and initiated an international architectural competition to build on it. David Chipperfield offered the most convincing pitch, an elegant contemporary building adapted to the historical context that peers onto the street through large plate-glass windows. Bastian, a former assistant to Joseph Beuys, financed the project, which he calls a "townhouse for art." The blue-chip gallery Contemporary Fine Arts resides on the first two floors. The third floor is temporarily operated by Bastian's son, Aeneas, as a commercial gallery—but the space also shows parts of Céline, Heiner, and Aeneas Bastian's high-profile private collection at least twice a year: from Joseph Beuys' drawings and Andy Warhol's polaroids to the works of young unknown artists.

Collectors:
Céline & Heiner Bastian

Address:
Am Kupfergraben 10
10117 Berlin
Germany
Tel +49 30 20673840
info@galeriebastian.com

Opening Hours:
Thurs–Fri: 11am–5pm
Sat: 11am–4pm

55   Sammlung Boros
*Roughly 700 works of contemporary art in an
extensively refurbished bunker*

G

Collectors:
Christian & Karen Boros

Address:
Bunker, Reinhardtstrasse 20
10117 Berlin
Germany
Tel +49 30 27594065
info@sammlung-boros.de
www.sammlung-boros.de

Opening Hours:
Thurs: 4 –7:30pm
Fri–Sun: 10am–4:30pm
Only guided tours with prior
online registration. Special tours
available by e-mail appointment.

This is one of the most spectacular places for a private collection of zeitgeisty art. It took Karen and Christian Boros four years to transform a former air-raid bunker, a historic monument in Berlin-Mitte, into their private museum. On top of this colossus they built a luxurious penthouse. Ad-man Boros, who has offices in Wuppertal and Berlin, has been collecting contemporary art since the 1990s. Since 2008 the collection has exhibited groups of works by twenty contemporary artists, who have operated within a given space. Many of them, like Olafur Eliasson, Cosima von Bonin, or Tomás Saraceno, created very tailored site-specific works. The remodeling of the Boros bunker—which was used in East Germany as a warehouse for exotic fruits, and then as a techno club after the Wall came down—took both time and money. Architect Jens Casper had to remove a number of walls to transform 120 small rooms into eighty larger ones that take up 3 000 square meters.

56 Salon Dahlmann
A Finnish collector and the revival of the salon tradition in Berlin

You simply can't ignore Berlin. The Finnish collector Timo Miettinen is convinced of this. In 2010 he acquired, together with his three sisters, an impressive historical building in Berlin-Charlottenburg. The technology company owner initiated a salon with rotating exhibitions on the building's first floor. Since 2004 he has collected—together with his wife, the architect Iiris Ulin—international contemporary art with a focus on Germany and Finland. At the Marburger Strasse 3 address he also presents works from his collection, ranging from Albert Oehlen and Björn Dahlem to Marianna Uutinen. At the center of his interest, however, is his Salon Dahlmann—named after the home's previous owner—which hosts openings that are always well attended. Miettinen also regularly invites young curators to have a fresh look at other scenes and collectors.

G

Collectors:
Timo Miettinen & Iiris Ulin

Address:
Marburger Strasse 3
10789 Berlin
Germany
Tel +49 30 21909830
info@salon-dahlmann.de
www.salon-dahlmann.de

Opening Hours:
Sat: 11am–4pm
And by appointment.

57 Sammlung Arthur de Ganay
Architectural, city, and landscape photography in an extraordinary Berlin loft

Once a month, on an entire floor of a spacious loft converted in 2006 from an old jelly factory in Berlin-Kreuzberg, photography fans swarm to hear Arthur de Ganay lead a tour through his remarkable collection overlooking the river Spree. The collection's nucleus is comprised of works by Becher students like Candida Höfer, Thomas Ruff, and Thomas Struth. But conceptual photographers also play a role—Lewis Baltz or Hiroshi Sugimoto, for example—and younger positions are given ample room. When de Ganay, a Paris-born architect, moved to Berlin, in 2001, he had been collecting for eight years. Now he's not just interested in bringing together works of art and making them publicly accessible; he also wants to push the medium of photography into equal standing with painting. Considering the immense caliber of his collection, photography stands quite the chance.

Collector:
Arthur de Ganay

Address:
Köpenicker Strasse 10a
10997 Berlin
Germany
info@collectionarthurdeganay.com
www.collectionarthurdeganay.com

Only guided tours with prior e-mail registration. Every first Saturday of the month from 2–4pm.

58   Sammlung Barbara und Axel Haubrok—Haubrokprojects

Contemporary avant garde instead of government vehicles in Berlin-Lichtenberg

Collectors:
Barbara & Axel Haubrok

Address:
Herzbergstrasse 40–43
10365 Berlin
Germany
Tel +49 172 2109525
info@haubrok.org
www.haubrok.org

Opening hours vary depending on exhibition. Please check the website for most current information.

Barbara and Axel Haubrok like art they don't immediately grasp. Perhaps this is why the Berlin couple, who moved from the Rhineland, has managed since 1988 to compile one of the most progressive collections of contemporary art in all of Germany. Their focus is clearly on contemporary minimalist and concept art, with works by exactly thirty international artists, including Christopher Williams, Carol Bove, and Wade Guyton. Understatement instead of extravagance: since 2005, the Haubroks have been organizing sophisticated exhibitions in their showroom at Strausberger Platz. Looking for a new challenge, in April 2013 they started to show their collection in rooms on the premises of a 20 000-square-meter compound of a former car-dispatch garage in Berlin-Lichtenberg. Where there once stood official vehicles of former GDR ministries now flourishes a new cultural center with workshops, warehouses, and exhibit spaces.

G

59   Sammlung Hoffmann

International contemporary art in a collector's private residence

Collectors:
Erika & Rolf Hoffmann

Address:
Sophie-Gips-Höfe, Staircase C
Sophienstrasse 21
10178 Berlin
Germany
Tel +49 30 28499120
info@sammlung-hoffmann.de
www.sammlung-hoffmann.de

Only guided tours with prior registration, every Saturday from 11am–4pm.
Closed through August and between Christmas and New Year.

They were among the first to head to Berlin after the Fall of the Wall to make their personal collection of art available to the public. Erika and Rolf Hoffmann, from Mönchengladbach, had been collecting German and American artists such as Günther Uecker, Frank Stella, or Bruce Nauman for some time. When they moved to Berlin, in the mid-1990s, they had long since sold their textile company. They acquired a former sewing-machine factory in Berlin-Mitte, entirely renovated it, and then moved into two of its floors. And now they have created something of a ritual in the German capital: every Saturday small groups of visitors in grey felt slippers push through the spacious private rooms, led by young, laid-back guides. Once a year the rooms are switched out with new works. Fresh acquisitions from Poland, Japan, or China have shifted the collection's focus ever more eastward. Since her husband's death, in 2001, Erika Hoffmann has been actively leading the project herself.

60   Jarla Partilager
In-depth mid-career exhibitions by known contemporaries

Who knows what the word *partilager* means? People familiar with Swedish, that's who: it means "outlet sale." But what does that have to do with art? The Swedish financial advisor Gerard De Geer collects high-quality, expensive contemporary works, like that of British video artist Phil Collins, Dutch installation artist Mark Manders, or Danish super-star Olafur Eliasson. Back in Stockholm, De Geer used to display works in his collection in a former warehouse outlet, before inaugurating a showroom in Berlin under the same name, with a Thomas Scheibitz retrospective, in fall 2011. The Berlin location, a bright, sky-lit room on the fourth floor of a gallery building on Lindenstrasse, is well chosen. De Geer wants to slow down the hype by presenting just one artist a year. Following the Scheibitz show: Thomas Schütte.

G

Collector:
Gerard De Geer

Address:
Lindenstrasse 34, 4th Floor
10969 Berlin
Germany
Tel +49 30 20188543
visit@jarlapartilager.org
www.jarlapartilager.org

E-mail appointment only.

61   Kienzle Art Foundation
Exciting rediscoveries far from the mainstream

Even in the Berlin art scene he is seen as an individualist, which says a lot. Jochen Kienzle collects and displays non-mainstream works of art, like those by painter Klaus Merkel, who in the 1980s worked exclusively in a limited gray palette. Or work by Josef Kramhöller, a painter and performance artist who committed suicide in 2000, at age thirty-one. Acknowledged as a talent by fellow artists, Kramhöller was pretty much ignored by the art market. With Jack Goldstein and Franz Erhard Walther, the collection also includes well-known names. Jochen Kienzle's parents collected modernist works, and already as a high-school student he purchased his first work of art at Art Basel, and went on to study art history. In 2010 the former gallerist opened the Kienzle Art Foundation, and his engagement in the Berlin scene has earned him much credit. The Kienzle Art Foundation works closely with curators organizing exhibitions, film screenings, and discussion forums.

Collector:
Jochen Kienzle

Address:
Bleibtreustrasse 54
10623 Berlin
Germany
Tel +49 30 89627605
office@kienzleartfoundation.de
www.kienzleartfoundation.de

Opening Hours:
Thurs–Fri: 2–7pm
Sat: 11am–4pm
And by appointment.

Berlin is like a magnet:

it draws young artists from Tel Aviv, Buenos Aires, or New York as well as foreign collectors and patrons, who can still find undiscovered spaces with provisional charm. The most recent example: the Kindl-Zentrum für zeitgenössische Kunst, in a former brewery in Neukölln, which has been opening step-by-step since the fall of 2014. A bustling and broadly branched international art scene gathers in Berlin. They meet at openings in the galleries of Berlin-Mitte, Charlottenburg, or Kreuzberg. The current focal point is the area around Potsdamer Strasse. Institutional contemporary art exhibitions can be found above all at the Hamburger Bahnhof and at the Kunst-Werke Berlin (KW), on Auguststrasse, but the Martin-Gropius-Bau also always attracts visitors with prestigious exhibitions, like Ai Weiwei und Walker Evans. C/O Berlin, a photography institution popular with Berlin's younger crowd, moved from east to west in the fall of 2014, into the former Amerika Haus, across from the Bahnhof Zoo train station. A bit further southwest of the city center you will find the Haus am Waldsee, in Zehlendorf, which offers exciting exhibitions of international artists living in Berlin. Since 1998, the Berlin Biennale has been enriching contemporary discourse with new artistic positions. But one need not wait two years; new impulses can always be found. Almost every evening, art enthusiasts can participate in intellectually stimulating events—artist talks, performances, or video screenings. And the art market? Since 2004, the Gallery Weekend, which takes place around May 1, attracts hundreds of international collectors to the city. Via VIP shuttle or bike, visitors can hit about fifty galleries. And at the start of the fall art season, in September, there's Art Berlin Contemporary (ABC). Founded in 2008, it sees itself as something quite other than a traditional art fair, such as its predecessor, Art Forum Berlin, which held its last edition in 2010. This much is clear: a regular visit to Berlin is mandatory for all art fans.

Nicole Büsing & Heiko Klaas

53   Kunstsaele Berlin
*Two exciting private collections and a gallery
together on one bel étage*

G

Collectors:
Geraldine Michalke &
Stephan Oehmen

Address:
Bülowstrasse 90
10783 Berlin
Germany
Tel +49 30 81801868
info@kunstsaele.de
www.kunstsaele.de

Opening Hours:
Wed–Sat: 11am–6pm
And by appointment.

Typical Berlin: two non-Berlin art collectors split a space with a new gallery and a hip platform for cultural events. Since the beginning of 2010 this renovated apartment hosts works from the Bergmeier and Oehmen collections. The Halle-born Geraldine Michalke, born Bergmeier, has amassed her collection over twenty-five years. The broad spectrum encompasses German Informel and young Leipzig photographers. Stephan Oehmen, an anesthetist from the Rhineland, started his collection with Dieter Krieg, a painter of the New Figuration movement. He now complements his existing collection with works by artists like Bogomir Ecker or Gert & Uwe Tobias. Bergmeier and Oehmen also show treasured finds of fellow collectors. With the enterprising concept-art gallery Aanant & Zoo and their event program as an added extra, the Kunstsaele has since long become a hip meeting place in western Berlin.

63　ME Collectors Room Berlin/
　　　Stiftung Olbricht

*A curiosity cabinet of existential themes from
the Renaissance to now*

G

The body, eros, and transitoriness: existential topics at
the center of the collection owned by Thomas Olbricht,
a physician and heir to the Wella fortune. Olbricht was
influenced by his great-uncle Karl Ströher's passion for collecting. Moreover, he loves extremities: Cindy Sherman
meets the grand-style painter Jonas Burgert; Marlene
Dumas meets Andres Serrano. Since 2010 the collection
has been on display at a Düttmann & Kleymann-designed
building on Auguststrasse in Berlin-Mitte. The ground
floor houses a café, a shop, and a lounge; the remaining
1 300 square meters are reserved for exhibition space. The
core of Olbricht's subjective *Wunderkammer* is formed by
over 200 objects, dating back to the Renaissance and Baroque periods. The ME Collectors Room quickly became
a space for dialogue with other collections and discourse
over art in general. The "ME," by the way, is an acronym
for "moving energies."

Collector:
Thomas Olbricht

Address:
Auguststrasse 68
10117 Berlin
Germany
Tel +49 30 86008510
info@me-berlin.com
www.me-berlin.com

Opening Hours:
Tues–Sun: 12–6pm

Collector:
Marc Barbey

Address:
Steinstrasse 12
10119 Berlin
Germany
Tel +49 30 84711947
info@collectionregard.com
www.collectionregard.com

Opening Hours:
Fri: 2–6pm (closed on public
holidays)
And by appointment.

64   Collection Regard
*Overlooked photography of the twentieth century
with a focus on Berlin*

It all began with a fortuitous discovery: a few years ago
French photography collector Marc Barbey found a convo-
lute of negatives by the German photographer Hein Gorny
(1904–1967). Since then he has administered the estate of
the underappreciated photojournalist and commercial
photographer. In 2011 Barbey showed the first part of the
collection, Gorny's images of war-ravaged Berlin, accompanied by art historical research. Connoisseurs of photography were impressed. Since 2005, Barbey, a software
entrepreneur and nephew of the Magnum photographer
Bruno Barbey, has been focused on growing the Collection
Regard. He is endowed with a sharp instinct for other overlooked twentieth-century talents. Stylish vintage furniture
from Scandinavia provides for a relaxed atmosphere in
his Berlin-Mitte apartment, where not only exhibitions
take place but also regular artist talks, guided tours, and
movie screenings.

G

Collectors:
Joëlle & Eric Romba

Address:
Berlin, Germany
Tel +49 30 89398917
info@rocca-stiftung.de
www.rocca-stiftung.de

Visitation permitted only
occasionally. Please inquire
by e-mail.

65   Rocca Stiftung
*A thematically structured collection of
contemporary art in a villa*

Joëlle Romba brings the best possible conditions to building her own art collection. The art historian, curator, collection consultant, and art dealer garnered experience
in a Berlin gallery and as the Berlin representative of the
auction house Sotheby's. For the past ten years she and her
husband, Eric, a lawyer, have acquired around 150 works
of contemporary art, ranging from Gregor Hildebrandt,
Thilo Heinzmann, and Wolfgang Tillmans, to Matti Braun
and Charlotte Posenenske. The thematic foci of the collection—photorealistic painting, architecture in art, and the
rethinking of art historical models—lends the collection
structure and conceptual clarity. The Rombas present their
treasures in a villa dating back to the turn of the century
in Berlin-Nikolassee. Visitors are welcome by appointment.

66   Sør Rusche Sammlung
*A traditional collection of Old Masters meets
contemporary art*

G

Thomas Rusche is a fourth-generation collector. The textile
entrepreneur's great-grandfather drove a horse and car-
riage through the Münster region buying antiques from
farmers. His grandfather collected old paintings, and his
father focused on Old Masters of the seventeenth century. He took his son to auctions and museums, and at age
fourteen Thomas Rusche acquired his first work of art. Today, the collection boasts over 2 500 works from over 500
artists, located at the family estate in the Westphalian city
of Oelde, and, at a second location, in an Art Nouveau
apartment in Berlin-Charlottenburg. The focus of the
collection is now on contemporary painting, with works
by Marlene Dumas, Daniel Richter, Matthias Weischer,
or Martin Eder, among others. Rusche bought their pictures early and before the artists were well-known—a fact
of which he remains proud.

Collector:
Thomas Rusche

Address:
Berlin, Germany
m.kuehn@kleidungskultur-soer.de
www.kleidungskultur-soer.de

Visitation permitted only
occasionally. Please inquire
by e-mail.

67   Safn
Iceland's best, in Berlin

Collector:
Pétur Arason

Address:
Levetzowstrasse 16
10555 Berlin
Germany
Tel +49 30 39839285
berlin@safn.is

Bergstaðastræti 52
101 Reykjavík
Iceland
Tel +354 891 9694
safn@safn.is

www.safn.is

Opening Hours:
Berlin
Fri–Sat: 1–5pm
And by appointment.
Reykjavík
By appointment only.

Having taken various forms in the Icelandic capital of Reykjavík since 2003, Safn (Icelandic for "collection") opened a second location—this time in Berlin's Hansaviertel—in March 2014. Both spaces show artists from the 1 200-work-strong collection of Pétur Arason and his wife, Ragna Róbertsdóttir, who also happens to be one of Iceland's most prominent artists. That collection spans Minimal and Conceptual Art heroes like Donald Judd, Lawrence Weiner, and Carl Andre. But Safn Berlin takes a less-expected tack: **G** the gallery-style ground-floor space focuses on the couple's deep knowledge of the Icelandic art scene and has undertaken an ambitious project of exposing some of country's most exciting artists, like Kristján Guðmundsson, Hreinn Friðfinnsson, and Sigurður Guðmundsson, to an international audience. It actualizes a role long held by Arason and Róbertsdóttir as prime ambassadors for the small Nordic island to the world writ large.

68   Sammlung Schürmann
Art and antagonism in a collection growing since 1972

Collectors:
Gaby & Wilhelm Schürmann

Address:
Berlin, Germany
visit@schuermann-berlin.de

Visitation permitted only
occasionally. Please inquire
by e-mail.

Gaby and Wilhelm Schürmann's collection has been part of their lives for four decades. Wilhelm Schürmann, a photographer, describes the moment of confronting a new artwork as being like "sudden enlightenment." For the collector couple, this is where the value of art truly lies: in asking us to continuously modify our own set of values. They find this kind of edginess in the works of renowned artists like Martin Kippenberger or Cady Noland, as well as in the unsettling works of Monika Baer or Michael E. Smith. Continuously expanding since 1972, the Schürmann's collection is housed in a private Berlin apartment and shown to interested parties occasionally upon request.

69   Sammlung Christian Kaspar Schwarm
*A young private collection of conceptual and
political art*

Christian Kaspar Schwarm describes his collection, not even a decade old, as a constant movement between two thematic poles or, more precisely, as an oscillation between two dimensions: "romanticism" and "hardness." The romanticism here doesn't imply the historical cultural movement but rather stands for the contemporary interpretation of emotion and desire, which characterizes, for example, the work of David Horvitz. In addition to more than one hundred works of this artist alone, this collection includes work groups by additional conceptual artists Fiona Banner, Jonathan Monk, Peter Piller, or Slavs and Tatars, selectively complemented by stronger sculptural positions, such as the ones advanced by Nina Canell or Michael E. Smith. Whenever he can, Schwarm enjoys giving tours to art lovers through his home, in Berlin-Kreuzberg.

G

Collector:
Christian Kaspar Schwarm

Address:
Berlin, Germany
collection@cks.xyz

Visitation permitted only occasionally. Please inquire by e-mail.

70   Sammlung Springmeier
*International contemporary art on an entire storey
of a Berlin building*

Giovanni Springmeier lives with his collection. Since the 1990s the doctor has been purchasing contemporary art, from Phyllida Barlow to Liam Gillick, from Michael Kunze to GCC and Uri Tzaig. When Springmeier occasionally opens his private rooms for visitors, they immediately get a sense of his enthusiasm for artistic positions and for the elaborate staging of his comprehensive collection of all media, which is summed up under the general theme *Man and His Complexities.* The holy alliance between art and life has long been passed down to his teenage children: in their rooms you'll not find standard teenager posters but rather works by Karin Sander, John Baldessari, and Jochen Lempert. A guest will walk some fifty meters from the entrance to the back bedrooms—a course peppered with international art and design objects.

Collector:
Giovanni Springmeier

Address:
Berlin, Germany
homecollection@springmeier.eu
www.springmeier.eu

Visitation permitted only occasionally. Please inquire by e-mail.

71 Sammlung Ivo Wessel
Profound and humorous German and international video and concept art

Collector:
Ivo Wessel

Address:
Berlin, Germany
email@ivo-wessel.de

Visitation permitted only occasionally. Please inquire by e-mail.

Ivo Wessel is a fixture of the Berlin art scene. He's a frequent guest at podium discussions, a favorite interview partner when the topic is private collections, and, together with Olaf Stüber, an organizer of the successful monthly film-screening series *Videoart at Midnight,* at Kino Babylon. This all makes sense, as the main focus of the software developer's collection is video art. Wessel owns work by artists of his generation, such as Bjørn Melhus, Stefan Panhans, or Tracey Moffatt, all of which lean toward the dreamily surreal. He also collects works of concept art by the likes of Karin Sander, Via Lewandowsky, or Sven Johne. For Wessel, how the work is shown is not important. His private rooms, located on a former military property, have more of a "warehouse feel than exhibit space." If you want to visit, arrange a personal tour with Ivo Wessel himself.

G

72 Wurlitzer—
Berlin-Pied-à-Terre Collection
An intimate view on emerging and established European artists

Collectors:
Gudrun & Bernd Wurlitzer

Address:
Berlin, Germany
gudrun.wurlitzer@artitious.com

Visitation permitted only occasionally. Please inquire by e-mail.

Gudrun and Bernd Wurlitzer fell into collecting somewhat by chance. While the pair has actively purchased works from artists' friends for several decades, it wasn't until a more recent move to Berlin that they began collecting in earnest. Faced with the numerous empty walls Berlin is famed for offering its transplants, Gudrun and Bernd Wurlitzer turned to those old friends and many more new acquaintances to help fill in the gaps. The collection now counts works by Alicja Kwade, Dirk Bell, Michail Pirgelis, Roe Ethridge, Jeppe Hein, Manfred Pernice, and Jonathan Meese, among others, in its ranks. But it has remained a rather private affair: architect Gudrun Wurlitzer and her art adviser husband invite art enthusiasts to the very Berlin *pied-à-terre* that spurred the collection forward in the first place on a by-appointment basis. Interested guests can also preview the space on their recently launched platform for young artists, Artitious.

73   Karin und Uwe Hollweg Stiftung
*Fluxus, Informel, and Pop live in discreet
Hanseatic ambience*

Businessman Uwe Hollweg and his wife, Karin, a painter, have been collectors since the early 1970s. They are
known in Bremen as patrons and supporters of the local
Kunsthalle. That the private collectors only sometimes
open their collection to visitors is a bit of Hanseatic understatement. But whoever does manage to nab one of the
very rare appointments will discover a fine collection in
G a historic trading house not far from the Kunsthalle. The
collection bears the strong imprint of the collector couple's eclectic tastes, with works ranging from British Pop-
Art pioneer Richard Hamilton to those by Dieter Roth
and Wols and the melancholic paintings of Bremen's local
art hero, Norbert Schwontkowski. The couple also owns
an impressive collection of artist's books. Chairs and sofas
add to the cozy ambience. "I find it very important that
our guests have the opportunity to sit down and be comfortable," says Karin Hollweg.

Collectors:
Karin & Uwe Hollweg

Address:
Altenwall 6
28195 Bremen
Germany
office@hollweg-stiftung.de

By appointment only.

74   Museum Biedermann
*International contemporary art from the Neue Wilde
to the present*

When she was eighteen years old, Margit Biedermann trad-
ed a pack of cigarettes and a watch for her first artwork. By
the end of the 1970s, she had started to collect more seri-
ously: the Neue Wilde for example, which today comprises
a large part of her collection, as well as abstract and figurative painting, prints, and sculpture from roughly 150 contemporary artists. The medical-technology businesswoman also collects works by artists who investigate the dia-
lectic between materiality and surface, most prominently
the British sculptor David Nash. The Museum Biedermann
opened in 2009 in a former movie theater in the town of
Donaueschingen. The structure was painstakingly renovated, and to it was added an elegant minimalist extension—
room enough for Biedermann to present groupings of her
collection at regular intervals.

Collector:
Margit Biedermann

Address:
Museumsweg 1
78166 Donaueschingen
Germany
Tel +49 771 8966890
info@museum-biedermann.de
www.museum-biedermann.de

Opening Hours:
Tues–Sun: 11am–5pm

In 2012, we published the first edition of this handy companion to private yet publicly accessible art collections worldwide. With the art world in constant flux, we knew from the beginning that this would become an ongoing project, with subsequent editions to follow. In the course of research and preparation for the second and third volumes, we continuously stumbled upon exciting stories, innovative projects, and other publications we wanted to share with our readers. Since including all of these findings in the Art Guide would exceed the scope of our travel-friendly pocket format, we decided to launch the BMW Art Guide Blog, **an interactive platform featuring all the additional material** we could not fit into our book, accessible by anyone, anywhere. As an additional place for thoughtfully curated content, the blog provides enough space to talk about individual collection visits, publishes personal interviews with collectors from around the world, and offers background information and insights into the topics that keep the art world buzzing. You can also find out more about the making of the Art Guide and receive further up-to-date book recommendations, hand-picked from our editors. With illustrated posts published on a regular basis, we aim for quality of content rather than quantity of posts, in order to generate material that dives deeply into the world of collecting. If you always wanted to know why a former French mining-town is moving into the art radar, why a bottle of sake once helped collector Donald M. Hess acquire a beloved art work, and what Hans Ulrich Obrist thinks about the *BMW Art Guide by Independent Collectors*, follow our link to explore: www.bmw-art-guide.com.

The Blog has been selected by the German Design Award 2015 and received a special mention in the category Excellent Communications Design—Audiovisual and Digital Media.

Independent Collectors

75   Fürstenberg Zeitgenössisch
Innovative young art infiltrates princely pomp

Collectors:
Christian & Jeannette
zu Fürstenberg

Address:
Am Karlsplatz 7
78166 Donaueschingen
Germany
Tel +49 771 229677563
info@fuerstenberg-
zeitgenoessisch.com
www.fuerstenberg-
zeitgenoessisch.com

Opening Hours:
April–November
Tues–Sat: 10am–1pm, 2–5pm
Sundays and public holidays:
10am–5pm

Expectations are high: The aristocratic couple Christian and Jeannette zu Fürstenberg are creating a collection by seeking "young, emerging artists who have distinguished themselves in recent years by new formal languages and concepts, and in so doing have influenced the international discourse." Moritz Wesseler, the well-connected director of the Kölnischer Kunstverein, advises the couple. Since 2011 contemporary art has gradually been replacing the hunting trophies, goblets, and uniforms normally seen in **G** a princely setting. Rising stars like Dirk Bell, Julian Göthe, or Kris Martin are already represented with their own artist rooms or interventions. The collection features regular thematic exhibitions of current positions.

76   Schloss Wendlinghausen
Contemporary art in the stately rooms and surrounding park of a moated castle

Collectors:
Elisabeth & Joachim von Reden

Address:
Schloss & Gut Wendlinghausen
32694 Dörentrup
Germany
Tel +49 5265 6407
ereden@hotmail.com
www.schloss-wendlinghausen.de

By appointment only.

This is the place where the legendary liar Baron von Münchhausen visited his cousin Hilmar von Münchhausen: a grand, moated castle that the Westphalian nobleman built in the Weser Renaissance style in the early seventeenth century. Since the mid-eighteenth century, the castle and estate have been owned by the von Reden family. Current owners Elizabeth and Joachim von Reden operate an organic vegetable business and are avid collectors and supporters of contemporary art. Since the early 1980s they have presented a portion of their collection and work by guest artists in the castle itself. Since 1988 they have also utilized the property's vast park and its collection of rare botanicals. Visitors are invited to linger at works like Christoph Keller's *Regenmaschine* (Rain Machine), a red living-unit by Atelier van Lieshout, or— a new acquisition—a pavilion by the artist duo Heike Mutter and Ulrich Genth.

77 Kunsthalle HGN
*With the gaze of a globetrotter: figurative painting,
sculpture, and photography in Duderstadt*

G

"I find myself in the pieces—collecting is a reflection of my development," says Hans Georg Näder, head of a medical technology company headquartered in Duderstadt, in Lower Saxony. During the many business trips he takes around the world, Näder consistently visits exhibitions and galleries—and especially likes to acquire non-European art. Twenty years ago he began building his ever-growing collection, focused on figurative painting, sculpture, and photography, and which now ranges from Neo Rauch to Dan Flavin to Sylvie Fleury. The roughly 650-square-meter Kunsthalle HGN, in Duderstadt, opened in 2011 and presents two exhibitions annually. Five staggered levels give the building the character of an open workshop. Näder also shows parts of his collection at the local Hotel zum Löwen and in the former Bötzow brewery, in Berlin.

Collector:
Hans Georg Näder

Address:
Karl-Wüstefeld-Weg
37115 Duderstadt
Germany
info@kunsthallehgn.de
www.kunsthallehgn.de

Please check the website
for most current information
on opening hours.

Collectors:
Dirk Krämer & Klaus Maas

Address:
Güntherstrasse 13–15
47051 Duisburg
Germany
Tel +49 203 93555470
mail@museum-dkm.de
www.museum-dkm.de

Opening Hours:
Sat–Sun: 12–6pm
Every first Friday of the month
from 12–6pm
And by appointment.

78   Museum DKM
An eclectic collection from antiquity to the present

Germany is becoming a nation of non-profiteers, with over 350 new foundations established each year. Dirk Krämer and Klaus Maas include their own Museum DKM under this motto. The two collectors have been involved with art for over twenty years, along the way encouraging the responsible behavior of private collectors vis-à-vis the public. They established their foundation in 1999, and ten years later they opened a private museum designed by Swiss architect Hans Rohr. Their collection covers a wide array of areas: from **G** ancient art through classical photography to contemporary art—particularly Concrete and Conceptual positions like Jan J. Schoonhoven or Ai Weiwei. Krämer and Maas also administer the estate of the German sculptor Ernst Hermanns, an important representative of Concrete Art.

Collectors:
Ulrich & Sylvia Ströher

Address:
Innenhafen Duisburg
Philosophenweg 55
47051 Duisburg
Germany
Tel +49 203 30194811
office@museum-kueppersmuehle.de
www.museum-kueppersmuehle.de

Opening Hours:
Wed: 2–6pm
Thurs–Sat: 11am–6pm
Sundays and public holidays:
11am–6pm

79   MKM Museum Küppersmühle
Masterpieces of German painting in an impressive mill in Duisburg's harbor

"Of all the major German collectors, they are the quietest," the weekly newspaper *Die Zeit* wrote about the Darmstadt-based collector couple Sylvia and Ulrich Ströher, in July 2005. What made a lot of noise, however, was the Wella heirs' purchase of the Duisburg construction magnate Hans Grothe's collection, comprised of 700 works of prominent names, such as Gerhard Richter, Georg Baselitz, and Anselm Kiefer. This collection was added to the Ströher's own 800-piece corpus, mostly featuring abstract painting of the postwar period. The Grothe purchase came with an added bonus: a 1908-erected mill and silo complex that had been converted into a museum by Herzog & de Meuron in 1999. Roughly two-thirds of the 3 600-square-meter exhibition space, spread over three floors, is reserved for the collection. The remaining area provides space for the three or four temporary exhibitions per year.

80   JaLiMa Collection
*Young contemporary art at a new collectors hotspot
in Düsseldorf*

That a good neighborhood creates productive synergy is
not only true in economics. In September 2012 Jan-Holger
Arndt and his wife, Mariam, opened their Düsseldorf exhibition space not only in the same building, but even on
the same floor as Gil Bronner's collection, Philara. This allows for joint openings. Arndt, a lawyer from Hamburg,
and his German-Persian wife, a doctor from Oldenburg,
G set out in their inaugural exhibition, *Life in the Woods—
Aspects of Escapism,* the standards of what JaLiMa hopes to
achieve in the future: exhibitions of young contemporary
art drawn from the collection, supplemented by—where
it makes sense—loans from other collectors and galleries.
What remains is the question of the collection's unusual
name, JaLiMa. It's an endearing compression of the German phrase "Jan liebt Mariam": Jan loves Mariam.

Collectors:
Jan-Holger & Mariam Arndt

Address:
Walzwerkstrasse 14
40599 Düsseldorf
Germany
info@jalimacollection.com
www.jalimacollection.com

Opening Hours:
Sat: 2–5pm
And by appointment.

81   Philara—Sammlung
zeitgenössischer Kunst
*A dynamically growing collection of young art
in all media*

Art instead of file folders: the former Leitz factory in
Düsseldorf-Reisholz retains the charming atmosphere of
historical industrial architecture. It has been the center
of Gil Bronner's activities since 2007. The busy real-estate
developer from Düsseldorf feels bound to art on several
levels: he owns a building containing seventy artist studios, the largest in the city; he organizes exhibitions four
times a year; he endows artist stipends; and he adds to his
collection, Philara, seemingly without pause. Bronner
buys works that capture him emotionally and aesthetically.
Trendy installations by Terence Koh or Björn Dahlem can
be found next to works from young Leipzig painters, such
as Tilo Baumgärtel. Since the current showroom is only
large enough to display parts of the collection, Bronner
plans to move into a former glazier's workshop by 2016,
where 1 800 square meters offer enough space for a museum, a café, and a rooftop terrace with a sculpture garden.

Collector:
Gil Bronner

Address:
Walzwerkstrasse 14
40599 Düsseldorf
Germany
info@philara.de
www.philara.de

Opening hours vary depending on
exhibition. Please check the website for most current information.

82   Julia Stoschek Collection
An ambitious young collector lasered-in on media art

Collector:
Julia Stoschek

Address:
Schanzenstrasse 54
40549 Düsseldorf
Germany
Tel +49 211 5858840
besuch@julia-stoschek-collection.net
www.julia-stoschek-collection.net

Opening Hours:
Sat–Sun: 11am–6pm
And by appointment.

For the young collector Julia Stoschek, opening a private museum in 2007 was the climax of her rapid collecting career: one day while taking a walk, the 1975-born heiress came across a historic landmark factory building. Today it holds one of the most extensive private collections of media art in Germany. After undergoing complex modifications by the Berlin-based architecture firm Kuehn Malvezzi, the reinforced-concrete building shows a smattering of videos, installations, and photographs spread across its multiple **G** floors. The 2 500 square meters represent a veritable Who's Who of the international media-art scene, with annual exhibits that include Douglas Gordon through Thomas Demand to Pipilotti Rist or Andreas Gursky. Stoschek is also devoted to up-and-coming stars, like the Frenchman Cyprien Gaillard, or the Hawaii-born Paul Pfeiffer.

83   Kunstwerk—Sammlung
Alison & Peter W. Klein
Contemporary and Aboriginal art in a remodeled factory

Collectors:
Alison & Peter W. Klein

Address:
Siemensstrasse 40
71735 Eberdingen-Nussdorf
Germany
Tel +49 7042 3769566
kunstwerk@sammlung-klein.de
www.sammlung-klein.de

Opening Hours:
Sun–Fri: 11am–5pm

They don't follow art market trends. Alison and Peter W. Klein, who live just outside Stuttgart, buy what they like: photography of the Helsinki school, paintings by Karin Kneffel, works of the American photo-artist Gregory Crewdson, but also works by younger, emerging artists. Over nearly thirty years, the Swabian and his American wife have brought together 1 500 works of contemporary painting and photography. They regularly travel to Australia, which is why contemporary Aboriginal art constitutes a second pillar of their collection. Klein sold his company, which made clutch systems, in 2007, and a year later opened this private museum, which occupies a spacious 1 000 square meters in Nussdorf—the town where Klein was once the largest employer.

84   Kunstraum Alexander Bürkle
*Monochrome painting and Minimal Art in dialogue
with younger artists*

G

Established in 2004, the Kunstraum Alexander Bürkle is located in northern Freiburg on the premises of the electronics wholesale company Alexander Bürkle. The collector, Paul Ege, the third-generation head of the company, founded in 1900, has a clear guideline: "A collection should not be a mere accumulation. I think the strength of a collection lies in its unique focus." Based on this principle, three to four internationally staffed exhibitions are shown annually in the nearly 1 000-square-meter art space, which is committed to the neutrality of the white cube. Classics of Minimalism like Fred Sandback, Donald Judd, or—in the electronics industry, almost a must—light artist Dan Flavin, meet younger artists like the Swiss painter Adrian Schiess, known for his radical monochrome art.

Collector:
Paul Ege

Address:
Robert-Bunsen-Strasse 5
79108 Freiburg
Germany
Tel +49 761 5106606
kunstraum@alexander-buerkle.de
www.kunstraum-alexander-buerkle.de

Opening Hours:
Tues–Fri: 11am–5pm
Sundays and public holidays:
11am–5pm

Collector:
Franz Armin Morat

Address:
Lörracher Strasse 31
79115 Freiburg
Germany
Tel +49 761 4765916
eva.morat@morat-institut.de
www.morat-institut.de

Opening Hours:
Sat: 11am–6pm
And by appointment.

85   Morat-Institut für Kunst & Kunstwissenschaft

An excellent print collection, African tribal art, and an extensive library

At the Morat-Institut für Kunst und Kunstwissenschaft, in Freiburg, the focus is on research. The institute organizes symposiums, publishes catalogue raisonnés, and oversees a library with around 50 000 volumes. The institute boasts the largest collection of works by the Viennese painter Carl Schuch, and earns additional points with an extensive print collection featuring work by Giorgio Morandi, Max Beckmann, and Albrecht Dürer. Treasures like a complete set of prints by Francisco de Goya, or high-quality West African sculptures are often requested on loan by other museums. The foundation resides in a 1950s light-flooded shed-roof hall. Since early 2010 the institute has tried to streamline and decelerate, focusing exclusively on its own collection rather than cultivating special exhibitions.

G

Collectors:
Andrea & Markus
von Goetz und Schwanenfliess

Address:
Hamburg, Germany
office@vgs-art.com

E-mail appointment only.

86   Sammlung Blankenburg

Contemporary art in a charming historic building in Hamburg-Winterhude

A spacious apartment with Parisian charm in the Winterhude district of Hamburg—this is where Andrea and Markus von Goetz und Schwanenfliess live with their art. On her birthday in 2006 the sociologist and young artists' patroness wished for her first work: a large-scale watercolor by Hanna Nitsch. That was the starting point for the collection Blankenburg, named after the family farm in Lower Saxony. Meanwhile, the collection, which focuses on young contemporary art and, increasingly, on representatives of the 1980s, includes roughly one hundred works, from Rinus van de Velde, Ralf Ziervogel, Werner Büttner, and Georg Baselitz to Oda Jaune. "For me, the works function like antennas with two ends," says Andrea von Goetz und Schwanenfliess. "The one end with reception to the outside world and to the unseen, and the other end to one's own world, the soul, the dark, the hidden realm of one's own self."

87   Deichtorhallen Hamburg—
      Sammlung Falckenberg
Positions of social criticism in German and
American contemporary art

G

Irony, social criticism, and the grotesque: Harald Falckenberg's art collection is essentially about resistance. Over
the past twenty years, the Hamburg-based businessman
has assembled around 2 000 works of art, mainly by German and American contemporary artists who use biting
sarcasm to hold a mirror up to society's ills. Paul McCarthy,
Andreas Slominski, Martin Kippenberger, and Paul Thek
are just some of his favorites. Since 2001 Falckenberg has
shown his collection on some 6 000 square meters of a
former rubber factory in Hamburg-Harburg, called the
Phoenix Hallen, cleverly altered by the architect Roger
Bundschuh. Unconventional temporary exhibitions and
guest appearances by other private collections makes it
one of the most important spaces for contemporary art.
Starting in 2011 the Sammlung Falckenberg has cooperat-
ed closely with the Deichtorhallen Hamburg, which is now
in charge of overall business operations.

Collector:
Harald Falckenberg

Address:
Phoenix-Hallen
Wilstorfer Strasse 71, Gate 2
21073 Hamburg
Germany
Tel +49 40 32506762
sammlungfalckenberg@
deichtorhallen.de
www.sammlung-falckenberg.de

Opening Hours:
Thurs, Fri: 6pm
Sat: 3pm
Sun: 12pm, 3pm and 5pm
Only guided tours with prior
registration.

88   Sammlung Wemhöner

Selected exhibits of an expansive collection in the
East Westphalian city of Herford

Collector:
Heiner Wemhöner

Address:
Planckstrasse 7
32052 Herford
Germany
Tel +49 5221 770210
www.sammlung-wemhoener.com

By appointment only.

"The art I encounter and surround myself with improves my quality of life. It gives me strength and inspires me," says Heiner Wemhöner. In spring of 2014 the business-man from the East Westphalian city of Herford presented around ten percent of his collection, compiled since the late 1990s, in Berlin's Osram-Höfe, the former home of one of Europe's largest lightbulb factories. This was the first time he exhibited his collection publicly—and apparent-   **G** ly he enjoyed it. Now Heiner Wemhöner or his curator, Philipp Bollmann, guide interested art lovers through his company building in Herford, where around sixty works are on display: photographs by Isaac Julien, sculptures by Stephan Balkenhol, works on paper by Richard Serra, and also works by Chinese artists, such as Zhou Tiehai or Yang Fudong. If there's time, the tour can be extended to Wemhöners private sculpture park, with works by Antony Gormley and Tony Cragg.

89   Stiftung Museum Modern Art Hünfeld— Sammlung Jürgen Blum

Circa 3 000 works of Concrete, Constructivist, and
Conceptual Art

Collector:
Jürgen Blum

Address:
Hersfelder Strasse 25
36088 Hünfeld
Germany
Tel +49 6652 72433
Tel +49 151 40470183
info@museum-modern-art.de
www.museum-modern-art.de

Opening Hours:
Tues–Sun: 3–6pm
And by appointment.

It's not an outpost of the Museum of Modern Art in New York City, but the Museum Modern Art Hünfeld is well worth the detour. Thanks to the German-Polish artist and collector Jürgen Blum, the small Hessian city near Fulda has a stellar private museum, with roughly 1 000 square meters of exhibition space, in a historic landmark building—a former gas plant. His collection brings togeth-er the East and the West, Concrete Art and conceptual thought, starkly reduced forms, and intellect. Along the way it highlights works by the Polish avant garde. Now a foundation, the collection's exhibition administration has been taken over by the city of Hünfeld. Additionally, the artist Günter Liebau was appointed an external curator to organize temporary exhibitions of contemporary art of various strains. A sculpture garden brings the presenta-tion outdoors.

90 Sammlung Würth

From the Middle Ages to the present: art at fifteen sites in Europe

"Art at Würth should not take place in an ivory tower, but in everyday life; it should be experienced close to the workplace," says company president Reinhold Würth. Since the 1960s, the owner of a wholesaler for assembly and fastening materials has amassed a comprehensive collection of art—from the Middle Ages through the modern period to the present—comprised of roughly 16 000 works. In 1991 the Museum Würth opened at the company's headquarters, in Künzelsau. Then, in 2001, the Kunsthalle Würth was opened in Schwäbisch Hall. Today, fifteen exhibition spaces inside innovative architectural structures are located at various European locations of the Würth Group, from Norway to Spain. The temporary exhibitions shown here are drawn from the collection. Works from Pablo Picasso to Gerhard Richter, from Paul Gauguin to Alex Katz—and the largest compilation of works by Christo and Jeanne-Claude in central Europe—mark the impressive range of the Würth Collection.

G

Collector:
Reinhold Würth

Address:
Würth Museum
Reinhold-Würth-Strasse 15
74653 Künzelsau-Gaisbach
Germany
Tel +49 7940 152200
museum@wuerth.com
www.kunst.wuerth.com

Opening hours vary depending on exhibition. Please check the website for most current information.

91 Sammlung Froehlich

An impressive group of works by German and American art stars

He was a blood-brother to Joseph Beuys. He was a regular at Andy Warhol's Factory. He met with Donald Judd at the artist's Texas studio. Josef Froehlich, a Stuttgart industrialist originally from Austria, does not just buy art; he also cultivates close relationships with artists. His life as a collector began with a run-in with Joseph Beuys at Documenta 7 in 1982. There, Froehlich helped him with his action *7000 Eichen*. Beuys thanked him with a work of art. A variety of important German and American artists—Gerhard Richter, Rosemarie Trockel, or Bruce Nauman—have since all found their way into the collection. Sammlung Froehlich comprises around 300 works and has been shown at the Tate Modern in London and the Museum of Modern Art in New York City. Since 2009 it has been housed in the architecturally adventurous building on the premises of Froehlich's Stuttgart firm.

Collectors:
Josef & Anna Froehlich

Address:
Kohlhammerstrasse 20
70771 Leinfelden-Echterdingen
Germany
Tel +49 711 753944
froehlich@sammlung-froehlich.de
www.sammlung-froehlich.de

By appointment only.

Art and architecture often make harmonious and attractive allies.

Many private collectors take great pains to find the appropriate architectural framework for their art. Some of them commission the careful renovation of historical buildings; others erect brand new ones. The documenta-tested Berlin-based architect-trio Kuehn Malvezzi, for example, transformed a former picture-frame factory in Düsseldorf into a multi-functional enclosure for Julia Stoschek's media-art collection. The Norwegian collector couple Venke and Rolf A. Hoff, on the other hand, discovered a former caviar factory, enveloped in ocean mist at the Lofoten, for their art, commissioning the art-aficionado Oslo architecture firm Element for its striking remodeling. Some collectors even open their private homes and apartments by appointment. For visitors, it's interesting to see how the living environment engages in a dialogue with art. Munich-based Karsten Schmitz, of Stiftung Federkiel, commissioned the artist group Famed to transform his office apartment on the premises of the Leipziger Baumwollspinnerei, with minimal intervention, into a habitable *Gesamtkunstwerk*. Art collectors frequently have a clear preference for good design: Alexander Ramselaar lives with his art collection and avant-garde furniture in a historic townhouse in Rotterdam, where well-stocked bookshelves serve as a room divider. It is ideal, of course, when collectors are able to commission their favorite architects to create new spaces for their art. This is the case with the collection of Bernard Arnault, who hired star architect Frank O. Gehry to create a spectacular building with interlaced glass-facade elements located in the middle of the Bois de Bologne, providing a new landmark for Paris. With the honeycomb-shaped building The Broad, designed by architects Diller Scofidio + Renfro, which opens in Los Angeles in 2015, the American billionaire and philanthropist Eli Broad leaves a similarly extravagant monument to posterity.

Nicole Büsing & Heiko Klaas

Collector:
Karsten Schmitz

Address:
Leipziger Baumwollspinnerei
Spinnereistrasse 7
04179 Leipzig
Germany
sammlung@federkiel.org
www.federkiel.org/sammlung

Visitation permitted only
occasionally. Please inquire
by e-mail.

92   Arbeitswohnung Federkiel
*A former working-class apartment as subtly
ironic Gesamtkunstwerk*

The Munich economist Karsten Schmitz is no stranger to
Leipzig. As an art collector and founder of the Stiftung
Federkiel—whose mission is the preservation of Leipzig's
Baumwollspinnerei as a location for galleries, studios, and
institutional exhibition—Schmitz is among the most important private sponsors of this Leipzig art center. His own
apartment, a former working-class home on the premises,
is for the collector both a place to generate ideas and an   **G**
exhibition space. But he also uses it regularly to accommodate collector friends, artists, or scholars. He invited
the Leipzig artist-group Famed to use the apartment and
its furniture as artistic material to create a permanent
intervention. The result is an ironic narrative installation
that runs through all of the rooms, providing a cheeky
visual link between them.

Collectors:
Anette & Udo Brandhorst

Address:
Kunstareal München
Theresienstrasse 35A
80333 Munich
Germany
Tel +49 89 238052286
presse@museum-brandhorst.de
www.museum-brandhorst.de

Opening Hours:
Tue–Wed: 10am–6pm
Thurs: 10am–8pm
Fri–Sun: 10am–6pm

93   Museum Brandhorst
*Art stars of the late twentieth century housed
in a dazzling new space*

The vibrant, shimmering façade of 36 000 ceramic rods
in twenty-three varying shades has a magnetic effect on
people. Nearly 350 000 visitors were attracted to the Museum Brandhorst in 2009, the year it opened. But perhaps
its success also lies on what is inside: nowhere in Europe
will you find more works by Andy Warhol—represented
by no less than one hundred pieces. Among the other
highlights are works by Gerhard Richter, Ed Ruscha, and
Cy Twombly, to name just a few. Located in the heart of
Munich's art quarter, this distinctive building—designed
by Sauerbruch Hutton—quickly became one of the most
popular exhibition spaces in all of Germany. The 700-work
collection belongs to Henkel heiress Anette Brandhorst
and her husband, Udo, who began assembling it in the
1970s. They found a comfortable home for the collection in
Munich, and the state of Bavaria covers building-mainte-
nance costs. The Brandhorsts' foundation is endowed with
120 million euros, which guarantees a deep source of funds
for purchasing new work at the highest level.

94   Sammlung Goetz
Impressive architecture for international contemporary art

Before she began concentrating on her own private collection, in 1984, Ingvild Goetz had been a gallerist for fifteen years. With around 5 000 works by over 300 artists, she now ranks among the most important private collectors of contemporary art in Germany. She started out with Arte Povera. Then came works by American artists of the 1980s and the Young British Artists of the 1990s, as well as some German stars. Names like Richard Prince, Tracey Emin, or Rosemarie Trockel are represented prominently. Since 1993 the collection has been housed in a cube constructed of frosted glass and birchwood, designed by the Swiss architects Herzog & de Meuron. In January 2014, Goetz donated 375 works of media art and her stylish private museum to the Free State of Bavaria. She nevertheless remains a passionate collector and director of the museum.

G

Collector:
Ingvild Goetz

Address:
Oberföhringer Strasse 103
81925 Munich
Germany
Tel +49 89 95939690
info@sammlung-goetz.de
www.sammlung-goetz.de

Opening Hours:
Thurs–Fri: 2–6pm
Sat: 11am–4pm
By telephone appointment only.

95   Alexander Tutsek-Stiftung
The use of glass as a material in international contemporary art

The challenging goal of the Alexander Tutsek-Stiftung, founded in 2000, is to push the fascinating material of glass out of the niche of "applied art." The internationally oriented collection and exhibition space focuses on the deployment of this fragile material in post-World War II and contemporary art. Its aim is to sensitize the broader public to "the subtle, abstract, and transcendent themes" that are suited specifically to an expression in glass. The foundation's seat, in a national landmark Art Deco mansion in Munich-Schwabing, was once the private residence and studio of the German sculptor Georg Albertshofer, and now hosts annual exhibits of glass sculptures. Since 2008 the foundation has also been supporting contemporary photography.

Collectors:
Alexander Tutsek &
Eva-Maria Fahrner-Tutsek

Address:
Karl-Theodor-Strasse 27
80803 Munich
Germany
Tel +49 89 343856
info@atstiftung.de
www.atstiftung.de

Opening Times:
Tues, Wed: 10am–2pm
Thurs, Fri: 2–6pm
Closed on public holidays.

96   The Walther Collection
Highbrow contemporary photographic art in the midst of the Swabian provinces

G

Collector:
Artur Walther

Address:
Reichenauer Strasse 21
89233 Neu-Ulm/Burlafingen
Germany
Tel +49 731 1769143
info@walthercollection.com
www.walthercollection.com

Opening Hours:
Thurs–Sun: 11am–5pm
Only guided tours with prior registration.

Additional exhibition locations:
New York, United States of America, p. 204

This is the tale of a man who went out to discover the world and returned to his hometown with a museum. Artur Walther worked as an investment banker on Wall Street. But in 1994 the then forty-five year old made a clean break and began to focus on art. More specifically, on photography. He went on African journeys with the former Documenta director Okwui Enwezor to gather his extensive collection of African photographic art. Positions from Asia and Western artists, such as August Sander or Bernd and Hilla Becher, complete the collection. After all this, Walther returned, and on his parents' property he erected a clear white cube with a 500-square-meter main gallery to display his finds. Two regional-specific houses also serve as exhibition spaces. The grand opening in Neu-Ulm was in 2010; an outpost in New York City was launched a year later.

97   Herbert-Gerisch-Stiftung
*Contemporary sculpture in the park, current art
in the villa*

The mythical land of Arcadia apparently lies in the middle of Schleswig-Holstein, in the city of Neumünster. There you'll find a dreamy sculpture park founded by Brigitte and Herbert Gerisch. There, among the property's series of intricate paths, ponds of water lilies, and fields of forget-me-not flowers, you discover contemporary sculptures by Bogomir Ecker, Olaf Nicolai, or Ian Hamilton Finlay. The foundation was established in 2001 with the mission of transforming a once overgrown park into an international sculpture garden of high repute. The founders have lived in the modern mansion on the adjacent property since the 1960s, when they bought the run-down Villa Wachholtz and renovated it back to splendor. In 2007 both the mansion and the park opened their doors to the public. Since then, temporary exhibitions by artists like Carsten Höller or Yehudit Sasportas have taken place in Villa Wachholtz and in the former swim hall of Villa Gerisch.

G

Collectors:
Brigitte & Herbert Gerisch

Address:
Brachenfelder Strasse 69
24536 Neumünster
Germany
Tel +49 4321 555120
kontakt@gerisch-stiftung.de
www.herbert-gerisch-stiftung.de

Opening Hours:
Wed–Sun: 11am–6pm
And by appointment.

98   Museum Insel Hombroich
*Two thousand years of art in harmony with nature
and the landscape*

The idyllic Museum Insel Hombroich, today operated by the city of Neuss and the state of North Rhine-Westphalia, was founded by a Düsseldorf real estate agent and arts patron. In 1982 Karl-Heinrich Müller (1936–2007) bought twenty-five hectares of wild meadow snaking alongside the river Erft. In 1994 he acquired an adjacent former NATO missile base. Today, visitors to the Museum Insel Hombroich stroll through this vast terrain, passing along the way sculptures by Per Kirkeby or Eduardo Chillida, eventually running into Erwin Heerich's modest brick pavilions. Müller assembled his collection based solely on his personal tastes, thus one also discovers African fetishes and centuries-old Chinese artifacts alongside works by Lovis Corinth, Yves Klein, or Gotthard Graubner.

Collector:
Karl-Heinrich Müller

Address:
Minkel 2
41472 Neuss
Germany
Tel +49 2182 8874000
museum@inselhombroich.de
www.inselhombroich.de

Opening Hours:
April–September
Mon–Sun: 10am–7pm
October
Mon–Sun: 10am–6pm
November–March
Mon–Sun: 10am–5pm

99   Langen Foundation
*European and Asian art presented in a fascinating
building by Tadao Ando*

G

Collectors:
Marianne & Viktor Langen

Address:
Raketenstation
Hombroich 1
41472 Neuss
Germany
Tel +49 2182 570115
info@langenfoundation.de
www.langenfoundation.de

Opening Hours:
Mon–Sun: 10am–6pm

A highlight for architecture fans: the Langen Foundation fits perfectly into the spaciousness of the former NATO missile base on the island of Hombroich. For founder Marianne Langen, who died in 2004, the minimalist building, made of exposed concrete by the Japanese architect Tadao Ando, is the most important work of art she ever acquired. Together with her husband, Viktor Langen, she began to compile a collection of modernist work at the beginning of the 1950s, now numbering roughly 300 works of art from Max Ernst and Paul Klee to Pablo Picasso. The second focus is on a collection of Japanese artworks quite unique to Europe: nearly 500 scrolls, Shoji screens, and sculptures from across eight centuries. The collectors' motto: *Art is not luxury; it is necessity.* The 1 300-square-meter exhibition space is used to show contemporary art in dialogue with the permanent collection.

G

100   Gratianusstiftung
*Plentiful space for artifacts from the Paleolithic
to the present*

A comprehensive view of the world: the Reutlingen-based collector couple Hanns-Gerhard Rösch and Gabriele Straub offer a concise overview of the world's art history in a modernized mansion from 1904. The collectors mix epochs and genres in thirteen rooms on two floors. The spectrum runs from Paleolithic tools through African tribal art, and from Columbian shamanic figures to precious East Asian artifacts and works by modernists like Henri Matisse, Giorgio Morandi, or Paul Klee. The collectors are brave enough to leave their shows up for a longer duration. The current exhibition, with works by Raimer Jochims, a Städel School professor emeritus, runs until 2015. With his abstract works on board and paper, Jochims offers a contemporary interpretation of the collection's motto: *Color as the substance of painting, of visible reality, and of sight itself.*

Collectors:
Hanns-Gerhard Rösch &
Gabriele Straub

Address:
Gratianusstrasse 11
72766 Reutlingen
Germany
Tel +49 7121 490177
info@gratianusstiftung.de
www.gratianusstiftung.de

Opening Hours:
Mon: 2–6pm
Thurs: 6–8pm (only every
first Thursday per month)
And by appointment.

101   Stiftung für konkrete Kunst
*Concrete Art by over one hundred artists
in a former factory building*

The Stiftung für konkrete Kunst, in Reutlingen, is not a place that rushes masses of people through its halls. Instead, personalized art education is the foundation's core mission. Each visitor is guided individually through the exhibition by either the collector, Manfred Wandel, or by the director, Gabriele Kübler. Theo van Doesburg's 1924 definition of Concrete Art supplies the collection's motto: *There is nothing more concrete or more real than a line, a color, or a plane.* Wandel's private collection forms the foundation's core, joined by additional bodies of work and archives. The three floors in a former cheesecloth factory are straightforwardly designed for an industrial feel. But Concrete Art is not a dogma: in special exhibitions these works are placed in relation to Bauhaus furniture or Russian icons.

Collector:
Manfred Wandel

Address:
Eberhardstrasse 14
72764 Reutlingen
Germany
Tel +49 7121 370328
skk.kuebler@t-online.de
www.stiftungkonkretekunst.de

Opening Hours:
Wed, Sat: 2–6pm
And by appointment.

102   Sammlung Siegfried Seiz
*Figurative painting from the last decade
of East Germany*

Collector:
Siegfried Seiz

Address:
Reutlingen, Germany
info@sieger-seiz.de

Visitation permitted only
occasionally. Please inquire
by e-mail.

As soon you hear the phrase "painting in East Germany,"
Socialist Realism comes to mind—and you head for the
door. But business executive Siegfried Seiz's Reutlingen-
based collection shows that there was another, non-official
kind of figurative painting in East Germany. Sixty-six primarily large-format paintings by twenty-three artists have
found a comfortable home in his 600-square-meter exhibition space, built out of a former factory. The art historian   **G**
Gisold Lammel pointed Seiz to artist studios in Berlin,
Dresden, Leipzig, and Halle, which he visited during the
last decade of the GDR. Alongside early pictures by Neo
Rauch, Seiz's collection holds unexpected works, like some
wildly expressive paintings by Klaus Killisch, or the realist
punk portraits by Clemens Gröszer.

103   Messmer Foundation/
Kunsthalle Messmer
*Concrete and Constructivist Art, plus the estate
of Swiss painter André Evard*

Collector:
Jürgen A. Messmer

Address:
Grossherzog-Leopold-Platz 1
79359 Riegel am Kaiserstuhl
Germany
Tel +49 7642 9201620
info@messmerfoundation.com
www.messmerfoundation.com

Opening Hours:
Tues–Sun: 10am–5pm

His life is defined by art and design. In 2005 Jürgen A.
Messmer, a former manufacturer of premium writing
utensils, established the Messmer Foundation in memory
of his deceased daughter, Petra. In 2009 he opened the
Kunsthalle Messmer in a former brewery in Riegel am
Kaiserstuhl. Across 900 square meters he exhibits works
from his trove of 1 000 paintings and sculptures in thematic and monographic groupings in up to three shows a
year: classics like Paul Klee and Otto Freundlich, inspiring
figures of Concrete Art like Max Bill or Victor Vasarely, as
well as numerous younger positions. Loans from other art
institutions broaden the exhibitions' scope. A central pillar
of the Messmer collection is the nearly complete estate of
the little-known Swiss painter André Evard (1876–1972),
which Messmer acquired in 1979 and has shown regularly
ever since.

104   Schauwerk Sindelfingen
A cool, remodeled factory with first-class international contemporary art

G

For him, beauty has a lot to do with purity and the harmony of form and color, says the Swabian businessman Peter Schaufler. His company, Bitzer, which makes refrigerator compressors, is among the world's market leaders. Schaufler and his wife, Christiane Schaufler-Münch, are known as reserved people. In fact, until the opening of their private museum, Schauwerk Sindelfingen, in summer 2010, only a few people had even known that they had started to build their private collection, one of the largest in Germany, as early as the late 1970s. The surprise was thus all the more: a 6 500-square-meter exhibition space where visitors can see top-quality works by artists like Donald Judd, Frank Stella, Imi Knoebel, John Armleder, or Sylvie Fleury, and an equally impressive collection of photography, which boasts works by the most important of the Becher students, as well as international giants like Nobuyoshi Araki or Vanessa Beecroft.

Collectors:
Peter Schaufler &
Christiane Schaufler-Münch

Address:
Eschenbrünnlestrasse 15/1
71065 Sindelfingen
Germany
Tel +49 7031 9324900
fuehrungen@schauwerk-sindelfingen.de
contact@schauwerk-sindelfingen.de
www.schauwerk-sindelfingen.de

Opening Hours:
Sat–Sun: 11am–5pm
Tues, Thurs: 3–4:30pm
(guided tours)

Despite the proliferation of art flippers across the globe and an ever-more monetized art market, collecting art remains a pursuit that extends beyond the purely economic realm. Buying a work of art is only the first step; patronage is the goal. Museum shows and biennials wouldn't happen without the many works that have been supported, sight unseen, owing to the lasting relationships and trust that exist between collector and artist. Varied models of patronage abound, of course. For instance, that of London supermarket heir Alex Sainsbury, who—despite his family's already-enviable collection and the wing his father donated to the National Gallery—wanted to delve deeper into contemporary art. To do so, he opened Raven Row, in 2009. Sainsbury located his exhibition space and residency program in an eighteenth-century edifice just bordering the city, near Whitechapel Gallery. It quickly became an important point of reference for Londoners because of its ongoing residency program and exhibitions of notable contemporary artists. Collectors like Patrizia Sandretto Re Rebaudengo use their deep institutional affiliations to help slingshot their chosen artists' careers. Art-world darlings David Ostrowski, Ned Vena, and Pamela Rosenkranz, whom Sandretto Re Rebaudengo began collecting in their early days, were recently placed in *Beware Wet Paint*, at London's Institute of Contemporary Art (ICA), in fall 2014. Some collectors, like Francesca von Habsburg, take a multi-level approach. Her foundation, Thyssen-Bornemisza Art Contemporary (TBA21), funds scores of artist projects for biennials and other exhibitions worldwide, as well as residencies and international trips for its artist-recipients. The exhibition space TBA21–Augarten, in Vienna, is also used for consistently first-class shows of supported artists. It even housed Ragnar Kjartansson and friends, for a month-long performance of *The Palace of the Summerland*, in 2014. Regardless of the methods they use, patrons like these are indispensible when it comes to helping make the art world spin.

Alexander Forbes

105 Sammlung Schroth/
Stiftung konzeptuelle Kunst
Concrete and Minimalist Art in a former school

Collector:
Carl-Jürgen Schroth

Address:
Filzenstrasse 6
59494 Soest
Germany
Tel +49 2921 14177
info@sammlungschroth.org
www.sammlungschroth.org

Opening hours vary depending on exhibltion. Please check the web-site for most current information.

Carl-Jürgen Schroth discovered his interest in Constructivism in art class. But first he got a degree in mechanical engineering and then focused on expanding the family business, in the city of Arnsberg, in Sauerland. Schroth devoted his entire professional career to the development of better safety belts, but in his free time he was drawn ever closer to art. He began building a collection in the 1980s, with a focus on Concrete Art and Post-Minimalism, in- **G** cluding artists that were interested in scientific and mathematical investigations like light, space, and perception: Daniel Buren, François Morellet, or Victor Vasarely, in addition to younger positions. Periodically throughout the year Schroth opens the collection to the public in his private home—a former school building erected around 1900, in the city of Soest, in North Rhine-Westphalia. In spring 2016, the collection will move into the extension of the Kunstmuseum Wilhelm-Morgner-Haus.

Collector:
Grässlin Family

Address:
Museumstrasse 2
78112 St. Georgen
Germany
Tel +49 7724 9161805
info@sammlung-graesslin.eu
www.sammlung-graesslin.eu

By appointment only.

106 Sammlung Grässlin—
Kunstraum Grässlin & Räume für Kunst
*An extraordinary collection with
a Black Forest backdrop*

Ever since the Grässlin family established the Räume für Kunst, in 1995, the city of St. Georgen has become obsessed with art. Every weekend the art-going crowd streaks through the vacant shops and factory floors elected to temporarily house artworks by figures like Albert Oehlen, Reinhard Mucha, Isa Genzken, or Cosima von Bonin. A tour of the impressive collection starts at the Kunstraum Grässlin, opened in 2006, and leads through the long-faded economic miracle of the 1960s, which is when the previous Grässlin generation began collecting Art Informel. Since the 1980s, their children have been adding contemporary works to the collection. Artist Martin Kippenberger also knew that St. Georgen breathed art, ever since he began coming to the Black Forest to recuperate from his excesses. Today, the Grässlins are among the largest holders of Kippenberger's works.

G

107 DasMaximum—KunstGegenwart
An attractive permanent exhibition of eight German and American artists

"It was always important for me to be in a dialogue with artists," says Heiner Friedrich. The former gallerist, collector, patron, and international art networker, who has lived in New York City since 1971, is co-responsible for such important projects as the Dia Art Foundation and Walter de Maria's Land-Art icon *The Lightning Field.* With his private museum in Traunreut, in southern Bavaria, Friedrich brings top artists to the city of his youth. Across more than 4 000 square meters you'll find works by Andy Warhol, Georg Baselitz, John Chamberlain, Dan Flavin, Imi Knoebel, Walter de Maria, and the nearly forgotten painter Uwe Lausen. An entire hall is dedicated to the early work of light artist Dan Flavin. Typical for the pioneering Friedrich: the collection is permanently on display, but opening hours change according to the shifting seasonal light.

Collector:
Heiner Friedrich

Address:
Fridtjof-Nansen-Strasse 16
83301 Traunreut
Germany
Tel +49 8669 1203713
mail@dasmaximum.com
www.dasmaximum.com

Opening Hours:
April-October
Sat–Sun: 12–6pm
November-March
Sat–Sun: 11am–4pm
Closed in December.

108   Sammlung Gunter Halke
Contemporary art in a cool, modernist house
at Lake Constance

Collector:
Gunter Halke

Address:
Überlingen, Germany
halke@web.de

E-mail appointment only.

If they are convinced of an artist, they immediately buy entire work groups. For example, photo-series by Tobias Zielony or Elad Lassry. The Überlingen-based orthodontist Gunter Halke and his wife passionately collect young art. And it may well raise political or social issues. A large showcase work of Josephine Meckseper is placed right in the entrance hall of their light-flooded house. "The criteria are a mixture of spontaneity, enthusiasm, and a certain **G** training of the eye," they say. "We try to be stubborn and deaf and often find without searching. We are eager to see whether the collection still looks fresh and justifiable twenty years from now." If you want to get to know the collection, you'll receive an extensive tour of its various rooms, running across works by André Butzer, Andy Hope 1930, or Günther Förg, among others.

109   Sammlung FER Collection
Minimal and Conceptual Art since the 1960s
as an intellectual challenge

Collectors:
Friedrich E. Rentschler &
Maria Schlumberger-Rentschler

Address:
Magirus-Deutz-Strasse 16–18
89077 Ulm
Germany
Tel +49 731 3885478
maria.schlumberger@fer-collection.de
www.fer-collection.de

Only guided tours with prior
online registration.

Friedrich E. Rentschler collects art that inspires thought, whether it's American Minimalism by Carl Andre or Sol LeWitt, Conceptual work by Robert Barry, or Italian Arte Povera by Giulio Paolini. Younger artists like Sylvie Fleury or Mathieu Mercier also find their way into the collection of this pharmaceutical entrepreneur—which has been growing constantly since 1960. This Ulm-based collection could be characterized by its discerning selectivity and its collector's subsequent courage for early purchase. Since 2009 Rentschler has shown his treasures at the award-winning Ulmer Stadtregal, a former factory building turned into lofts, workshops, and cultural institutions in the western part of the city. With a little luck, you can catch a tour by Rentschler himself, who will explain why he doesn't just collect with his eye but also with his brain.

110 Kunsthalle Weishaupt
Geometric American and European art since the 1960s

G

Siegfried Weishaupt likes to point out that he collects by instinct. His father, Max, had good contacts in the Ulm School of Design. Like his father, Siegfried was inspired by director Max Bill and interested in the connections between aesthetics and mathematics. In his early acquisitions, in the mid 1960s, the young engineer focused on Concrete and Geometric Art by professors at the Ulm School, such as Josef Albers. Later, travels to the US opened his eyes to Color Field Painting, like the works by Mark Rothko. Under the guidance of his daughter, the art historian Kathrin Weishaupt-Theopold, the Kunsthalle Weishaupt has acquired some more contemporary positions, like Markus Oehlen, Robert Longo, or Liam Gillick. Works from the collection are regularly shown in a transparent glass building in the center of Ulm.

Collectors:
Siegfried & Jutta Weishaupt

Address:
Hans-und-Sophie-Scholl-Platz 1
89073 Ulm
Germany
Tel +49 731 1614360
info@kunsthalle-weishaupt.de
www.kunsthalle-weishaupt.de

Opening Hours:
Tue–Wed: 11am–5pm
Thurs: 11am–8pm
Fri–Sun: 11am–5pm

111 Museum Ritter—
Sammlung Marli Hoppe-Ritter
Square-centered geometric abstraction from the twentieth and twenty-first century

Almost everyone knows the infamous square-shaped Ritter Sport chocolate bar. Marli Hoppe-Ritter, the grandchild of the company's founder, took this basic form as the starting point for her art collection. Kazimir Malevich defined the square in 1915 as "the first step of pure creation in art"; a small drawing by the Russian Constructivist forms the basis of the collection. Geometric-constructive works from Joseph Albers, Johannes Itten, and the Zurich Concrete artists to the Zero Group form the collection's inner core. Add to this a few younger artists like Gerold Miller or Paola Pivi, and the consistent 900-work collection progresses further into the present. Swiss architect Max Dudler constructed a modernistic limestone cube on the chocolate company's Waldenbuch property. Since its inauguration, in 2005, the Museum Ritter has staged three to four exhibitions annually, derived from the collection.

Collector:
Marli Hoppe-Ritter

Address:
Alfred-Ritter-Strasse 27
71111 Waldenbuch
Germany
Tel +49 7157 535110
besucherservice@museum-ritter.de
www.museum-ritter.de

Opening Hours:
Tues–Sun: 11am–6pm
And by appointment.

113

112

Great Britain

114–117

G

112 Chatsworth
*A ducal collection facilitates art historical dialogue
from antiquity to the present*

Collectors:
Duke & Duchess of Devonshire

Address:
Bakewell
Derbyshire DE45 1PP
Great Britain
Tel +44 1246 565300
www.chatsworth.org

Opening Hours:
March–December
Mon–Sun: 11am–5:30pm

The breathtaking landscape of the Peak District in Derbyshire and the palatial manor house may be the biggest attractions for visitors to the country estate of Chatsworth. Between ancient sculptures, valuable furniture pieces and aristocratic portraits of centuries past, the twenty-first century has also entered the collection. The 12th Duke of Devonshire, Peregrine Cavendish, passionately continues his family's 500-year-old collecting tradition, which over the generations has compiled one of the most important art collections in Europe. The Duke and his wife have carefully added works of contemporary art, design, and ceramics, by artists such as Allen Jones, Edmund de Waal, and Nicola Hicks. A small suite of rooms is entirely devoted to the contemporaries, and in the spacious garden, between the decorative hedges, one can find sculptures by Richard Long, Elisabeth Frink, and William Turnbull.

113   Jupiter Artland
*A sculpture garden where art is anything
but parked and forgotten*

In 1999 Robert and Nicky Wilson bought the historic Bonnington House and its surrounding property. Since then, monstrous exotic flowers have begun to bloom, courtesy of *Love Bomb,* by Marc Quinn. And Charles Jenck's *Life Mounds* have transformed part of the grounds into wavy terraces. Such alterations have come about because the couple has engaged internationally acclaimed sculptors and installation artists—Anish Kapoor, Jim Lambie, or Antony Gormley—to build works specifically for their garden. The works fit seamlessly into the landscape; some, like Andy Goldsworthy's *Stone House,* spur an art double take. Jupiter Artland is closed during the winter. The lively dialogue the collectors demand of their art garden cannot flourish when the garden is barren of natural life.

Collectors:
Robert & Nicky Wilson

Address:
Bonnington House Steadings
Wilkieston
Edinburgh EH27 8BB
Great Britain
Tel +44 1506 889900
enquiries@jupiterartland.org
www.jupiterartland.org

Opening Hours:
May 15–September 28
Thurs–Fri: 10am–5pm
And by appointment.
Online registration required.

114 Dairy Art Centre
Art across nearly 4 000 square meters, in an industrial building, in the heart of London

Collectors:
Frank Cohen & Nicolai Frahm

Address:
7a Wakefield Street
Bloomsbury
London WC1N 1PG
Great Britain
Tel +44 20 7713 8900
contact@dairyartcentre.org.uk
www.dairyartcentre.org.uk

Opening Hours:
Wed–Fri: 10am–5pm
Sat: 11am–5pm
Sundays and public holidays:
11am–5pm

In a backyard between the old townhouses of Bloomsbury, contemporary art has made its home in an old industrial milk-depot. The young Dairy Art Centre is the project of two art connoisseurs who met over ten years ago at a dinner: Nicolai Frahm, a Danish art collector, and Frank Cohen, one of the most active English collectors. The latter had been showing his collection under the name Initial Access, in the Midlands city of Wolverhampton. After **G** several years of hunting for suitable premises in London, the opening of the joint-venture exhibition space was finally celebrated in April 2013, with a John Armleder show, followed by thematic group shows and stellar solo exhibitions by the likes of Julian Schnabel and Yoshitomo Nara. Artworks from the two owners' collections form the basis of the exhibitions, complemented by loans and commissions.

115 David Roberts Art Foundation
A foundation with a focus on the avant garde from all media

Collector:
David Roberts

Address:
Symes Mews
London NW17JE
Great Britain
Tel + 44 20 73833004
info@davidrobertsartfoundation.com
www.davidrobertsartfoundation.com

Opening Hours:
Thurs–Sat: 12–6pm
Tues–Wed: by appointment

In 2012 the David Roberts Art Foundation (DRAF) was pulled from the posh West End of London to a former furniture factory in vibrant Camden Town. The Scottish collector acquires art from British and international contemporaries, including photography by Ed Ruscha, paintings by Miriam Cahn, Gerhard Richter, Anselm Kiefer, and Louise Bourgeois, alongside important works by Martin Creed, Thomas Houseago, and Martin Kippenberger. While the collection and its throng of important names occupy part of the premises, the remaining area is charged with a different task: housing current artists' projects. Whether artistic interventions, movie nights, or panel discussions, all is welcome, as long as the platform hosts exciting forays into contemporary art.

116   Saatchi Gallery
Whether as collector or gallerist, he puts
Young British Artists first

Charles Saatchi is known as a man who makes artists. Born in Iraq, he's been collecting for over forty years. The Young British Artists thank him for assisting their stratospheric rise in the 1990s. The founder of the Saatchi & Saatchi advertising agency has a second passion as a gallerist. In the beginning, he was interested in artists like Andy Warhol or Donald Judd, whose work has been in Saatchi's private

G London museum since 1985. A few years later he acquired a cornucopia of works by Damien Hirst, Tracey Emin, or Jake & Dinos Chapman, making the graduates of Goldsmiths College a flourishing brand name. His collection, which since 2008 has been housed in a classically restored building by the architecture firm Alford Hall Monaghan Morris, counts among the world's largest. This remains true, even though he gave part of it to the British government, and over 140 works were destroyed in a 2004 fire.

Collector:
Charles Saatchi

Address:
Duke of York's HQ
King's Road
London SW3 4RY
Great Britain
www.saatchi-gallery.co.uk

Opening Hours:
Mon–Sun: 10am–6pm

117   Zabludowicz Collection, London
A collection in the unconventional ambiance of a church

After studying art, Anita Zabludowicz began, in 1994, to amass a private collection, placing young, international, untested positions at the center. Her husband, Poju Zabludowicz, the Finnish financier, preferred to collect more established names. Given this combination, one finds in the couple's 2 000-work collection of videos, photographs, drawings, and installations stars like Vanessa Beecroft or the Swiss duo Fischli/Weiss—as well as artists like Tom Burr or Ryan Gander, whose complex subject matters are less prevalent. The main exhibition space in London is located in a nineteenth-century Methodist church, where—in addition to the location in New York—large parts of the collections have been shown since 2007. The third site, on the Finnish island Sarvisalo, is reserved exclusively for artist residencies, but once a year visitors can admire works by leading artists created in situ.

Collectors:
Anita & Poju Zabludowicz

Address:
176 Prince of Wales Road
London NW5 3PT
Great Britain
info@zabludowiczcollection.com
www.zabludowiczcollection.com/
london

Opening Hours:
Thurs–Sun: 12–6pm
And by appointment.

Additional exhibition locations:
New York, United States
of America, p. 207

The exclusive center, the elegant West, the hip East, or the up-and-coming South: in **London,** contemporary art has developed its own urban coordinates, according to which you can plan your art escapades. In the West, long distances must be traversed between institutions, such as the Serpentine Galleries, in Hyde Park, the Saatchi Gallery, and the Institute of Contemporary Arts (ICA). But in Mayfair and St James's—within the vicinity of the Royal Academy of Arts (RA)—the most prominent auction houses and galleries, such as Pace, Hauser & Wirth, David Zwirner, and Sprüth Magers, are huddled between designer boutiques and grand hotels that offer high tea. Super-dealer Larry Gagosian established an impressive exhibition hall near King's Cross station, in addition to his gallery in Mayfair, while north of Oxford Street, around Eastcastle Street, you can find another hotspot for contemporaries: the Fitzrovia district, which is now home to more than twenty-five galleries, including Alison Jacques and Carroll/Fletcher. The East End of London is not solely a hipster and media hub: from the Old Street Roundabout, near where Victoria Miro and Modern Art are located, galleries like Maureen Paley and scores of artists' studios spread from Shoreditch to Hackney Wick. Any visit to the East should include the Whitechapel Gallery, with its cutting-edge exhibitions. In the Southeast, with the exception of White Cube Gallery, on Bermondsey Street, close to the iconic Tate Modern, there are few commercial galleries. There are, however, the art schools Camberwell College of Arts and Goldsmiths, which feature graduate shows each summer. In between these is the non-commercial South London Gallery. Following a visit there you can round off a fine summer evening at Frank's Bar, surrounded by art students, on the roof of a parking garage in Peckham, overlooking the annual sculpture exhibition *Bold Tendencies*—and the London skyline.

Anne Reimers

Collector:
Dakis Joannou

Address:
Filellinon 11, Nea Ionia
14234 Athens
Greece
Tel +30 210 2758490
info@deste.gr
www.deste.gr

Open only during exhibitions.
Please check the website for
most current information.

118   Deste Foundation for Contemporary Art
*A renowned collection with a flair for color
and provocation*

While walking through New York's East Village in the
1980s, Greek Cypriot industrialist Dakis Joannou passed
by the International With Monument Gallery, saw Jeff
Koons's *One Ball Total Equilibrium Tank,* and bought it. This,
anyway, is the legendary tale of how Joannou began his collection of contemporary art, today acknowledged as one of
the most important in the world and shown in museums
like the Palais de Tokyo, in Paris, and the New Museum, in
New York. Joannou's Deste Foundation, established in 1983,
aims to be a "container" for culture, an idea suggested by
the design of the foundation's main entrance: a giant wood-
en crate similar to those used to transport works of art.
Since 1999 the foundation has been supporting young artists through the bi-annual 10 000 euros Deste prize, whose
recipients include Anastasia Douka and Eirene Efstathiou.

119   The George Economou Collection
German art in Greece

Greek ship-owner George Economou has a penchant for German art. His collection, which has been expanding rapidly since the late 1990s (the *Economist* says at a rate of roughly a new picture every two days), offers in-depth insights into modern art in Germany, with a focus on art movements like Expressionism or Neue Sachlichkeit (New Objectivity). But the coverage does not end with modernism; it also includes artists ranging from Anselm Kiefer and Georg Baselitz, to Neo Rauch and Andreas Gursky. "All my purchases of contemporary art have a strong historic element," says Economou. Alongside his interest in artists like Ellsworth Kelly, Cady Noland, or Jenny Saville, is concept art of the postwar period. Since 2011, two to three exhibitions have been organized annually in his exhibition space in Athens.

Collector:
George Economou

Address:
Kifissias Ave. 80, Marousi
15125 Athens
Greece
Tel +30 210 8090519
info@economoucollection.com
www.thegeorgeeconomoucollection.com

Opening Hours:
Mon–Fri: 10am–6pm

G

120   Frissiras Museum
3 500 contemporary figurative paintings

"In our age, art has a right to pure madness. Assuming a defensive position against the prevailing artistic atmosphere, I made my personal aesthetic choices and embraced contemporary painting with an anthropocentric slant." With his bold statement, Greek lawyer and passionate collector Vlassis Frissiras explains how he became the proud owner of over 3 500 contemporary paintings of the human figure. "Anything else leaves me indifferent," he told the *Athens News,* where he also stated that he has some form of erotic relationship to all his paintings, adding: "I decided right away that I wanted the paintings to be anthropocentric. That's my character—it is monomaniacal and very focused." The Frissiras Museum includes, of course, a number of Greek artists, such as Yannis Moralis and Diamantis Diamantopoulos, as well as Europeans like David Hockney and Frank Auerbach.

Collector:
Vlassis Frissiras

Address:
Monis Asteriou 3 & 7, Plaka
10558 Athens
Greece
Tel +30 210 3234678
info@frissirasmuseum.com
www.frissirasmuseum.com

Opening Hours:
Wed–Fri: 10am–5pm
Sat–Sun: 11am–5pm

121   Herakleidon—Experience in Visual Arts
The perfect place for mathematicians with an eye for art

Collectors:
Paul & Anna-Belinda Firos

Address:
Herakleidon 16, Thissio
11851 Athens
Greece
Tel +30 210 3461981
info@herakleidon-art.gr
www.herakleidon-art.gr

Please check the website
for most current information
on opening hours.

Few visual motifs have found the commercial success of
Dutch graphic artist M. C. Escher's interlocking patterns of
nature and geometry, mathematics and architecture. The
consequence of Escher's ubiquity is that almost anyone, no
matter how unversed in art, can recognize his work when
they see it. Lesser known, however, is exactly where to do
so. That one of the largest collections of Escher's work is
located in Athens, Greece, in a neoclassical building next
to the Acropolis, may come as a surprise. Yet Paul and   **G**
Anna-Belinda Firos's collection, aside from the impressive
gathering of Escher prints, shows a general predilection
for mathematical and geometrical patterns: Op Art pioneer Victor Vasarely and American engraver Carol Wax
are both extensively represented. The institution also organizes exhibitions of earlier moderns like Edgar Degas,
Edvard Munch, and Henri de Toulouse-Lautrec.

122   Portalakis Collection
International art in the heart of the business district

Collector:
Zacharias Portalakis

Address:
Pesmazoglou 8, 8th Floor
10559 Athens
Greece
Tel +30 210 3318933
info@portalakiscollection.gr
www.portalakiscollection.gr

Opening Hours:
Wed: 12–8pm
Sat: 11am–3pm
And by appointment.

The typical art lover might not go to the business district
to look for art, but, then again, the eighth floor of Zacharias Portalakis's brokerage company, located directly
across from the former location of the Athens Exchange,
is not your typical location. A self-made broker, Portalakis
once told the *National Herald,* "All of the money I made
is now colors." He started buying Greek artists at the end
of the 1980s and then moved on to expatriated Greeks,
such as Jannis Kounellis and Theodoros Stamos, the latter
of whom he is the world's foremost collector. It was not
always so: when Portalakis first met Stamos, the baffled
collector says he did not understand the work. Instead, he
let his eight-year-old daughter choose a painting for her
father's burgeoning collection, which today counts such
international stars as Lucio Fontana, Christopher Wool,
and Richard Prince among its highlights.

123   Vorres Museum
*3 000 years of Greek history
and postwar Greek art*

G

In the small town of Paiania, just east of Athens, the Vorres Museum strives to preserve Greek national heritage by covering 3 000 years of the nation's history. The nearly 6 000 works in the collection are divided into two sections: an impressive folk art collection, exhibited in four reconstructed village houses, and a museum of contemporary Greek art, featuring paintings and sculptures by Greek artists from the second half of the twentieth century, including Lucas Samaras and Vlassis Caniaris. The sheer diversity of the collection reflects the personality of its owner, Ian Vorres, a Greek expatriate who lives in Canada and whose notable past endeavors include art critic, liaison between Canada and Greece, biographer of Russian grand duchess Olga Alexandrovna, and even mayor of Paiania.

Collector:
Ian Vorres

Address:
Diadochou Konstantinou 1
19002 Paiania
Greece
Tel +30 210 6642520
mvorres@otenet.gr
www.vorresmuseum.gr

Opening Hours:
Sat–Sun: 10am–2pm
And by appointment.

124

Hungary

H

124 Vass Collection
*Hungarian and international abstraction,
Constructivist and Concrete Art*

Collector:
László Vass

Address:
Vár Utca 3–7
8200 Veszprém
Hungary
Tel +36 88 561310
info@vasscollection.hu
www.vasscollection.hu

Opening Hours:
May–October
Mo–Sat: 10am–6pm
November–April
Mo–Sat: 10am–5pm

In keeping with the Budapest cordwainer tradition, the name László Vass is known as a hallmark of quality and elegance in men's handmade leather shoes. Less well known—but no less refined—is the Vass art collection, preserved in the castle district of Veszprém, a small town of history and lore located 100 kilometers from Budapest. Incidentally, Veszprém is also known as "the city of queens": for centuries, Hungary's female royals were crowned by the local bishop. Vass began collecting contemporary Hungarian art in the 1970s and, influenced by an encounter with artist Jenö Barcsay, initially focused on native Constructivist Art and abstraction. He then turned to the same positions on an international level, assembling a collection of roughly 600 works by artists like Max Bill, Josef Albers, Manfred Mohr, Sean Scully, and Günther Uecker.

Iceland

125

125 Hafnarborg—The Hafnarfjordur
Centre of Culture and Fine Art
*Icelandic art of the twentieth century, plus plentiful
special exhibitions*

No matter if it's in Berlin, New York, or Venice, Icelandic art has great appeal. And whoever wishes to trace Icelandic art to the homeland of elves and mountain trolls should begin in the Hafnarborg–The Hafnarfjordur Centre of Culture and Fine Art. In 1983 the pharmacist couple Sverrir Magnússon and Ingibjörg Sigurjónsdóttir donated their extensive collection of Icelandic modern art, and their private home, to the small town near to Reykjavík. An extensive cultural center was developed around the building and opened in 1988. Almost every month there is a new special exhibition that focuses mainly on Icelandic art. Today the ever-expanding collection includes 1 400 works. Icelandic artists living outside their home country, such as Ragnar Kjartansson, Egill Saebjörnsson, or Olafur Eliasson, have all had exhibitions there. Eliasson has the home-game advantage: he grew up in Hafnarfjörður.

Collectors:
Sverrir Magnússon &
Ingibjörg Sigurjónsdóttir

Address:
Strandgata 34
220 Hafnarfjörður
Iceland
Tel +354 585 5790
hafnarborg@hafnarfjordur.is
en.hafnarborg.is

Opening Hours:
Wed: 12–5pm
Thurs: 12pm–9pm
Fri–Mon: 12–5pm

126; 127

India

I

126   Devi Art Foundation
*The spectrum of Indian contemporary art
in one family collection*

Collectors:
Lekha & Anupam Poddar

Address:
Sirpur House, Plot 39
Sector 44, Gurgaon
India
Tel +91 124 4888177
info@deviartfoundation.org
www.deviartfoundation.org

Opening Hours:
Tues–Sun: 11am–7pm

Businesswomen Lekha Poddar began collecting art in the 1970s, concentrating on work that highlighted domestic Indian art. Her son Anupam Poddar has since broadened the scope of the family collection by harnessing work from the Asian subcontinent: Pakistan, Bangladesh, and Sri Lanka, as well as from Afghanistan, Tibet, and the Middle East. His main interest is in experimental artists of his own generation whose genre-bending artworks mirror the vision of India. Examples range from Sudarshan Shetty through Subodh Gupta or Jagannath Panda, all the way to Sakshi Gupta. Also represented are the Iranian Golnaz Fathi and Kuwaiti Hamra Abbas. The Devi Art Foundation, in Gurgaon, near New Delhi, displays a large part of its collection in the family's company building, completed in 2008.

127   The Kiran Nadar Museum of Art
150 years of Indian art

One of the first private museums in India was opened in New Delhi in 2010. Kiran Nadar not only aims to make her twenty-year-old collection publicly accessible, but to increase the quality of India's museum culture while doing so. A large part of Nadar's program is dedicated to education for schoolchildren and university students. Ninety percent of the roughly 450 artworks are from India, while the remainder comes primarily from Pakistanis and from Indian artists who live abroad. In the museum's 1 600 square meters, visitors find key works by well-known Indian modernists, such as Raja Ravi Varma or Maqbul Fida Husain, the "Picasso of India." Alongside these are works by a pioneering group of Bombay artists who worked together in the 1940s, as well as art by contemporaries like Anish Kapoor, Bharti Kher, or Raqib Shaw.

Collector:
Kiran Nadar

Address:
145, DLF South Court Mall, Saket
New Delhi 110017
India
roobina.karode@hcl.in
www.knma.in

Please check the website
for most current information
on opening hours.

128

128   OHD Museum of Modern &
Contemporary Indonesian Art
A private collection with museum-level Indonesian art

Collector:
Oei Hong Djien

Address:
Jl. Jenggolo 14
Magelang 56122
Central Java
Indonesia
Tel +62 293 362444
info@ohdmuseum.com
www.ohdmuseum.com

Opening Hours:
Wed–Mon: 10am–5pm

Quite an accomplishment: since the 1980s former physician Oei Hong Djien has assembled roughly 3 000 works of Indonesian art. The result is a stellar overview of abstract and figurative painting, print, sculpture, photography, installation, and video art. The collection spans from the European-educated Prince Raden Saleh (1811–1880) to pioneer artists of the twentieth century, such as Affandi, S. Sudjojono, Hendra Gunawan, Widayat, and Soedibio. Notable are European artists like Rudolf Bonnet or Walter Spies, both of who played important roles in Balinese modern art. Roughly half of the collection is comprised of contemporary artists, among them Entang Wiharso, Heri Dono, Nasirun, Nyoman Masriadi, and Rudi Mantofani. For some of them, the culture of the Wayang, or "shadow play," has been an important factor in their works. The collection is housed in three beautiful two-storey buildings in the city of Magelang.

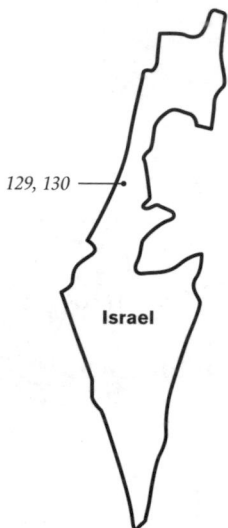

129, 130 —

Israel

129   Igal Ahouvi Art Collection
*International and Israeli contemporary art
in an university context*

With around 1 600 works, the international investor Igal
Ahouvi owns one of the largest private art collections in
Israel. It includes some 750 pieces of art by international
artists, from Andy Warhol and Christopher Williams to
Marlene Dumas. The second focus of the collection is on
Israeli contemporary art, with 850 works by artists such
as Sigalit Landau or Elad Lassry. Beginning in early 2014,
Ahouvi began showing his collection at the Genia Schreiber University Art Gallery, in a planned series of twelve
thematic exhibitions over a period of four years. This offers
an ideal opportunity for both students and the broader
public to engage in a substantive, critical encounter with
major works of contemporary art. The academic character
of the exhibition rooms creates a dispassionate context for
reflection and analysis.

Collector:
Igal Ahouvi

Address:
The Genia Schreiber University
Art Gallery
Entin Square, Tel Aviv University
54 Haim Levanon Street
Tel Aviv 69978
Israel
Tel +972 3 6408860
igalahouviartcollection@gmail.com

Opening Hours:
Sun–Wed: 11am–7pm
Thurs: 11am–9pm
Fri: 10am–2pm

Tel Aviv is an acclaimed place not only for art fans, but also

for architecture enthusiasts: roughly 4 000 buildings are built in the Bauhaus or International Style. An audio tour of the White City and a visit to the Bauhaus Center Tel Aviv should also be on everyone's agenda. The Tel Aviv Art Museum (TAM), founded in 1932, houses art of all periods, from the Old Masters to contemporary, in its historic building, built in the 1970s, and in the geometric modulated Herta and Paul Amir Building, which opened in 2011. Also part of the TAM but run virtually independently is the Helena Rubinstein Pavilion, which specializes in innovative exhibition formats of contemporary Israeli and international art. The Herzliya Museum of Contemporary Art focuses on art with a social and political dimension, often by Arab and Palestinian artists. Established in 1998 as a nonprofit space, the Center for Contemporary Art (CCA), with its three exhibition spaces and an auditorium, is a home for all those interested in video art, experimental film, and performance. The Sommer Contemporary Art gallery, opened in 1999 and located in a 1920s building at the top of Rothschild Boulevard, shows internationally renowned Israeli artists like Yael Bartana and Yehudit Sasportas. Other members of Sommer's program like Tom Burr and Thomas Zipp make the gallery an equally important showcase for international artists as well. This is much the same at Dvir Gallery, in the hipster neighborhood Florentin, whose program includes Claire Fontaine and Douglas Gordon as well as Israeli artists like Omer Fast and Ariel Schlesinger. The Chelouche Gallery for Contemporary Art, which moved into the west wing of Tel Aviv's famously historic Twin House in 2010, shows Michelangelo Pistoletto and William Kentridge, among other greats. The final amazing thing about Tel Aviv: from nearly every nook of the city the sea is just a few blocks away.

Nicole Büsing & Heiko Klaas

130   SIP Shpilman Institute for Photography
Highlights from the history of photography from the Bauhaus to Israeli avant garde

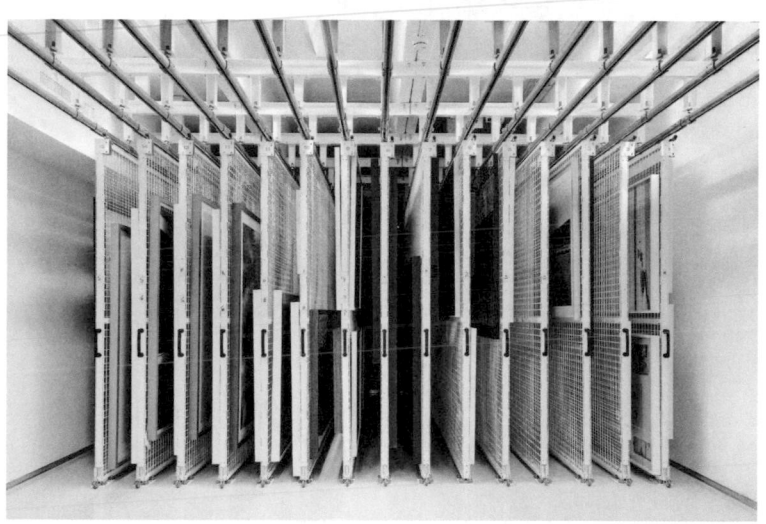

Collector:
Shalom Shpilman

Address:
27 Shoken Street, 3rd Floor
Tel Aviv 66532
Israel
Tel +972 3 7283737
info@thesip.org
www.thesip.org

Opening Hours:
Thurs: 4–8pm
Fri–Sat: 10am–2pm

A radical step: at the age of sixty the Israeli entrepreneur Shalom Shpilman sold his company to devote, during the second part of his life, his "intellectual and financial resources one hundred percent to photography." Established in 2010, the SIP Shpilman Institute for Photography, sprawled across 700 square meters, presents an ever-growing collection that captures the medium in all its diversity: from the Bauhaus to Man Ray and Hans Bellmer, all the way to Thomas Ruff, Hiroshi Sugimoto, and young Israeli photographers like the rising star Assaf Shaham. Of the works, sixty-five percent are by international artists, and the remaining thirty-five percent are from Israel. Regularly scheduled artist talks, lectures, and discussions make SIP an important address for photo fans from Israel and abroad.

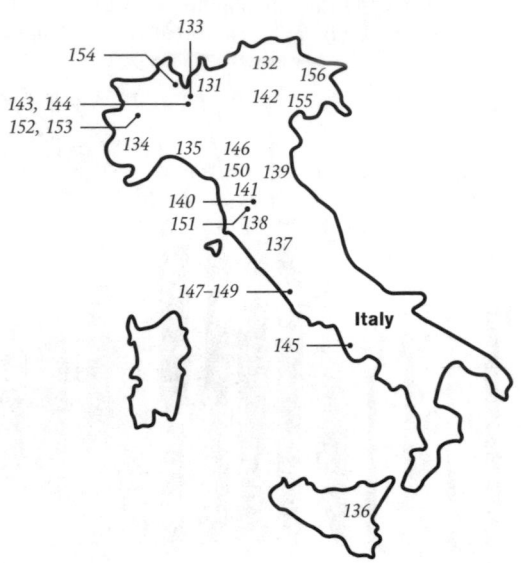

131 ALT Arte Lavoro Territorio
Arte Contemporanea—
Spazio Fausto Radici
Industrial archeology meets contemporary aesthetics

The exhibition space ALT, near Bergamo, in northern Italy, is a testimony to the friendship between Tullio Leggeri, an architect and builder, and Fausto Radici, a one-time professional skier and businessman. The two men had shared a passion for contemporary art; they dreamed of opening their collections to the public. To this end, they bought the former headquarters of Italcementi, an old cement factory, and gave it it a new lease on life. Opened in 2009 and dedicated to Radici, who died in 2002, the ALT exhibition space shows part of the founders' own collections as well as new site-specific projects. Among the artists included are Enrico Castellani, Joseph Beuys, Maurizio Cattelan, Shirin Neshat, Vanessa Beecroft, Wim Delvoye, Carsten Höller, and Paul McCarthy.

Collectors:
Tullio Leggeri & Fausto Radici

Address:
Via Gerolamo Acerbis 14
24022 Alzano Lombardo
Italy
Tel +39 035 4536730
info@altartecontemporanea.it
www.altartecontemporanea.it

By appointment only.

132   ADN Collection
*Contemporary art and architecture in the vineyards
of South Tyrol*

Collector:
Antonio Dalle Nogare

Address:
Via Rafenstein 19
39100 Bolzano
Italy
Tel +39 0471 971626
info@adncollection.it
www.adncollection.it

By appointment only.

A visit to the ADN Collection is already worthwhile because
of the beautiful landscape and sophisticated architecture.
For the construction of the vineyard-encircled building,
which houses both the collection and the private rooms of
Antonio Dalle Nogare, a mountain was hollowed out and
the pink porphyry stone was reused as a building material.
This is how local architects Walter Angonese and Andrea
Marastoni impressively managed to insert the building
harmoniously into the landscape. Dalle Nogare, who began collecting thirty years ago, focuses on Minimal and
Conceptual Art. In his collection, positions of the 1960s and
1970s stand in dialogue with younger contemporary artists.
The works are displayed in three main halls; additionally,
there are three "black boxes" for the presentation of videos
and a project room for temporary presentations.

133   Fondazione Pietro Rossini
Large-scale sculptures in a landscaped park

Collector:
Alberto Rossini

Address:
Via Col del Frejus 3
20836 Briosco,
Monza and Brianza
Italy
Mob +39 335 5378472
info@fondazionepietrorossini.it
www.fondazionepietrorossini.it

By telephone appointment only.

Just north of Milan is a park that fuses modern and contemporary sculpture, architecture, and landscape. It is, in
fact, an open-air museum, founded in 2010 by entrepreneur
Alberto Rossini and his wife, Luisa, in memory of their son
Pietro. Alberto Rossini's interest in art began in the 1950s.
Several large sculptures are located in the park, some of
them developed as site-specific projects. Among the artists
are important Italian names of the postwar period, including Fausto Melotti, Pietro Consagra, or Giulio Turcato, as
well as international names such as Dennis Oppenheim,
César, Erik Dietman, or Nobuho Nagasawa. A pavilion in
the park used for exhibitions was designed by James Wines
of the New York architecture firm Site—one of the largest
agencies in the field of green architecture.

134 Collezione La Gaia
*Minimal Art, Conceptual Art, and Arte Povera
in Piedmont*

When Bruna Girodengo and Matteo Viglietta began collecting art, at the end of the 1970s, they did so "on tiptoe and with a big desire to learn." Initially the pair bought modern works—their first acquisition a 1918 collage by Giacomo Balla—but they soon turned their attention to art from the 1960s to the present. Today the collection counts nearly 1 200 pieces, including a significant group by Arte Povera artists like Alighiero Boetti, Giuseppe Penone, and Michelangelo Pistoletto, which are placed in a "conversation" with more contemporary works by the likes of Bill Viola, Anish Kapoor, and Tony Cragg. Among Girodengo and Viglietta's recent acquisitions, always selected via their personal preferences, are works by Bas Jan Ader, David Hammons, Sanja Iveković, Robert Gober, Roman Ondák, and Christian Rosa.

Collectors:
Bruna Girodengo &
Matteo Viglietta

Address:
Strada Monte Gaudio 13
12022 Busca
Italy
Tel +39 0171 945900
info@collezionelagaia.it
www.collezionelagaia.it

Visitation permitted only
occasionally. Please inquire
by phone or e-mail.

135 Fondazione Pier Luigi e
       Natalina Remotti
*A marriage in the name of art, and a collection
in a former church*

Since their wedding nuptials, at the end of the 1960s, Pier Luigi and Natalina Remotti have been collecting contemporary art. "We have always looked for artists who are experimenting with a new language but who do not yet command exorbitant prices," says Natalina Remotti. "A collector must recognize an artist before the market does." Their collection includes works by Francesco Vezzoli, Vanessa Beecroft, and Nico Vascellari and has a special slant toward photography. Their foundation was opened in 2008 in a former church renovated by the artist Alberto Garutti. There they present their collection and organize exhibitions with additional artists they appreciate. "Our collection has grown quite nicely because my husband and I agree on things," Natalina Remotti says. "It's often happened that I've shown him a work of art at a fair and he says, 'I just bought that.'"

Collectors:
Pier Luigi & Natalina Remotti

Address:
Via Castagneto 52
16032 Camogli, Genoa
Italy
Tel +39 0185 772137
info@fondazioneremotti.it
www.fondazioneremotti.it

Opening Hours:
Sat–Sun: 11–6pm
And by appointment.

136   Fondazione Brodbeck
*Contemporary art in a post-industrial complex—
in the shadow of a volcano*

Collector:
Paolo Brodbeck

Address:
Via Gramignani 93
95121 Catania
Italy
Tel +39 095 7233111
info@fondazionebrodbeck.it
www.fondazionebrodbeck.it

By appointment only.

The 6 000-square-meter industrial complex in the neighborhood of San Cristoforo, in Catania, used to be a factory for producing licorice and processing nuts. It has
also served as a garrison, a storage facility, and joinery.
Now it is home to Fondazione Brodbeck, founded by industrialist Paolo Brodbeck in 2007, which aims to transform the region into an international art nexus. So far
the commitment has entailed the renovation of a section
of the industrial area and a chance to rethink the entire
neighborhood. Brodbeck's collecting is equally sweeping:
Arte Povera and Gruppo Forma, as well as international
artists like Louise Bourgeois, Tony Cragg, and Julian Opie.
With an eye to the future, Brodbeck supports young artists through a residency program, which has hosted João
Maria Gusmão and Pedro Paiva, whose works have found
their way into Brodbeck's esteemed compendium.

137   Il Giardino dei Lauri
Contemporary blue chips in the Umbrian countryside

Born into a family of art collectors, Massimo Lauro came
in contact with art at a young age. He was love-struck by
his parents' enthusiasm and eventually began collecting.
Knowing he could not compete with his parents' stately
compilation, he began, in the 1990s, garnering the work of
a younger generation. Today the collection Massimo Lauro
and his wife, Angela, have amassed in their Umbrian countryside residence boasts more than 300 works of established
contemporary artists like Urs Fischer, Jeff Koons, Allora &
Calzadilla, Takashi Murakami, and Fischli/Weiss. Some
sculptures are installed in the garden: a hulking metallic
hand by Piotr Uklanski, and an unsettling sculpture of a
hanged child by Maurizio Cattelan, which shocked some
of Milan's city dwellers in 2004. A neon rainbow by Ugo
Rondinone glows over wandering garden visitors, asking,
Where Do We Go from Here?

Collectors:
Massimo & Angela Lauro

Address:
Località San Litardo
ss Umbro Casentinese Km 79
06062 Città della Pieve
Italy
Tel +39 3409669052
elda@ilgiardinodeilauri.it
www.ilgiardinodeilauri.it

Opening Hours:
Fri–Sat: 10am–1pm,
3:30–6:30pm
And by appointment.

138   Sensus—Luoghi per l'Arte
Contemporanea
Space as leitmotif in a 1960s building

"Collecting has always been a priority for me. As a child
I was already collecting things that triggered my imagination. I used them to create my own world." This is how
insurance broker Claudio Cosma explains the motivation
behind his passion of the last thirty years. "My greatest
satisfaction," he says, "is to assist in the creation of works,
to exchange ideas with artists to such an extent that these
works would not exist without me." This approach is re-
flected in the name of Cosma's showroom in Florence,
which refers to perception: Sensus. Opened in December
2012, on the ground floor of a 1960s building, and then
expanded into the first level in April 2013, the collection's
overarching theme is the relationship between art and its
surrounding space. Along with Italian artists like Fabrizio
Corneli, Angelo Barone, and Maurizio Nannucci are Asian
representatives like Maitree Siriboon or Yuki Ichihashi.

Collector:
Claudio Cosma

Address:
Viale Gramsci 42
50132 Florence
Italy
info@sensusstorage.com
www.sensusstorage.com

Opening Hours:
Fri–Sat: 6–8pm
And by appointment.

139   Fondazione Dino Zoli
Twentieth-century Italian art in a multifunctional museum

Collector:
Dino Zoli

Address:
Viale Bologna 288
47100 Forlì
Italy
Tel +39 0543 755770
info@fondazionedinozoli.com
www.fondazionedinozoli.com

Opening Hours:
Mon–Fri: 10am–1pm, 4–7pm

The Fondazione Dino Zoli, located in the city of Forlì, in the central-north district Emilia-Romagna, calls itself a "dynamic museum." Rightly so: opened by local industrialist Dino Zoli in 2007, the foundation not only houses his exquisite collection of modern art, but also a vibrant series of talks, music events, fashion shows, and book launches, with a particular attention paid to the region. The foundation's connection to the surrounding locale is also evidenced by exhibitions of paintings by Mattia Moreni, an artist in Emilia-Romagna. The collection as a whole lends a visual excursus of twentieth-century Italian art, featuring established names like Alberto Magnelli, Mimmo Paladino, and Fabrizio Plessi, as well as those lesser known internationally but beloved in Italy: Salvatore Fiume and Emilio Scanavino.

140   Castello di Ama per l'Arte Contemporanea
Site-specific installations for a dual passion: art and wine

Collectors:
Marco & Lorenza Pallanti

Address:
Località Ama
53013 Gaiole in Chianti, Siena
Italy
Tel +39 0577 746031
info@castellodiama.com
arte@castellodiama.com

E-mail appointment only.

One thing is essential for the vintner couple Marco and Lorenza Pallanti: the uniqueness of place. This is true of their wines, of course, whose uniqueness is owed the soil's inherent qualities, but as well as of their art collection, which is exclusively comprised of site-specific installations. Since 2000 they have invited artists once a year to install work on their vineyard estate. The project was created in collaboration with Lorenzo Fiaschi of the Galleria Continua in San Gimignano. The first artist was Michelangelo Pistoletto, who set up a four-meter-high tree with a mirror hidden inside of it—a trademark of the artist—in the basement of the Villa Pianigiani. After Pistoletto, many other well-known artists, such as Daniel Buren or Ilya and Emilia Kabakov, came and dealt with this unique space in a striking way.

141 Collezione Nunzia e Vittorio Gaddi
International contemporary art in the city and country

Tuscan notary Vittorio Gaddi has been collecting contemporary art since the beginning of the 1990s. His first work was the sculpture *The Daughter of the Sun,* by the Italian artist Giò Pomodoro. After this, his attention shifted to more international and emerging art. Today, Gaddi owns around 350 works by artists such as Olafur Eliasson, Carsten Höller, or Wade Guyton. His interest is triggered less by a specific style or medium than by an artist's contemporaneity. From the very outset Gaddi wanted to have his collection publicly accessible. Today it is divided among a 1920s Art Nouveau mansion, in the city of Lucca, and in two old farmhouses nestled in the countryside. One of these adjacent houses was intended as a country chalet but was gradually taken over by art. The other was renovated for the collection in summer 2012.

Collectors:
Nunzia & Vittorio Gaddi

Address:
Viale Carducci 627
55100 Lucca
Italy
Tel +39 0583 587748
info@collezionegaddi.com
www.collezionegaddi.com

By appointment only.

142 La Casabianca
Graphic art from the 1960s to the 1990s

Aspiring collectors with insufficiently deep pockets can always turn to works on paper for beauty and value. Giobatta Meneguzzo turned to exactly such work in the 1970s, and his decisions have paid off. Today he possesses a distinguished collection of more than 1 200 works by 700 international artists spanning from the 1960s to the 1990s. His collection, in La Casabianca, is housed in a seventeenth-century palace—replete with a library—in a small town in the Veneto region. The collection's artworks are grouped together by movement and, all told, evidence a tight spectrum: Minimalism and Pop, Conceptual Art and Transavanguardia. All the works are hung salon style—and without labels—so that visitors approach the works with an unbiased eye.

Collector:
Giobatta Meneguzzo

Address:
Largo Morandi 1
36034 Malo
Italy
Tel +39 0445 602474
info@museocasabianca.com
www.museocasabianca.com

Opening Hours:
Sun: 10am–12:30pm, 3–6:30pm
And by appointment.

How commercial may a biennial be? And how culturally engaged may an art fair be? Contemporary art fairs have become events that go far beyond their commercial function. Sections arranged by well-known curators, panel discussions, artists talks, and performances are all based on a model initiated by ArCo Madrid, in the 1980s, and which MiArt artistic director Vincenzo de Bellis has recently defined as "a process of biennializing the art fair." Biennials, on the other hand, have always claimed to be purely cultural events. Even mentioning "the art market" can cause waves of outrage. Yet, it goes without saying that biennials have a significant effect on the career and market-value of the artists they exhibit. Though some people still idealize biennials as events free of business and commerce, it is worth remembering that until 1968 the Venice Biennale had a sales office, and it is no secret that, even today, gallerists make deals during opening days.

What art fairs and biennials do have in common is the roles they play in

proliferation at the global level; almost every single week, an art fair takes place somewhere in the world. Participation in these fairs is fundamental for a gallery's business and reputation, even though it requires significant financial expenditure. Accordingly, biennials are sprouting in the most remote places: from Dakar to Kochi, from Montevideo to Sapporo. Some critics have complained about this proliferation, questioning the need for yet another biennial. Undoubtedly both developments must be considered a side effect of globalization and the concomitant growth of interest in contemporary art. "The structure of the art world today is similar to a profiterole: it started out small and is expanding to fill demand," says curator Francesco Bonami. "To put a limit on the number of art events that should exist is like putting a limit on the size of a profiterole."

Silvia Anna Barrilà

143   Fondazione Opera
Contemporary art meets toys and antiques

Collectors:
Guido Galimberti &
Donatella Picenelli

Address:
Piazza San Marco 1
20121 Milan
Italy
info@operadv.com
www.operadv.com

E-mail appointment only.

If you're the son of a passionate collector who had already purchased works by Lucio Fontana and Piero Manzoni in the 1960s, the probability that you'd fall in love with art at an early age is pretty high. This is precisely what happened to Guido Galimberti. He was twenty years old when he acquired his first work of art: *Flowers,* by Andy Warhol, which he paid for in installments. For years he had worked as a financial consultant but considered art his passion. In 2007 he transformed his hobby into his profession and became an art consultant. Galimberti's handling of art is playful and provocative, combining works of contemporary artists like Nedko Solakov and Pascale Marthine Tayou with Asian antiques or toys. You will find, for example, a top hat by Giulio Paolini next to a Japanese samurai helmet, or a cube by Stuart Arends next to an antique Chinese vase.

144   Collezione Peruzzi
Prints and multiples from Arte Povera to today

Collector:
Vittorio Peruzzi

Address:
Collezione Peruzzi
20133 Milan
Italy
Mob +39 3484937953
collezioneperuzzi@collezioneperuzzi.it
www.collezioneperuzzi.it

E-mail appointment only.

Graphic art is often falsely viewed as a second-class art. But in order to master the praxis of printing, one must precisely control the materials. The results some artists achieve are amazing. When Milanese engineer Vittorio Peruzzi first became interested in prints and multiples, in the 1970s, the reason was primarily economic: these works were usually less expensive than unique works. Today he has put together an extraordinarily coherent collection of some of the best prints and multiples by selected artists. Lucio Fontana's series *Teatrini* was the first work Peruzzi purchased, followed by prints by Enrico Castellani and Alberto Burri, as well as by Arte Povera artists like Gilberto Zorio or Giuseppe Penone. Among contemporary artists, the collector appreciates the work of Maurizio Cattelan and Vanessa Beecroft.

145   Fondazione Morra Greco
*International contemporary art in the historic
heart of Naples*

The Neapolitan palace that houses the foundation of dentist Maurizio Morra Greco has contained art for centuries. It was used in the seventeenth century as an exhibition hall by the Caracciolos, the royal family of Avellino. Today, works by Italian artists such as Roberto Cuoghi and Diego Perrone are represented, as are those of international names such as Mark Dion or Manfred Pernice. "I started to buy antiques at the age of fourteen," says Morra Greco. "Then I understood that contemporary art is an expression of my time." The artists of Greco's collection not only draw the zeitgeist to Naples, they also provide a connection to the city: the foundation regularly invites artists to create site-specific works. One of the most spectacular was an installation by the German artist Gregor Schneider, who transformed the basement of the palace into a shadowy labyrinth.

Collector:
Maurizio Morra Greco

Address:
Largo Avellino 17
80138 Naples
Italy
Tel +39 081 210690
info@fondazionemorragreco.com
www.fondazionemorragreco.com

Please check the website
for most current information
on opening hours.

146   Collezione Maramotti
From prêt-à-porter to contemporary art

Achille Maramotti, founder of fashion group Max Mara, was not only the inventor of prêt-à-porter in postwar Italy, he was also an enthusiastic collector of art. His focus was on painting—above all, Transavanguardia—but he also collected works by international stars Julian Schnabel and Alex Katz, of whom he was the first European collector. Sharing Maramotti's collection with the public dates back thirty years: initially it hung in the corridors of the Max Mara factory. When production was moved to accommodate company expansion, the factory was turned into a museum that exhibited 200 of Maramotti's 600-work trove. Though he passed away in 2005, Maramotti's three children have continued to buy and commission works by young artists for their family's collection, such as those by Jacob Kassay and Kara Tanaka.

Collector:
Maramotti Family

Address:
Via Fratelli Cervi 66
42124 Reggio Emilia
Italy
Tel +39 0522 382484
info@collezionemaramotti.org
www.collezionemaramotti.org

Opening Hours:
Thurs–Fri: 2:30–6:30pm
Sat–Sun: 10:30am–6:30pm
By appointment only.

147   Fondazione Giuliani
Contemporary flair with blue-collar neighbors

I

Collectors:
Giovanni & Valeria Giuliani

Address:
Via Gustavo Bianchi 1
00153 Rome
Italy
Tel +39 06 57301091
info@fondazionegiuliani.org
www.fondazionegiuliani.org

Opening Hours:
Tues–Sat: 3–7:30pm
And by appointment.

Over the past few years, Rome's contemporary art scene has boomed. Among the most notable events have been the inauguration of a branch of Gagosian Gallery and the opening of Museo Nazionale Delle Arti Del XXI Secolo (MAXXI). But beneath all the glitz, Giovanni Giuliani and his wife, Valeria, discreetly opened their impressive private foundation in 2010—a white cube in the basement of a housing project in the neighborhood of Testaccio. The area alone is worth a visit: a working-class district with strong character that offers an attractive nightlife. The Giulianis, who began collecting at the end of the 1980s, now maintain nearly 400 works, primarily sculptures and installations by artists including Cyprien Gaillard, Mona Hatoum, Alicja Kwade, and Nedko Solakov, as well as work by figures of Arte Povera and Conceptual Art.

148   Casa Musumeci Greco
An historic apartment for contemporary art
in central Rome

Visiting the Roman house of Ines Musumeci Greco—a
former art writer and gallerist—means not only visiting
a collection of works by contemporary Italian and international artists—Nico Vascellari, Luisa Rabbia, Jonathan
Monk, Pascal Marthine Tayou, or Chen Zhen—but entering a private apartment where life meets art, and where
modernity meets history. Greco's apartment is located
inside Palazzo Bernini, a stately address in the heart of
the historic center, once home to Baroque architect Gian
Lorenzo Bernini and a temporary residence of the Scottish
novelist Sir Walter Scott. Renovated with an eye toward its
idiosyncrasies, the apartment regularly hosts artists' talks
and lectures, evincing Ines Musumeci Greco's preference
for a direct, daily relationship with artists and their work.

Collectors:
Ines & Giuliano Musumeci Greco

Address:
Via Della Mercede 11
00187 Rome
Italy
inesmusumeci@hotmail.com

E-mail appointment only.

149   Nomas Foundation
Nomadism and otherness against the force
of homogeneity

The word *nomas* is Latin for "nomad." This is how the
Romans described the Saharan Berbers, who spoke neither Latin nor Greek and opposed any foreign attempt
to suppress their culture and identity. The Rome-based
collectors Raffaella and Stefano Sciarretta were inspired
by this concept of nomadism and otherness when they
opened their foundation in 2008. Here they present their
expansive collection, complemented by exhibitions, talks,
and seminars. One of their goals is to offer residencies to
support young artists with their projects. The Sciarrettas
began to collect in the 1990s—at first Italian Pop Art, and
then international contemporary works. Today they own
about 700 artworks by 300 artists, among them Rossella
Biscotti, Alexandre Singh, and Ryan Gander.

Collectors:
Raffaella & Stefano Sciarretta

Address:
Viale Somalia 33
00199 Rome
Italy
Tel +39 06 86398381
info@nomasfoundation.com
www.nomasfoundation.com

Opening Hours:
Tues–Fri: 2:30–7pm

150   Collezione Gori—Fattoria di Celle
Site-specific art nestled in the Tuscan hillside

Collector:
Giuliano Gori

Address:
Via Montalese 7
51030 Santomato di Pistoia
Italy
Fax +39 0573 479486
info@goricoll.it
www.goricoll.it

Only guided tours with prior
registration by e-mail.

The beauty of the Tuscan countryside is known the world over. And at Fattoria di Celle, near Pistoia, the region's natural beauty is complemented by the profundity of art. It is here that Giuliano Gori, since the 1980s, has been inviting international stars like Robert Morris, Sol LeWitt, Richard Serra, or Daniel Buren to create site-specific works in the park surrounding his majestic residence. Each artist chose a location after carefully sizing up the local elements and conditions and allowing the local charm and history of the Tuscan region—birthplace of the Renaissance—to win them over. When you visit the Collezione Gori, be sure to bring the right shoes and a genuine interest: more than thirty years of collecting have amassed an extensive collection that can take several hours to visit.

151 Depart Foundation
Young American art in Tuscany and Rome

Since 2005, Pierpaolo Barzan has collected primarily young American art. "At first I was driven by the desire to build a collection that reflects my generation," Barzan explains. "So I was interested in artists like Sterling Ruby, Joe Bradley, and Nate Lowman. After that, it was only natural to continue with the next generation." Meanwhile, the collector has acquired about 500 works, by artists such as Cory Arcangel, Grear Patterson, Lucien Smith, or Kour Pour. Parts of the collection are on display in his estate in Tuscany. In addition, Barzan regularly organizes exhibitions in collaboration with museums and institutions in Rome, such as the Museo d'Arte Contemporaneo Roma (MACRO). He also opened a project space in Los Angeles in September 2014, with which he aims to promote cultural exchange between artists from Europe and America.

Collectors:
Pierpaolo & Valeria Barzan

Address:
Via di Poggio Golo
53045 Montepulciano, Siena
Italy
info@departfoundation.org
www.departfoundation.org

E-mail appointment only.

152 Fondazione Sandretto Re Rebaudengo
Not just a collection; a foundation to promote the new

Thanks to a mix of institutional and private initiatives, the region of Piedmont has become an important hub for contemporary art in Italy. And among all the private ventures, perhaps the most well known is Fondazione Sandretto Re Rebaudengo, which was established in 1995 by the Italian grande dame of contemporary collecting, Patrizia Sandretto Re Rebaudengo. The foundation prides itself on the early recognition of talented artists who have achieved international acclaim since the 1990s, like Californian multimedia artist Doug Aitken, for example. Among Sandretto Re Rebaudengo's more recent acquisitions are works by Tauba Auerbach and João Onofre. But because the main aim of the foundation is to promote the work of young artists, it not only shows works from Sandretto Re Rebaudengo's collection, it also organizes thematic exhibitions and supports the production of work by artists just entering the fray.

Collector:
Patrizia Sandretto Re Rebaudengo

Address:
Via Modane 16
10141 Turin
Italy
Tel +39 011 3797600
info@fsrr.org
www.fsrr.org

Opening Hours:
Thurs: 8–11pm
Fri–Sun: 12–7pm

153   Videoinsight Foundation
Art and psychotherapy: a healing combination

Collector:
Rebecca Russo

Address:
Via Ferdinando Bonsignore
10131 Turin
Italy
Tel +39 3472390155
videoinsight@videoinsight.it
www.fasv.it

By e-mail appointment only.

Art can heal. That's the theory that psychotherapist and art collector Rebecca Russo stands behind and implements at her center Videoinsight. For her, a work must convey universal messages that relate to human needs; this principle has guided her collecting. Ten years ago she started to show art—mostly videos—to her patients. She uses it as a kind of Rorschach test for self-reflection. She also offers this method in the form of group therapy once a week to an interested art audience. One may also visit the monthly rotating exhibitions usually devoted to one artist. The collection includes, among others, Marina Abramović, Vik Muniz, and Thomas Ruff, as well as many artists from Asia, such as Filipino Ronald Ventura or Thai Natee Utarit.

154   Villa e Collezione Panza/
Fondo Ambiente Italiano (FAI)
Minimal Art in a neoclassical villa in dialogue with antique furniture and African art

Collector:
Giuseppe Panza di Biumo

Address:
Piazza Litta 1
21100 Varese
Italy
Tel +39 0332 283960
faibiumo@fondoambiente.it

Opening Hours:
Tues–Sun: 10am–6pm

When Giuseppe Panza di Biumo passed away, in 2010, the *Los Angeles Times* described him as "a Milanese businessman who was the first great international collector of postwar American art." In the mid-1950s, after a trip to America, di Biumo began acquiring art superheroes like Mark Rothko, Bruce Nauman, and Richard Serra. His collection holds a few Europeans but is comprised mostly of American Abstract Expressionist, Pop, Minimal, and Conceptual Art. Large parts of di Biumo's trove are now in museums like the Guggenheim in New York, and the Museum of Contemporary Art in Los Angeles. But an important group of works is still maintained in his neoclassical villa near Varese. One wing boasts light installations by Dan Flavin and James Turrell, and Minimal Art and Monochromes sit next to Renaissance furniture and African and pre-Columbian art, arrangements decided upon by di Biumo's own keen eye.

155   Francois Pinault Foundation/ Palazzo Grassi & Punta della Dogana
High art with an even higher profile

Luxury-goods magnate François Pinault is not only famous in the fashion world; he's also famed in the art world, as the owner of the auction house Christie's and as a collector of contemporary art. Since 2006 the fruits of his passion can be admired in Venice. Here, Pinault commissioned the Japanese architect Tadao Ando, first to modify the Palazzo Grassi and then, in 2009, the historic customs building Punta della Dogana, which is situated at the eastern tip of the Dorsoduro district. In both places he presents his collection in curated temporary exhibitions. Among the artists shown are Martial Raysse, Wade Guyton, Danh Vo, and Philippe Parreno. "That my collection can be appreciated by as many people as possible, especially by the younger generation," is how Pinault describes his mission as a collector. "With a bit of luck, it might change their lives. It opened me up."

Collector:
François Pinault

Addresses:
Palazzo Grassi
Campo San Samuele 3231
30124 Venice
Italy

Punta della Dogana
Sestiere Dorsoduro 2
30123 Venice
Italy

Tel +39 041 2719031
www.palazzograssi.it

Opening Hours:
Wed–Mon: 10am–7pm

Venice is known the world over for its extraordinary beauty and legendary canals. But in the context of art there is another reason for its fame: the Biennale. Every two years the art world gathers in the Giardini and at the adjacent Arsenale for the oldest and most prestigious art biennial in the world. Founded in 1895, the Venice Biennale has not lost one bit of its attraction and significance. But contemporary art in Venice no longer ends with the Biennale. The city has institutions such as Fondazione Bevilacqua La Masa, which promotes exhibitions of well-known international artists, such as Hiroshi Sugimoto and Simon Starling, among others, and also fosters emergent artists with a residency program. Another nonprofit organization is the Fondazione Giorgio Cini, which is committed to the promotion of Italian twentieth-century glass and, moreover, the restoration of the monumental site on the island San Giorgio Maggiore. It also hosts major exhibitions of contemporary art on occasion of the Biennale. Furthermore, there is the Fondazione Querini Stampalia, which owns a collection of Old Masters but also integrates contemporary art into its exhibition program. A recent addition to the Venetian art scene is the Fondazione Prada at Ca' Corner della Regina, established by fashion designer and art collector Miuccia Prada and her husband, Patrizio Bertelli, in 2011. It hosts important exhibitions, including the 2013 restaging of Harald Szeemann's historical show *When Attitudes Become Form*, first exhibited in 1969 at Kunsthalle Bern. And even if Venice is not a relevant center for the art market, there are some interesting galleries, such as the Galleria Michela Rizzo, Caterina Tognon, and the historical Galleria Il Capricorno, founded in 1970 by prestigious art dealer Bruna Aickelin—all of which attest to Venice being much more than "just" the Biennale.

Silvia Anna Barrilà

156   Prato d'Arte Collezione Marzona
*Land Art without borders: installations
in the Carnia mountains*

Collector:
Egidio Marzona

Address:
Villa di Verzegnis
33020 Verzegnis
Italy
Tel +39 0433 487779
carnia.musei@cmcarnia.regione.fvg.it

The park is open at all times.

It's a truism that many great ideas are conceived in conversation over a glass of wine with good friends on a mid-
summer's eve. This was surely the case with Prato d'Arte,
a sculpture garden founded in the late 1980s in the 400-
inhabitant town of Verzegnis, in northeastern Italy. The
two friends were German art dealer Konrad Fischer—an
early supporter of American Minimal and Conceptual
artists who was responsible for bringing many of them
to Europe—and Egidio Marzona, one of the world's most
important collectors of Conceptual, Minimal, Land Art,
and Arte Povera, who donated a large part of his collection to Berlin's Hamburger Bahnhof museum in 2002.
The sprawling Prato d'Arte Collezione Marzona contains
thirteen sculptures by the likes of Bruce Nauman, Richard
Long, Dan Graham, and Laurence Weiner, among others,
all nestled in the landscape of the mountainous region of
Carnia, from whence the Marzona family comes.

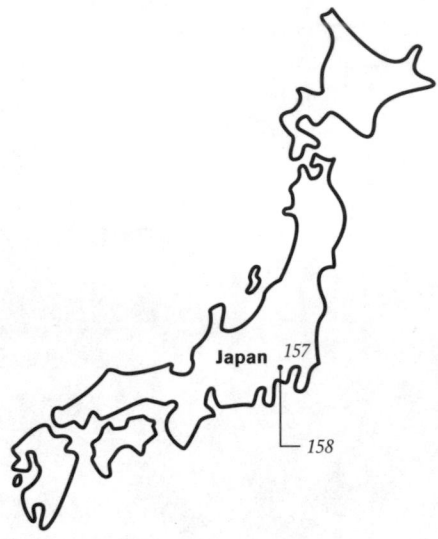

Japan *157*

158

J

157 Dream House
*High-quality Asian and international art
in an extravagant building*

A house made by an artist for art: Installation artist
Dominique Gonzalez-Foerster designed a colorful,
structurally eye-catching house for the collector Daisuke
Miyatsu. In and around the Dream House you'll find
works by Asian and international contemporary artists
like Yayoi Kusama, Yoshitomo Nara, Yang Jun, Lee Kit, or
Olafur Eliasson. Many of the works were designed particularly for the Dream House—where the telecommunica-
tions employee lives with his family. Media art is the main
focus of this roughly 300-work collection, spanning from
Yang Fudong or Cao Fei & Ou Ning, from China, through
American Tony Oursler, to Nina Fischer and Maroan
el Sani from Germany. Works from the video collection,
which began in 1994, are beamed upon request.

Collector:
Daisuke Miyatsu

Address:
3-3-17 Wakamiya
Ichikawa
Chiba Prefecture 272-0812
Japan
Fax +81 47 3321141

Visitation permitted only
occasionally. Please inquire
by fax or post.

158   Takahashi Collection
*One of the most important collections of Japanese
contemporary art in Japan*

J

Collector:
Ryutaro Takahashi

Address:
Tokyo, Japan
art@takahashiryutaro.com
www.takahashi-collection.com

Opening hours vary depending on
exhibition. Please check the website for most current information.

He's one of the most vital collectors of contemporary art in
Japan. Since 1997 the psychologist Ryutaro Takahashi has
concentrated on gathering together mainly Japanese paintings, drawings, videos, and small sculptures—now numbering more than 1 500 works. He acquired many of these
at a time when Japanese museums no longer could: subsequent the financial bubble-burst of the 1990s. Prominent
older artists in the collection are Yayoi Kusama—whose
works sparked Takahashi to begin collecting—as well as
Katsura Funakoshi, Yoshitomo Nara, Tomoko Konoike, or
Kenji Yanobe. Among the younger artists in his pool are
Ruriko Murayama and Mika Kato.

Luxembourg

159

L

159   Sammlung Majerus
Pointed contemporary concept art with critical potential

"Either you're a collector or you aren't," says Patrick Majerus, perhaps the only officer in the Luxembourg army with a distinct interest in contemporary concept art, primarily from Berlin. His collection attained international attention in 2010, when it was shown at the Kunstsaele Berlin. Majerus collects entire groups of works from just a few select artists of his generation, convinced that it is more important to collect deeply than broadly. Around thirteen artists, mostly between the ages of thirty and forty, including Alicja Kwade, Tim Berresheim, Katja Novitskova, Dominik Sittig, Michael E. Smith, and Sven Johne, share the walls in Majerus's remodeled private home, which, as one might guess, does not keep fixed opening hours. Instead, he likes to personally guide like-minded art enthusiasts through his collection from time to time.

Collector:
Patrick Majerus

Address:
Luxembourg City, Luxembourg
m@jerus.lu

Visitation permitted only
occasionally. Please inquire
by e-mail.

Mexico

160

M

160 Fundación Jumex Arte Contemporáneo
*Young Latin American and international
contemporary art at its best*

Collector:
Eugenio López Alonso

Addresses:
Museum:
Miguel de Cervantes Saavedra 303
Col. Ampliación Granada
Mexico-City C.P. 11529
Mexico

Gallery:
Via Morelos 272
Col. Santa María Tulpetlac
Ecatepec de Morelos C.P. 55400
Mexico

Tel +52 55 57758188
info@fundacionjumex.org
www.fundacionjumex.org

Please check the website
for most current information
on opening hours.

Viva México! Since the end of 2013, when the Museo Jumex opened in the posh district of Polanco, Mexico City has become even more firmly established on the international art map. With its roof in the shape of a saw blade, this building, designed by British star architect David Chipperfield, his first in Latin America, is already worth a visit. The new headquarters of the largest collection of contemporary Latin American and international art on the continent, with 2 800 works, shows artists such as Francis Alÿs, Damián Ortega, Tacita Dean, or Danh Vo, in addition to international temporary exhibitions that travel to Mexico for the first time. Eugenio López Alonso, a colorful character and the sole heir of Jumex, the country's largest juice company, continues to present parts of his collection at the previous location, at Galería Jumex, on the company's premises outside the city.

167; 168
164
162, 163

Netherlands

165
166

161
169

N

161 Collectors House
*Cooperation between international collectors
and a city museum*

"Strength in unity," goes the saying. This is also the principle of the Collectors House, in Heerlen, a collaboration between the city museum Schunck, the Dutch collector Albert Groot, and several international collectors. Their shared goal is to show works of contemporary art that are otherwise rarely seen in public. The exhibitions at the Collectors House bring together works currently residing in different places—in the Netherlands, Hong Kong, or Romania—and put them in a constructive dialogue with each other. Among the artists shown have been Marina Abramović, Mircea Cantor, Hans Op de Beeck, and Cao Fei. At a time when culture and museums are experiencing drastic cutbacks, initiatives that combine public and private certainly offer an alternative solution.

Collector:
Albert Groot

Address:
Raadhuisplein 19
6411 Heerlen
Netherlands
Tel +31 45 5711525
info@collectorshouse.eu
www.collectorshouse.eu

Opening Hours:
Thurs–Sun: 1–5pm

162   Concordia Collection
Local and international artists in an historic house in Rotterdam

Collector:
Julian Oggel

Address:
Eendrachtsweg 57A
3012 LE Rotterdam
Netherlands
Tel +31 10 2409715
Mob +31 653 771561
julian.oggel@xs4all.nl

E-mail appointment only.

In one of the most beautiful streets of Rotterdam, between the lively Witte de Withstraat and the Boijmans Van Beuningen Museum, sits the home of Julian Oggel, a lawyer and the CEO of an investment firm. The house itself is worth a visit: built in 1860, it survived even the brutality of World War II. Oggel's collection, which he has been amassing since 2002, is eclectic and yet retains a strong connection to the city. This has much to do with the presence of local artists like Ron van der Ende and Marin de Jong, and of international artists who have produced work while here, such as Keith Haring and Ivan Chermayeff. Oggel has a preference for Pop Art but also owns works of Hyperrealism and Conceptual Art. Once the neighboring house is turned into luxury apartments, part of his collection will also be shown there.

N

163   Alexander Ramselaar Collection
A townhouse of young talent from Rotterdam, the Netherlands, and around the world

Collector:
Alexander Ramselaar

Address:
Rotterdam, Netherlands
art@alexander-ramselaar.com
www.alexander-ramselaar.com

Visitation permitted only
occasionally. Please inquire
by e-mail.

Rotterdam collector Alexander Ramselaar discovered his first artwork in a gallery on the way to work. He was immediately transfixed. After a longer period of collecting modern design, the real estate specialist, who now advises arts and cultural institutions, began to specialize in contemporary art. In his cozy townhouse, the hospitable collector presents art in his living room and bedrooms, in the stairwell, and even in the bathroom. Ramselaar, an avid traveler, collected first in the Rotterdam art scene and now does so internationally: Yael Bartana, Hans Op de Beeck, Guy Tillim, or Rossella Biscotti are just some of the talented artists in his collection. Moreover, after becoming frustrated by the massive cuts in the Dutch cultural budget, Ramselaar and a few other collectors established the Foundation C.o.C.A. to support young artists.

164 Museum Beelden aan Zee
*Modern and contemporary sculpture nestled
in the Netherlands' pristine dunes*

The Museum Beelden aan Zee is camouflaged so perfectly, you almost walk right past it. Located in the middle of sand dunes of the swanky seaside resort of Scheveningen, the entrance to the most important collection of sculptures in the Netherlands hides behind an exposed concrete façade. Though highly frequented tourist attractions—the spa hotel, the pier, or the casino—are right around the corner, the inside of the house that opened in 1994 is quiet. Under the leitmotif "man—the human image," Theo and Lida Scholten began in 1966 to bring together nearly 1 000 sculptures from all major art centers of the world. The spectrum ranges from Armando to Marc Quinn, all the way to Berlinde De Bruyckere. Every year three to four thematic and monographic exhibitions are curated from the collection.

Collectors:
Theo & Lida Scholten

Address:
Harteveltstraat 1
2586 EL The Hague/Scheveningen
Netherlands
info@beeldenaanzee.nl
www.beeldenaanzee.nl

Opening Hours:
Tues–Sun: 11am–5pm

N

165 Museum De Pont
*Masterpieces of contemporary art in the
spacious halls of a former wool mill*

Berlinde De Bruyckere, Roni Horn, Anri Sala, Fiona Tan, Rosemarie Trockel, Luc Tuymans, and Mark Wallinger—the Tilburg-based collection of the Museum De Pont, in the southern Netherlands, is remarkable. Since opening its doors, in 1992, around 700 works by international contemporary artists have come together to be presented in a 6 000-square-meter space. Benthem Crouwel Architects, from Amsterdam, renovated a wool mill from the 1930s so sensitively that one can still feel the industrial character of the building. The construction was made possible by Jan de Pont (1915–1987), a Tilburg businessman, who provided a large part of his estate for the promotion of contemporary art. Currently, the architects are working on a gentle "facelift": the beginning of 2015 welcomes a more visually striking entrance, and, in 2016, a new wing for film, video, and photography.

Collector:
Jan de Pont

Address:
Wilhelminapark 1
5041 EA Tilburg
Netherlands
Tel +31 13 5438300
info@depont.nl
www.depont.nl

Opening Hours:
Thurs–Sun: 11am–5pm

It can be difficult to acquire works by promising and in-demand artists in galleries, particularly if gallery owners prefer to place them exclusively in prestigious collections. Auctions, however, are a more democratic affair: everyone—as long as they have the money—can bid. Traditionally, works with one or more previous owners are offered, which means the secondary market is not necessarily the place to discover new artists. This is the task usually reserved for galleries, which often develop the careers of their protégés over long periods. But if and when a certain price level and corresponding popularity are attained, auction houses enter the picture, taking on the works of these artists and increasing their value. Recently a novel development has been observed: rising art stars that move **from a first solo show almost directly to the auction room.** Phillips, an auction house that specializes in contemporary art, regularly brings new names into the game. If the hammer price far exceeds the estimate in the catalogue, or if demand is very high—as in the recent cases of Oscar Murillo or Lucien Smith—works by these artists might appear in future prestigious evening auctions at Christie's and Sotheby's. New talents being signed by influential gallerists can also confirm their rising value. But investing in artists who have barely left university and whose prices have rapidly crossed the 100 000-dollar mark with an eye to future returns is a risky financial endeavor. It is difficult to predict whether an artist has the power and potential to build a compelling body of work over the decades ahead and to remain a permanent presence in the public eye. If the artist fails and the works remain unsold at auctions, this can have a negative effect on their price level. The basic premise remains: art is worth what someone is currently willing to pay for it.

Anne Reimers

166 Museum van Bommel van Dam
*An enthusiastic Dutch couple and
their personalized collection*

Collectors:
Maarten & Reina
van Bommel van Dam

Address:
Deken van Oppensingel 6
5911 AD Venlo
Netherlands
Tel +31 77 3513457
info@vanbommelvandam.nl
www.vanbommelvandam.nl

Opening Hours:
Tues–Sun: 11am–5pm

Maarten van Bommel acquired his first artwork at the age of sixteen. Later, as a stock trader, he continued growing his collection. From 1944 on, he and his wife, Reina van Dam, both now deceased, collected unsystematically: abstract Dutch painting of the Informel and CoBrA, but also African masks and Japanese woodcuts. After extensively seeking a suitable location to house their 1 000 works, they found it in 1969 in the city of Venlo: an ideal museum for their art and, next door, a residential bungalow. Through a connecting door, they could move freely between the two. Over the years, the collection has been added to by other collectors, and under the current director, Rick Vercauteren, it has become more contemporary and international.

N

167 KRC Collection
*Dutch and international artists with
a critical-political approach*

Collector:
Rattan Chadha

Address:
Voorschoten, Netherlands
info@krccapital.com
www.krccollection.com

Visitation permitted only
occasionally. Please inquire
by e-mail.

Curiosity aroused Rattan Chadha's enthusiasm for contemporary art. In the mid-1980s, he came across one of Andy Warhol's Campbell's Soup paintings and was shocked at the price: 50 000 dollars for an image of soup cans? Chadha wanted to understand the valuation, so for six months he studied Warhol. He became convinced of Warhol's artistic strategy, and bought the work. Born in India in 1949, the entrepreneur had founded—and then sold—the fashion label Mexx. His collection, one of the largest in the Netherlands, is located in spacious modern rooms behind the historic façade of an old silver factory near Leiden. It includes works by Candice Breitz, Thomas Hirschhorn, Erik van Lieshout, and Marc Bijl—all artists who have taken a critical stance towards contemporary politics and society.

168 Caldic Collectie
*Masterpieces of contemporary sculpture
in harmony with nature*

An estate in Wassenaar, near The Hague, is home to sixty-five sculptures in a park overflowing with natural abundance. The industrialist Joop van Caldenborgh, who acquired his first work of art as a teenager, is considered one of the most important art collectors in the Netherlands. His impressive sculpture garden, established in 1995, hosts major works by Anish Kapoor, Sylvie Fleury, Sol LeWitt, and Antony Gormley. Visits can be arranged via written appointment; visitors will be accompanied by an art historian. A visit offers a double experience: "The combination of art and nature sharpens the perception," Joop van Caldenborgh says. "One begins to look more consciously at both the artwork and at nature." A new museum is being built for this extensive collection of paintings, photography, video art, and installations—planned to open in 2016/17.

Collector:
Joop N.A. van Caldenborgh

Address:
Buurtweg 90
2244 AG Wassenaar
Netherlands
Tel +31 70 5121660
voorlinden@caldic.nl

Guided tours of the sculpture garden each Thursday from May to October. Please visit www.beeldentuinclingenbosch.nl to book your visit.

N

169 Bonnefanten Hedge House Foundation
Art from the 1960s to the present in a modern pavilion

Over the past few decades, the collectors Marlies and Jo Eyck have turned their castle Wijlre, in Limburg, which they acquired in 1981, into a *Gesamtkunstwerk*. The owners of a paint wholesale company began collecting abstract painting in the late 1960s. Over time they added other kinds of art. Today, their collection includes artists from Donald Judd and René Daniëls to Marlene Dumas. Sculptural works, mainly site-specific, can be found in the palace garden, such as a fallen tree by Giuseppe Penone. In 1999 the architect Wiel Arets designed a modern exhibition-pavilion of concrete, glass, and steel called The Hedge House. In 2012, Jo and Marlies Eyck entrusted the castle, the gardens, and the pavilion to the Bonnefantenmuseum in Maastricht, which organizes two annual exhibitions in the idyllic castle and guarantees the collection's endurance into the future.

Collectors:
Jo & Marlies Eyck

Address:
Kasteel Wijlreweg 1
6321 PP Wijlre
Netherlands
Tel +31 43 4502616
info@hedgehouse.eu
www.hedgehouse.eu/nl

Opening Hours:
Thurs–Sun: 11am–5pm
And by appointment.

170 — New Zealand

New Zealand

N

170   Gibbs Farm
A sculpture park in XXL format with monumental art in the grandness of nature

Collector:
Alan Gibbs

Address:
Kaipara Harbour
North Auckland Peninsula
New Zealand
info@gibbsfarm.org.nz
www.gibbsfarm.org.nz

By appointment only.
Please inquire via website.

It's as if giants had dropped their toys on green grass hills. At the Gibbs Farm sculpture park, opened in 1991, on the coast of New Zealand, art and nature correspond in a way that emphasizes the monumentality of both. Since the 1960s, entrepreneur Alan Gibbs has collected works by Richard Serra, Sol LeWitt, Andy Goldsworthy, George Rickey, and Daniel Buren—all artists known for grand outdoor gestures. But even art aficionados are amazed by the dimensions of these site-specific sculptures, some of which extend—in the case of Goldsworthy's *Arches*—into the water. It's not surprising that the park has become a visitor magnet. If you're looking to be one of them, however, book a tour as early as possible: Gibbs Farm is open to the public only one day a month.

171 —

Norway

173

— 172; 174, 175

N

171 Rolf A. Hoff Collection
*Contemporary art projects on an island
off the northern Norwegian coast*

This exhibition space is as close to the Arctic Circle as it could be. In the summer of 2013, the Norwegian art collectors Venke and Rolf A. Hoff opened their art space in a former caviar factory on the Lofoten. The Kaviarfabrikken Galleri is located in the picturesque fishing village of Henningsvær, the gateway to the northern Norwegian archipelago. The charming building was renovated by the Norwegian architecture firm Element. "Many international artists have visited us here," says Rolf A. Hoff, enthusiastically. "All of them love this place and want to come back." Equally popular is their Lighthouse, which the Hoffs offer as guest quarters. The collectors own works by Norwegian and international artists such as Bjarne Melgaard, Julieta Aranda, or Jack Goldstein, and they invite artists from all over the world to realize exhibitions in the 500-square-meter former factory.

Collectors:
Venke & Rolf A. Hoff

Address:
Henningsværveien 13
8312 Henningsvær
Norway
Tel +47 907 34743
contact@kaviarfactory.no
www.kaviarfactory.no

Opening Hours:
Mon–Sun: 10am–6pm
And by appointment.

172   Henie Onstad Kunstsenter (HOK)
*Modern art and exhibitions with contemporary artists
in spectacular architecture*

N

Collectors:
Sonja Henie & Niels Onstad

Address:
Sonja Henie vei 31
1311 Høvikodden
Norway
Tel +47 67 804880
post@hok.no
www.hok.no

Opening Hours:
Tues–Thurs: 11am–7pm
Fri–Sun: 11am–5pm

Sonja Henie (1912–1969) is considered one of the most successful figure skaters in history. Together with her third husband, Niels Onstad, a ship owner and art patron, she amassed a collection of modern art. In 1968 they opened the Henie Onstad Kunstsenter (HOK), high over the Oslo Fjord, south of the capital city. Norwegians Jon Eikvar and Sven Erik Engebretsen won the architectural competition, and erected a spectacular neo-expressionist structure that meshes nicely with the surrounding landscape. The building was extended in 1994, and again in 2003, and is now complemented by a sculpture park featuring works by Per Kirkeby and Tony Cragg, among others. Spread across 3 500 square meters, the HOK offers highlights of its collection, from Henri Matisse through Hans Hartung to Fernand Léger, as well as temporary exhibitions with contemporaries such as Ilya Kabakov, Omer Fast, or Olav Christopher Jenssen.

173   Kistefos-Museet
Prime public art park in the Norwegian woodlands

N The roughly 4 000-person Oppland municipality of Jevnaker is certainly not on the shortlist of art world hot-spots. But for lovers of large-scale sculpture and the great outdoors, Christen Sveaas's Kistefos sculpture park stands out. The largest publicly accessible sculpture park in all of Scandinavia, Kistefos currently features twenty-nine artworks, by the likes of Marc Quinn, Elmgreen, and Dragset, and Fernando Botero. The park is part of the Kistefos-Museet, which investor and industrialist Sveaas founded in 1996 to commemorate the Kistefos sawmill, which his grandfather built on the Randselva River in 1889. An Industry Museum now occupies that building, with the sculptures spread across the vast, pristine grounds. Open to the public twenty-four hours a day, 365 days a year, the works, from Olafur Eliasson's *Viewing Machine,* which looks out over the river, to Anish Kapoor's *S-Curve,* make Kistefos well worth the hour's trip north from Oslo.

Collector:
Christen Sveaas

Address:
Samsmoveien 41
3520 Jevnaker
Norway
Tel +47 61 310383
post@kistefos.museum.no
www.kistefos.museum.no

The park is open at all times.

174   Astrup Fearnley Museet
Major works of contemporary art in a new Renzo Piano building upon a fjord

Collector:
Hans Rasmus Astrup

Address:
Strandpromenaden 2
0252 Oslo
Norway
Tel +47 22 936060
info@fearnleys.no
www.afmuseet.no

Opening Hours:
Tues, Wed, Fri: 12–5pm
Thurs: 12–7pm
Sat–Sun: 11am–5pm

Norwegians seldom complain about strained finances. Oil and gas resources supply an influx of capital, and Oslo has become the most expensive city in the world. Perhaps this is why private museums are somewhat more grandiose in Norway than elsewhere, a fact perfectly illustrated by the brand new building of the Astrup Fearnley Museum, which was founded in 1993. Ship owner and collector Hans Rasmus Astrup commissioned none other than Italian architect Renzo Piano, who, at age seventy, remains one of the most in-demand architects in the world. A 4 000-square-meter exhibition space, built in 2012, reflects maritime flair in glass, steel, and wood in an exposed location on a fjord, housing entire work-complexes by well-known blue-chip artists such as Francis Bacon, Anselm Kiefer, Jeff Koons, Takashi Murakami, and Cindy Sherman. The collectors are also interested in young Norwegian art and, more recently, in newcomers from Asia and Latin America.

N

175   Ekebergparken—
Collection Christian Ringnes
A three-kilometer-long sculpture trail with a harbor view

Collector:
Christian Ringnes

Address:
Kongsveien 23
0193 Oslo
Norway
Tel +47 975 67165
info@ekebergparken.com
www.ekebergparken.com

The park is open at all times.

In the hills framing the Norwegian capital of Oslo an enchanting sculpture park is hidden among the trees. The Ekebergparken—pictured in the background in Edvard Munch's famous painting *The Scream*—is a public park featuring remains from the Stone, Bronze, and Viking Ages, established in the late eighteenth century. Since September 2013, visitors have been able to encounter more than thirty sculptures, by artists from Maillol to Tony Cragg and Lynn Chadwick. The transformation of this previously neglected park is the brainchild of the collector Christian Ringnes, whose foundation lent the artworks to the city after Oslo declined a donation. The art here enters a fascinating dialogue with nature: an aluminum couple by Louise Bourgeois floats between trees, and bronze muses, lost in thought, by Guy Buseyne and Salvador Dalí, are located between a pavilion by Dan Graham and installations by James Turrell and Jenny Holzer.

Poland

176 Art Stations Foundation
Polish and international art trends
in a consumer temple

P

Art and business are often seen as separate things. But this isn't the case for Polish businesswoman Grażyna Kulczyk, who says, "I have always known that I would not be satisfied by the division into being an entrepreneur by day, and an 'after-hours collector.' So I married the two, adopting the 50/50 philosophy." To this end, Kulczyk turned an old brewery, the Stary Browar in Poznań, into a complex comprising a shopping mall and an exhibition hall: the Art Stations Gallery. Her collection vaunts more than 400 works, including pieces by key Polish artists of the twentieth century, like Jacek Malczewski and Tadeusz Kantor; international names like Victor Vasarely and Sam Francis; and a smattering of contemporary photography. Kulczyk is also fascinated by artists who explore the coexistence of art, science, and technology, as seen in works by Olafur Eliasson or Loris Gréaud.

Collector:
Grażyna Kulczyk

Address:
Półwiejska 42
61-888 Poznań
Poland
Tel +48 61 8596122
office@artstationsfoundation5050.com
www.artstationsfoundation5050.com

Opening Hours:
Mon–Sun: 12–7pm

177 Michał Borowik Collection
*Young Polish art melding aesthetics
and content*

Collector:
Michał Borowik

Address:
Warsaw, Poland
contact@borowikcollection.com
www.borowikcollection.com

By appointment only.

P

"I collect artworks by young Polish artists in a variety of media. It gives me great pleasure to live with objects that reflect our times." This is how Michał Borowik describes his approach. When he chooses a piece to include in his discerning collection, he does so with an eye toward artworks that inject aesthetics with meaning. "I really dislike empty shells," he says, insisting at the same time that the artist's medium fit that message. This attitude has earned Borowik a place on the list of the world's fifty most interesting collections assembled by people under fifty years old, a list drawn up by American magazine *Modern Painters* in 2011. Among other artists, Michał Gayer, Magdalena Starska, and Michał Smandek are some of the young Polish artists one finds in Borowik's stunning assembly.

Portugal

178

178 Museu Colecção Berardo
One of Portugal's largest private collections in a public art center

P

Think big! José Berardo has achieved a lot. The son of farm workers, he had to leave school at age thirteen to work as an unskilled vineyard laborer. At age eighteen he immigrated to South Africa, and what followed was the ascent from fruit picker to owner of gold and diamond mines. Berardo went back to Portugal in 1986 and began his rule over a multinational consortium of companies. His museum-quality and thoroughgoing art collection mirrors his entrepreneurial self-confidence. From Cubism to the Becher School, nearly every art movement is represented. Special attention is paid to Portuguese artists like Helena Almeida or Pedro Cabrita Reis. Since 2007 the roughly 900 works are permanently exhibited at the public art center of Belém.

Collector:
José Berardo

Address:
Praça do Império
1449-003 Lisbon
Portugal
Tel +351 213 612878
museuberardo@museuberardo.pt
www.museuberardo.com

Opening Hours:
Tues–Sun: 10am–7pm

Qatar

179

179 Mathaf—Arab Museum of Modern Art
A royal collection spanning 200 years of Arab art

Collector:
Sheikh Hassan bin Mohamed bin
Ali Al Thani

Address:
Education City Student Center
Al-Luqta Street
Doha
Qatar
Tel +974 4402 8855
mathaf_info@qma.org.qa
www.mathaf.org.qa

Opening Hours:
Tues–Thurs: 11am–6pm
Fri: 3–8pm
Sat–Sun: 11am–6pm

The Art Newspaper once reported that Qatar is the world's biggest art buyer and has initiated some of the most important purchases of modern and contemporary art over the last few decades. Indeed Qatar's royal family has played an active role in acquisitions, with the aim of building a top-class collection for Qatar's growing network of museums. The latest of them is Mathaf, which is dedicated solely to Arab art. It opened in December 2010 thanks to the commitment of the Emir's son, Sheikh Hassan bin Mohamed bin Ali Al Thani, and thanks to the support of museum officials. The Sheikh began collecting in the 1980s and has amassed some 6 000 works, including pieces by artists throughout the Middle East, North Africa, and the Arab Diaspora, from 1840 to today.

Q

180, 181

180   The Cultural Foundation Ekaterina
*Russian and international contemporary art
in a pioneering private museum*

R

Ekaterina and Vladimir Seminikhin were among the first Russian collectors to open their collection to the public. In the catalogue to their first exhibition, in 2007, the couple wrote: "Those mysterious private collections that were treated with suspicion by both the state and society during Soviet times are now gradually stepping out of the shadows." The Seminikhins have been collecting international contemporary works since 2003, but they were such early supporters of the post-Soviet avant garde that the *Financial Times* deemed them "pioneers among Russian private collectors" and "the unofficial patron saints of Russia's contemporary arts scene." The Cultural Foundation Ekaterina consists of 800 works of Russian art, from Ivan Shishkin through Komar & Melamid to Dubossarsky & Vinogradov.

Collectors:
Ekaterina & Vladimir Seminikhin

Address:
Kuznetsky Most, 21/5
107996 Moscow
Russia
Tel +7 495 6215522
info@ekaterina-foundation.ru
www.ekaterina-fondation.ru

Opening Hours:
Tues–Sun: 11am–8pm

Despite of the omnipresent threat of censorship, Moscow has developed a vibrant contemporary art scene, thanks primarily to the support of Russian business tycoons and private collectors. The city's premier art center is the Garage Museum of Contemporary Art, founded in 2008, by collector Dasha Zhukova. Devoted to organizing exhibitions and fostering research and education, it is named after its first location, a former bus depot, built in 1926. Currently still located in a pavilion, the center is getting a makeover from Dutch architect Rem Koolhaas, who is renovating the famous 1960s Vremena Goda restaurant, which will become the museum's permanent home. Another active institution is V-A-C Foundation, established in 2009 by gas magnate Leonid Mikhelson, who aims to integrate Russian contemporary art into national and international discourse. Equally as committed to supporting Moscow's art scene are Russian collectors like Sergey Gridchin, who founded the Gridchinhall Art Center, in 2009, and Maria Baibakova, who launched Baibakov Art Projects, in 2008. Among the state-owned institutions is the Moscow Museum of Modern Art (MMOMA), which is spread out over four locations. More focused on the twenty-first century is the National Centre for Contemporary Arts (NCCA), an exhibition and research organization that was crucial for the reorganization of artistic life in Russia during the 1990s. Since 2008, the NCCA and the MMOMA have been organizing the Moscow International Biennale for Young Art, which is dedicated to artists younger than age thirty-five. Russia's largest biennial, however, is the Moscow Biennale of Contemporary Art, which was launched in 2005 and takes place in September, alongside the art fair Cosmoscow. As for Moscow's galleries, the most interesting programs are held by XL Gallery, Regina Gallery, Guelman Gallery, and Aidan Studio, all of which are located at Winzavod Centre for Contemporary Art, a former nineteenth-century brewery and later wine-bottling factory, now also home to a variety of artists' workshops and showrooms.

Silvia Anna Barrilà

181   Stella Art Foundation
An exhibition space for contemporary Russian art

Collector:
Stella Kesaeva

Address:
Skaryatinsky Pereulok, 7
121069 Moscow
Russia
Tel +7 495 6913407
info@safmuseum.org
en.safmuseum.org

Opening Hours:
Tues–Sun: 12–7pm

Since opening her gallery, in 2003, Stella Kesaeva, art collector and wife of the billionaire Igor Kesaev, has become an influential player on the Russian art scene. She was appointed commissioner for the 2011, 2013, and 2015 Russian Pavilions at the Venice Biennale, and in Moscow she runs a private space with works from her personal collection and elsewhere. The Stella Art Foundation consists of approximately 800 pieces, mainly by contemporary Russian artists like Ilya Kabakov, Andrei Monastyrski, Yuri Albert, and Oleg Kulik. But it also has some famed international types: Andy Warhol, Bill Viola, and Robert Mapplethorpe. Kesaevas's plans to build an art museum in a former bus depot in Moscow were foiled by bureaucratic hurdles.

182   Novy Muzei
*Soviet nonconformist art: the only alternative
to Socialist Realism*

Collector:
Aslan Chekhoyev

Address:
6-ya Liniya, 29
199004 St. Petersburg
Russia
Tel +7 812 3235090
info@novymuseum.ru
www.novymuseum.ru

Opening Hours:
Thurs–Sun: 12–7pm

If you think the only art movement in Russia before the end of the Soviet era was Socialist Realism, you need to visit the Novy Muzei in Saint Petersburg. It holds Aslan Chekhoyev's collection of the unofficial movements of **R** Russian modern art from the postwar era to the end of the twentieth century. After Josef Stalin died, in 1953, there was an underground wave of liberalization in the arts in Russia, and artists began experimenting, even if they could not exhibit. One famous episode of state repression of unsanctioned art was in 1974, when police broke up a show with a bulldozer and water cannons. Chekhoyev's collection is an important effort to direct public attention to works by artists like Lydia Masterkova, Lev Kropivnitsky, and Vladimir Nemukhin. Figures in their contemporary collection are artists like Oleg Kulik and the AES+F group, among others.

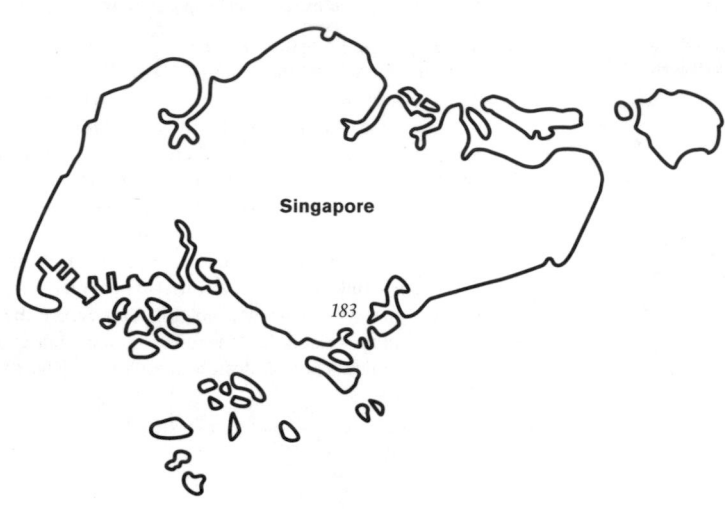

Singapore

183

183 The Private Museum
A collector's room—also for other collectors

The architect and real estate developer Daniel Teo began to collect art in the 1990s. His collecting intensified after 1994, when he teamed up with the Swede Björn Wetterling to open the Wetterling Teo Gallery in Singapore, one of the first international art galleries in Southeast Asia. Teo is particularly interested in Pop Art; the first work he acquired was by James Rosenquist. He also collects ink paintings and works by local artists. Alongside images by Roy Lichtenstein, Jim Dine, and Tom Wesselmann are those by Lim Tze Peng, Chua Ek Kay, and Kumari Nahappan. In 2008 he opened the Private Museum, where he exhibits his own collection—and that of fellow collectors. "I have met many collectors," Teo says, "and I would like to encourage more collectors to step forward to showcase their collections. It is an important way to establish relationships between artists, collectors, and the public."

S

Collector:
Daniel Teo

Address:
51 Waterloo Street, #02–06
Singapore 187969
Singapore
Tel +65 6738 2872
mail@theprivatemuseum.org
www.theprivatemuseum.org

Opening Hours:
Mon–Fri: 10am–7pm
Sat–Sun: 11am–5pm
And by appointment.

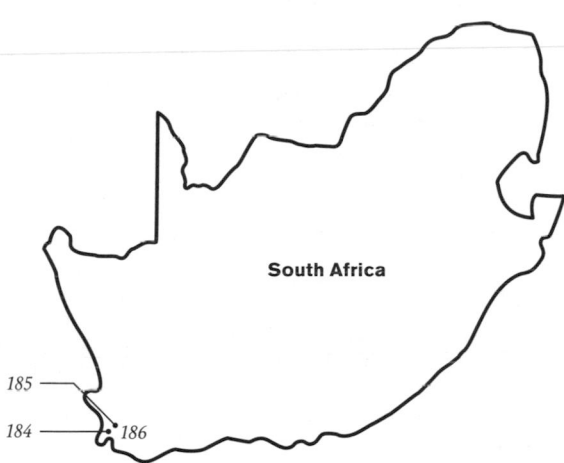

South Africa

185
184 — *186*

Collectors:
New Church Foundation

Address:
102 New Church Street
Tamboerskloof, Cape Town
South Africa
info@thenewchurch.co
www.thenewchurch.co

Opening Hours:
Tues, Thurs: 12–3pm
Sat: 11am–3pm

184 The New Church Museum
Contemporary African art as a mirror of society

The name "The New Church" does not refer to a church
as exhibition space but rather to the street upon which
the museum is located. What is church-like, however, is
the high degree of social commitment the museum has
taken on: according to its founding idea, the institution
is inspired by "the art's ability to facilitate the examina-
tion of society's values and norms, and believes that this
has tremendous social benefit." The New Church Museum
comprises a collection of about 450 works of contemporary
African art. Among them are works by renowned representatives such as Meschac Gaba, Willem Boshoff, and
Pieter Hugo. Two to three times per year, guest curators
work with the collection, occasionally bringing external
loans into dialogue. The museum is housed in a converted
Victorian house, which has been renovated to include a
minimalistic exhibition space at the rear.

S

185   The Hess Art Collection, Glen Carlou
Contemporary art for all and references to historical
and present-day Africa

Whether in his vineyards in California's Napa Valley or
in the Argentine Andes, cosmopolitan art-and-wine lover
Donald M. Hess fuses his passion for wine, contemporary
art, and art education in the South African Cape Town
region: "I truly believe contemporary art should be made
available to the widest possible audience," Hess says, "and
that collectors have a responsibility to make their collections accessible to the public to the best of their ability."
Everyone is welcome. No entrance fee. At his vineyard
Glen Carlou, in Klapmuts, not far from Cape Town, Hess
features work by artists like the British Andy Goldsworthy,
the South African Deryck Healey, and the Ivory Coast-
born painter Ouattara Watts, who lives in New York City.
Hess's collection of contemporary art reflects the rich cultural heritage of Africa.

Collector:
Donald M. Hess

Address:
Simondium Road
Klapmuts 7625
South Africa
Tel +27 21 8755528
welcome@glencarlou.co.za
www.glencarlou.co.za

Opening Hours:
Mon–Fri: 8:30am–5pm
Sat–Sun: 10am–3pm

Additional exhibition locations:
Salta, Argentina, p. 014
Napa, United States of America,
p. 203

186   Rupert Museum
South African art highlights since 1940
in a region known for its wine

A fire in their private home prompted collectors Huberte
and Anton Rupert to build a museum for their extensive
art collection. They found the right partner in Hannes
Meiring, an artist and architect from Cape Town. Meiring
decided upon a contemporary adaption of a simple seventeenth-century farmhouse. In 2005 the Rupert Museum
opened in South Africa's famous wine capital, Stellenbosch, and exhibits mainly South African art from 1940 to
2005 in a 2 000-square-meter space. Artists shown include
the New Objectivity landscape painter Jacobus Hendrik
Pierneef, the sculptor Anton van Wouw and the painter
Irma Stern, who was friends with the German Expressionists. Contemporary artists like William Kentridge have
also found their way into this large collection.

Collectors:
Huberte & Anton Rupert

Address:
Stellentia Avenue
Stellenbosch 7600
South Africa
Tel +27 21 8883344
rupertmuseum@remgro.com
www.rupertmuseum.org

Opening Hours:
Mon–Fri: 9:30am–4pm
Sat: 10am–1pm

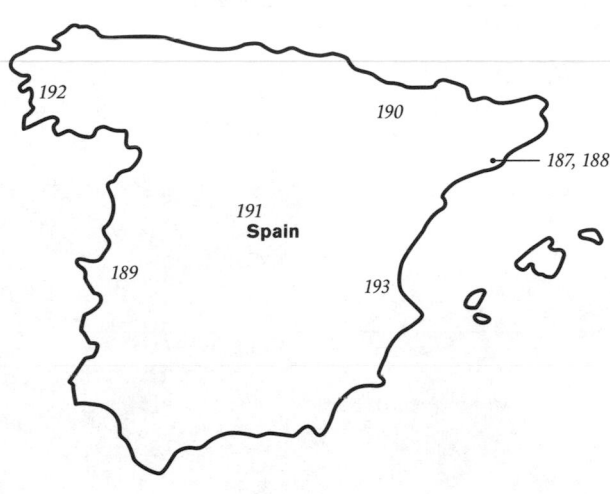

187 Fundació Suñol
Two rooms, two ideas: Spanish classics meet new art

Collector:
Josep Suñol

Address:
Passeig de Gràcia 98
08008 Barcelona
Spain
www.fundaciosunol.org

Opening Hours:
Mon–Fri: 11am–2pm, 4–8pm
Sa: 4–8pm
And by appointment.

Real estate mogul Josep Suñol's 1 200-work collection, opened in 2007, counts as one of the largest in Catalonia. Represented are the three great Spaniards of the twentieth century—Pablo Picasso, Joan Miró, and Salvador Dalí—as well as artists of the subsequent generation, including Antonio Saura, Antoni Tàpies, and Eduardo Chillida. The collection also holds works from Italy and Switzerland, like those by Giacomo Balla, Lucio Fontana, and Alberto Giacometti, and by a younger generation of artists, mostly from Catalonia. Two yearly exhibitions permit the public to warm to the collection. Nivell Zero, a second exhibition space with a separate entrance, leans toward to the radically contemporary: events that take place there have a laboratory or workshop feel. Exhibitions and a smattering of film and video screenings deal with current themes.

S

188   Fundació Vila Casas
*Three houses, three points of focus: painting, sculpture,
and photography*

The Catalonian pharmaceutical businessman Antoni Vila
Casas is fortunate to be able to show his foundation's extensive holdings of modern and contemporary art across
three architecturally interesting buildings in Catalonia.
The Museo Can Framis, in Barcelona, is located in a former
wool factory, replete with a new addition. Its 3 800 square
meters are devoted to painting. Over 350 sculptures are
housed at the Museo Con Mario, in a renovated cork factory
in Palafrugell on the Costa Brava. And not far from there,
at the Renaissance-era palace Palau Solterra, in Torroella
de Montgrí, is where Vila Casas shows 300 works from his
collection of photography. Catalonian art dominates, and
you don't find any superstar names. This has been changing
since 2010, however, with a rotating exhibition cycle that
has brought in the holdings of fellow collectors.

S

Collector:
Antoni Vila Casas

Addresses:
Museo Can Framis
Carrer Roc Boronat 116–126
08018 Barcelona, Spain
Tel +34 93 3208736

Museo Can Mario
Plaça Can Mario 7
17200 Palafrugell, Spain
Tel +34 972 306246

Museo Palau Solterra
Carrer de l'Església 10
17257 Torroella de Montgri, Spain
Tel +34 972 761976

www.fundaciovilacasas.com

Opening hours vary depending on
exhibition and season. Please
check the website for most current
information.

Moving pictures in the windows of chic boutiques, in dimly lit bodegas, or stylish tapas bars. Once a year, the Catalan metropolis

Barcelona transforms into a paradise for lovers of video

art. During the ten-day spring Loop Festival, artist videos are shown in approximately one hundred locations—sometimes in subtle locales, sometimes more prominently displayed. The three-day Loop fair, at the end of the festival, regularly attracts the international art community to the 1.8-million-inhabitant city. It is located in the rooms and suites of a four-star hotel, which are turned into "black boxes." This is perhaps the best opportunity to learn about local institutions and galleries. While the Museu Picasso and the Fundació Joan Miró focus on the art of these two superstars, complemented by smaller exhibitions, the Fundació Antoni Tàpies repeatedly distinguishes itself with a decidedly contemporary program that, in addition to its collection, shows artists ranging from Allan Kaprow to Jeanne Faust. Opened in 1995, the Museu d'Art Contemporani de Barcelona (MACBA), located in a blinding-white Richard Meier building, in the trendy Raval district, has an excellent collection of Spanish and international art from the 1950s to today. Temporary exhibitions are devoted to the latest trends but also to earlier avant-garde movements. Side glances at architecture, performance, dance, or film round off the program. From here it's just a few steps to one of the most exciting commercial galleries: Àngels Barcelona is specialized in conceptually charged and socially critical photography, film, and video art—for example, by Harun Farocki or the young Peruvian Daniela Ortiz. Director Emilio Álvarez is also a big inspiration for the local art scene: he's on the management team of the Loop, and his restaurant, Carmelitas, is a place to meet and casually look at video art while enjoying grilled artichokes and fresh octopus.

Nicole Büsing & Heiko Klaas

189   Centro de Artes Visuales/
Fundación Helga de Alvear
*One of the world's most important collections
of contemporary art*

Collector:
Helga de Alvear

Address:
Calle Pizarro 8
10003 Cáceres
Spain
Tel +34 927 626414
general@fundacionhelgadealvear.es
www.fundacionhelgadealvear.es

Opening Hours:
June–September
Tues–Sat: 10am–2pm, 6–9pm
Sun: 10am–2:30pm
October–May
Tues–Sat: 10am–2pm, 5–8pm
Sun: 10am–2:30pm

The German Helga de Alvear has lived in Madrid for over fifty years. There she runs a successful gallery with an international art program. But de Alvear does not just sell art to collectors; she has often been her own best client. This is how her roughly 2 800 works of art have been assembled: Joseph Beuys, Jeff Wall, Juan Muñoz, or Louise Bourgeois—the remarkable list could go on. Since 2010 Alvear has been incrementally revealing parts of her collection in the city of Cáceres, in southwestern Spain. Her collection is housed in a 3 000-square-meter patrician villa, redesigned by the highly sought Madrid architects Mansilla and Tuñón. A 7 000-square-meter addition has just gotten underway; the second phase of construction has just begun.

S

190 CDAN—Centro de Arte y Naturaleza/
Fundación Beulas
Spanish postwar painting and rotating exhibits
relating to landscape

Art and nature are the focus of activities of the CDAN–
Centro de Arte y Naturaleza/Fundación Beulas, opened
in 2006 near the northeastern Spanish city of Huesca. The
core of CDAN is formed by a private collection owned by
painter José Beulas, born in 1921. In the 1950s he began
collecting the work of friends and companions: primarily
regional landscape painters and sculptors, but also representatives of New Figuration and Informel, like stars
Antonio Saura and Antoni Tàpies. In 2000, Beulas converted all of his assets and property into a public foundation.
An organic, wavy building by star architect Rafael Moneo
houses the art center. The surrounding landscape is spectacular, and with the help of the foundation, it has been
blessed with land-art projects—eight so far—by artists including Richard Long, Per Kirkeby, and Ulrich Rückriem.

Collectors:
José Beulas & Maria Sarrate

Address:
Avenida Doctor Artero s/n
22004 Huesca
Spain
Tel +34 974 239893
info@cdan.es
www.cdan.es

Opening Hours:
April–October
Thurs–Fri: 6–9pm,
Sat: 11am–2pm, 6–9pm
Sun: 11am–2pm
November–March
Thurs–Fri: 5–8pm,
Sat: 11am–2pm, 5–8pm
Sun: 11am–2pm

191 OTR Espacio de Arte
Perpetual surprises in a manageable and
modern project space

The aim of this downtown Madrid art space, opened in
2008, is not just to present a collection. Located near the
Prado, the 300-square-meter OTR Espacio de Arte is dedicated to promoting young, not-yet-established art. Two to
three thematic exhibits annually investigate artistic questions that cross into architecture. José Antonio Trujillo
and Elsa López show the work from their own collection,
as well as that of guest artists. Spanish and Latin American positions dominate, among them Montserrat Soto
and Ernesto Neto. Artists like John Baldessari, Katharina
Grosse, and Rémy Zaugg are also represented in the collection, displayed in exhibitions that nicely fuse concepts
with sensual color.

S

Collectors:
José Antonio Trujillo & Elsa López

Address:
Calle de San Eugenio 10
28012 Madrid
Spain
info@espaciodearteotr.com
www.espaciodearteotr.com

By appointment only.

192   Fundación Rosón Arte Contemporáneo (RAC)
An award-winning concept-art collection far from the Spanish art-metropolises

Collector:
Carlos Rosón Gasalla

Address:
Padre Sarmiento 41
36002 Pontevedra
Spain
Tel +34 637 717172
info@fundacionrac.org
www.fundacionrac.org

By appointment only.

The Galician city of Pontevedra lies in the outermost region of northwest Spain. Here, you have to be brave to open an ambitious exhibition hall. Luckily, the Madrid-educated architect Carlos Rosón Gasalla is a risk-taker. His collection of 280 artworks from 160 Spanish and international artists opened on the ground floor of his house in 2007. It's not the simple artistic positions that triggered his passion to collect; rather, Gasalla favors art with conceptual and ironic leanings: work by Cildo Meireles, Karin Sander, and Liam Gillick, for example. Accolades have come quickly for the carefully curated exhibitions, which take place twice a year: in 2009 he received the collector award of the Madrid art fair ArCo. Rosón Gasalla's foundation also sponsors an artist-in-residence program, which has hosted artists such as Tania Bruguera and Caio Reisewitz.

193   Fundación Chirivella Soriano
Spanish painting since 1957 in a beautifully restored gothic palace

Collectors:
Manuel Chirivella Bonet &
Alicia Soriano Lleó

Address:
Calle deValeriola 13
46001 Valencia
Spain
Tel +34 196 3381215
info@chirivellasoriano.org
www.chirivellasoriano.org

Opening Hours:
Tues–Sat: 10am–2pm, 5–8pm
Sun: 10am–2pm

Notary Manuel Chirivella Bonet and his wife, Alicia Soriano Lleó, had been collecting art for over twenty years before they purchased a piece of property containing a dilapidated gothic palace in the oldest section of Valencia, in 2001. The permission to destroy the palace came a few days later. Apparently, a misunderstanding: the couple did not want to tear down the building; they wanted to restore it. They opened their collection—spread across 1 000 square meters—in 2005. The focus is on Spanish painting since 1957. That is the year both collectors were born, but the selection also serves an art historical purpose: in 1957 the followers of the Informel movement founded a breakaway artist group dedicated to new geometric abstraction and new kinds of figuration. Artists like Antonio Saura are well represented in the collection, which also shows more recent Spanish art.

S

Sweden

194

194 Wanås Foundation/Wanås Konst
Site-specific contemporary art on a castle estate in southern Sweden

Wanås castle in southern Sweden is a fortress from the fifteenth century. Charles and Marika Wachtmeister are the seventh generation to inhabit the residence. In 1987 Marika Wachtmeister began to exhibit sculptures on the sprawling grounds. Site-specific works by Jenny Holzer, Louise Bourgeois, Dan Graham, Ann Hamilton, Tadashi Kawamata, or Maya Lin are scattered across the estate. The Wanås Foundation is also known for its dense atmospheric sound works, such as an audio-walk by Janet Cardiff or an installation by Robert Wilson. Today, more than fifty permanently installed works comprise the continuously expanding outdoor collection. Since 2005, the spacious stable, built in 1759, has been used to house exhibitions. And since the Wanås castle is also the site of an eco-friendly agricultural business, guests who stroll around with map in hand looking at sculptures may just run into a few happy wandering cows.

S

Collectors:
Marika & Charles Wachtmeister

Address:
Box 67
289 90 Knislinge
Sweden
Tel +46 44 66158
info@wanaskonst.se
www.wanaskonst.se

Opening hours vary depending on exhibition and season. Please check the website for most current information.
The park is open daily from 8am–7pm.

200 —

196

195

197 199

Switzerland

201

198

Collectors:
Myriam Gebert Macconi &
Heinrich Gebert

Addresses:
Kunstmuseum Appenzell
Unterrainstrasse 5
9050 Appenzell
Switzerland
Tel +41 71 7881800

Kunsthalle Ziegelhütte
Ziegeleistrasse 14
9050 Appenzell
Switzerland
Tel +41 71 7881860

www.h-gebertka.ch

Please check the website
for most current information
on opening hours.

195 Kunstmuseum Appenzell/
Kunsthalle Ziegelhütte
*A perfect synthesis of the pristine with modern and
avant-garde architecture*

A must-see for architecture fans: inspired by the vision
of functional museum architecture—as the Swiss artist
Rémy Zaugg dreamed of—the architect-duo Annette Gig-
on and Mike Guyer built the Kunstmuseum Appenzell
(formerly: Museum Liner) in 1998, an architectural gem
in the Appenzell region. Right next to the museum, the
Heinrich Gebert Kulturstiftung opened a second house in
2003, the Kunsthalle Ziegelhütte, which was restored by
architect Robert Bamert and extended with an exhibition
hall. Wood, iron, brick, and exposed concrete are unified
in a successful synthesis of modernity and the local in this
multifunctional industrial monument. Up to six special
exhibitions a year showcase the broad range of the collection, from classic modernism to contemporary art, which
includes more than 1 000 works of the artists Carl August
and Carl Walter Liner, alongside 400 works by the likes of
Hans Arp, Frank Stella, or Beat Zoderer.

S

196   Kloster Schoenthal
Nature-inspired sculptures in a pristine landscape

There is a special place about fifty kilometers southeast of Basel in the gentle foothills of Swiss Jura. Basel-based entrepreneur and collector John Schmid has created a sculptural landscape with thirty-two works by Swiss and international artists around the former Schoenthal monastery. But urban art lovers had better exchange their fine shoes for rubber boots to walk the sculpture trail, which meanders through fifty hectares of fields, meadows, and forest. Twenty-four artists, from Richard Long to Roman Signer and Miriam Cahn, have engaged the natural environs with great sensitivity and realized works that meld perfectly into the landscape. Schmid, who maintains friendly relations with all the artists, acquired the estate and its landmark building in 1985.

Collector:
John Schmid

Address:
Schönthalstrasse 158
4438 Langenbruck
Switzerland
Tel +41 61 7067676
mail@schoenthal.ch
www.schoenthal.ch

The park is open at all times.

197   Museum Sammlung Rosengart
The crème de la crème of classic modernism:
Picasso, Klee, and friends

S

The Lucerne-based Rosengart collection inhabits a neoclassical building formerly owned by the Swiss National Bank. Carefully remodeled by the Basel architecture firm Diener & Diener, the building, finished in 2002, offers perfect conditions for this impressive collection of classic modernism. Art dealer Siegfried Rosengart (1894–1985) didn't just *collect* Pablo Picasso, Georges Braque, and Henri Matisse; he and his daughter Angela, who entered the family business at age sixteen, were actually close friends with all of them. And thus, "all the paintings were chosen with the heart," Angela Rosengart says. The ground floor is devoted to Picasso, and the first floor contains paintings by his contemporaries Fernand Léger and Wassily Kandinsky. In the secure basement, where bolted safes used to hold gold reserves of the Swiss national bank, a fine collection of Paul Klee works hangs gently illuminated.

Collectors:
Siegfried & Angela Rosengart

Address:
Pilatusstrasse 10
6003 Lucerne
Switzerland
Tel +41 41 2201660
info@rosengart.ch
www.rosengart.ch

Opening Hours:
April–October
Mon–Sun: 10am–6pm
November–March
Mon–Sun: 11am–5pm

198   Collezione Giancarlo e Danna Olgiati
*Avant-garde art of the twentieth and
twenty-first centuries on Lake Lugano*

Collectors:
Giancarlo & Danna Olgiati

Address:
Riva Caccia 1
6900 Lugano
Switzerland
Tel +41 58 8667214
mediazione@lugano.ch
www.collezioneolgiati.ch

Opening Hours:
Fri–Sun: 11am–6pm

Initially devoted to the German Expressionist avant
garde, in the early 1960s, the then-young lawyer Giancarlo
Olgiati began to direct his attention to the contemporary
art scene. In so doing, he discovered the artists of the Nou-
veaux Réalisme, whose work he began to collect systematically in the second half of the 1970s. Since 1985, his wife,
Danna Olgiati, a gallerist specialized in Italian Futurism,
has assisted his building up of the collection, which also
includes positions of Spatialism, Arte Povera, and the   **S**
latest tendencies of neo-abstraction. In 2012 the Olgiatis
gave the city a part of their collection on permanent loan,
which is now stored and presented in temporary exhibitions in an underground area in Lugano's Central Park.
The space's name, " 1," mirrors its location; it will be
managed as of autumn 2015 by the new cultural center
LAC Lugano Arte e Cultura.

199   Kunst(Zeug)Haus

*An extensive private collection of Swiss contemporary art
of the last thirty years*

Zurich-based lawyer Peter Bosshard and his wife, Elisabeth, started collecting art in the 1970s. They had just completed a two-year stay in New York City and returned to Switzerland, where they began a decades-long engagement with the contemporary art scene. Today, the Bosshards support artists and art projects, in addition to having accumulated roughly 5 000 works of their own. In May 2008 they opened an art center in a former arsenal in the city of Rapperswil. Zurich architects Isa Stürm and Urs Wolf meticulously transformed the long and bulky building into a spacious 2 600 square meters, providing enough room for three to four exhibits each year. Aside from established Swiss art stars like Silvia Bächli, Fischli/Weiss, or Roman Signer, younger positions such as Mario Sala or Yves Netzhammer have also found a comfortable home.

Collectors:
Peter & Elisabeth Bosshard

Address:
Schönbodenstrasse 1
8640 Rapperswil
Switzerland
Tel +41 55 2202080
info@kunstzeughaus.ch
www.kunstzeughaus.ch

Opening Hours:
Wed–Fri: 2–6pm
Sat–Sun: 11am–6pm

Basel's flagship is Art Basel, undisputedly the most important art fair in the world, held each year in mid-June. The elite of international collectors meet at Art Basel or at one of the half-dozen side fairs taking place simultaneously. Approximately 300 participating galleries at the main fair offer the most exquisite, most sensational—and, not least, most expensive—contemporary works for sale today. Given this spectacle, visitors are apt to overlook the city's expansive range of top-class art institutions: the Kunstmuseum, for example, together with its branch for contemporary art, the Museum für Gegenwartskunst, holds collections ranging from Lucas Cranach the Elder to Wolfgang Tillmans. Kunsthalle Basel, which specializes in young avant-garde positions, attracts visitors with its dependably fascinating program. New to the scene as of 2014 is the Haus für elektronische Künste (HEK), a center of excellence for "all art forms that express themselves through new technologies and media, and reflect upon them." Likewise forging new paths is the neighboring Schaulager, a hybrid combination of museum, art depot, and research facility, located in a polygonal building designed by the Basel architect super-duo Herzog & de Meuron, where art stars like Matthew Barney or Paul Chan are fêted with monographic exhibitions. In the **Basel** suburb of Riehen, the Fondation Beyeler scores big not only with its Renzo Piano architecture, which is perfectly suited to the surrounding landscape, but also with exhibitions of classical modernism, postwar art, and established contemporaries like Jenny Holzer and Jeff Koons. Interesting exhibitions of international and Swiss contemporary artists can also be found in the gallery Stampa. The Kunsthaus Baselland, in Muttenz, renowned for its discourse-friendly program, and the Vitra Design Museum, in Weil am Rhein, which resides in a deconstructivist building built by Frank O. Gehry, are additional worthwhile destinations outside the city.

Nicole Büsing & Heiko Klaas

Collectors:
Ernst & Hildy Beyeler

Address:
Baselstrasse 101
4125 Riehen, Basel
Switzerland
Tel +41 61 6459700
info@fondationbeyeler.ch
www.fondationbeyeler.ch

Opening Hours:
Wed. 10am–8pm
Thurs–Tues: 10am–6pm

200 Fondation Beyeler
*World-famous art in a building by Renzo Piano
outside of Basel*

His standards were always high. Ernst Beyeler, who died in 2010, turned his gallery in Basel into one of the most important addresses of the international art market. Together with his wife, Hildy, he built an impressive collection of Modernist, Abstract Expressionist, and Pop Art works. Paintings by Pablo Picasso, Mark Rothko, and Andy Warhol have all found a home here. In 1997, the collectors opened the Fondation Beyeler in their hometown of Riehen, on the outskirts of Basel. The elongated Renzo Piano building blends perfectly into the landscape. Every year the foundation stages three large exhibitions of modern or contemporary art. In 2008, Sam Keller, a former director of Art Basel and a hyper-connected art-world figure, became the foundation's director, lending a sense of continuity and inventiveness to the collection. If you think the Museum of Modern Art in New York City is too far to travel, a visit here might be just as good.

Collector:
Ruedi Bechtler

Address:
Via Castell 300
7524 Zuoz
Switzerland
Tel +41 81 8515253
info@hotelcastell.ch
www.hotelcastell.ch/art07

Open visitation during hotel
hours. Guided tours every
Thursday at 5pm.

201 Sammlung Ruedi Bechtler—
Kunst im Castell
*Contemporary art of the highest quality
in a truly cool hotel*

There are simply too many so-called art hotels showcasing works by unknown regional artists usually purchased in a blitz right before the hotel's grand opening. Hotel Castell, in Zuoz, in the Engadin region, however, goes about things differently. In the house and its surroundings, the visitor bumps into works by Pipilotti Rist, Tadashi Kawamata, Roman Signer, or Lawrence Weiner—most of them built specifically for the place. Hotel owner Ruedi Bechtler is an artist in his own right, and sensible enough not to feed his guests standard artistic fare. In 1955, his father, Walter A. Bechtler, started one of the largest Swiss art foundations, whose mission is to make contemporary art accessible. Its current president, Ruedi Bechtler, is deeply devoted to this goal. One of the hotel's highlights, James Turrell's *Skyspace,* offers the opportunity for a contemplative experience both night and day.

S

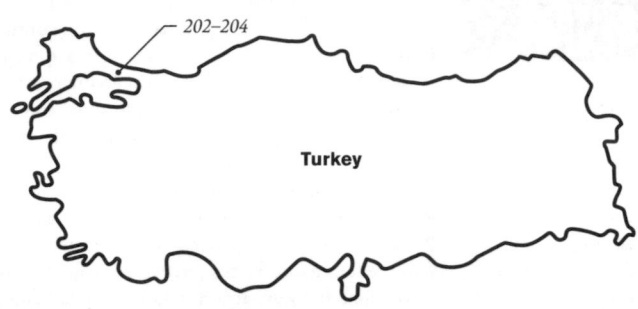

202–204

Turkey

202 Proje4L—Elgiz Museum of Contemporary Art
Influential Turkish and international contemporary art

Long before contemporary Turkish art came into the spotlight, Sevda and Can Elgiz knew its inherent worth. The couple has been eagerly collecting since the early 1980s, even knocking down walls of their own home to fit the artworks inside, as they told the American magazine *Art+Auction.* Initially they focused on Turkish artists; at the end of the 1990s they began to acquire works by international artists. The private Elgiz Museum—opened in 2001 as one of the first institutions for contemporary art in Turkey—now holds works by influential Turkish artists like Ömer Uluç and Güngör Taner, as well as that by international names like Tracey Emin and Barbara Kruger. In 2012, the museum was supplemented by 1 500 square meters of open-air, rooftop exhibition space.

T

Collectors:
Sevda & Can Elgiz

Address:
Meydan Sokak
Beybi Giz Plaza B Blok
Maslak
34398 Istanbul
Turkey
Tel +90 212 2902525
info@proje4l.org
www.elgizmuseum.org

Opening Hours:
Wed–Fri: 10am–5pm
Sat: 10am–4pm
Tues: by appointment only

The development of the art scene in **Istanbul** can be described in one word: speedy. Within the span of just a few years, Turkish contemporary art has moved into the international spotlight, and despite low support from the state, the metropolis has established itself as a major international art center. This is due foremost to the private sector, with corporations and banks generously subsidizing the city's art institutions. One example is a platform for contemporary art, Akbank Sanat Beyoğlu, founded in 1993, which is sponsored by a financial institution. So is Istanbul Modern, a private museum of modern and contemporary art established in 2004 by an industry group in a former warehouse on the Bosporus. Both institutions are located in the Beyoğlu district, considered one of the most important addresses of the local art scene. Here you'll find a smattering of young galleries, such as Pi Artworks, Non, Galerist, Galeri Nev, Rodeo, or Pirosmani. Additional art institutions reflecting the contemporary art scene in Istanbul are Santrallstanbul, located in a former power plant, the nonprofit center Salt, as well as Garaj, whose activities include exhibitions and publishing the magazine *Gist*. The Istanbul Biennial, launched in 1987, continues to make a decisive contribution to the development of the Istanbul art scene. Today, it's one of the most important art biennials, alongside Venice, São Paulo, and Sydney. It is held from mid-September to mid-November and starts at the same time as the annual art fair Contemporary Istanbul. Since September 2013 the city has also been home to the ArtInternational Istanbul, a new art fair that sees itself as a bridge between East and West and which has quickly established itself.

Silvia Anna Barrilà

203 Nesrin Esirtgen Collection
*Turkish and international artists reflecting
upon the present*

Collector:
Nesrin Esirtgen

Address:
İstiklal Caddesi Mısır Apt.
No:163 Kat 5 D: 17
Beyoğlu
34430 Istanbul
Turkey
Tel +90 212 2437853
info@nesrinesirtgencollection.com
www.nesrinesirtgencollection.com

Opening Hours:
Tues–Fri, Sun: 11am–6:15pm

Even as a child, Nesrin Esirtgen showed a keen interest in composition, form, and color. From this fascination a true passion has developed over time: for twenty years Esirtgen has been collecting contemporary Turkish art. In 2011, the businesswoman, active in the family's pharmaceutical company, opened an art space in the lively Beyoğlu district of Istanbul, in which she presents up to four temporary exhibitions a year. One of these is always devoted to her own collection, which includes—alongside national artists such as Mehmet Ali Uysal, Ali Kazma, and Ahmet Öğüt—international names such as Jaume Plensa, Ai Weiwei, Tony Cragg, and Mark Manders. Other exhibitions realized in the space are dedicated to young artists, who Esirtgen also supports by publishing monographs of their work.

204 Özil Collection
East and West, past and present in the heart of Istanbul

Collector:
Dağhan Özil

Address:
Ayazmadere Cad. 4
Fulya/Besiktas
34349 Istanbul
Turkey
Tel +90 212 2276852
eymur@ozilcollection.com
www.ozilcollection.com

By appointment only.

Istanbul is the place where East meets West. Art dealer and collector Dağhan Özil has been leveraging this knowledge since 1986, when he began exploring the interaction between Western and Turkish artists in his gallery, now headquartered in both Istanbul and Berlin. Özil's private collecting reflects his bifurcated interest: Islamic art, on the one hand; contemporary Western art stars, on the other. In 2007 Özil opened his private collection **T** to the public, atop his Istanbul gallery, showing around 250 works of contemporary art and 500 pieces of Islamic ceramics and bronzes, displayed in thematic rooms that highlight the legacy of the Islamic–Western past and today's understanding of international art, including works by Wim Delvoye, Sarah Morris, Gerhard Richter, Markus Lüpertz, and Jan Fabre.

205

Ukraine

205 Pinchuk Art Centre
Blue-chip contemporary in the first private museum in the former USSR

Within the span of a few years, Ukrainian billionaire Victor Pinchuk has asserted himself as one of the most powerful collectors on the international scene. He bought *Hanging Heart (Magenta/Gold),* by Jeff Koons, for a reported 23.6 million dollars, and *99 Cent II Diptychon,* by Andreas Gursky, for a reported 3.3 million dollars, setting a record price for both artists. Pinchuk has purchased other million-dollar artworks by the likes of blue-chip stars Peter Doig and Takashi Murakami. He reveals it all at his very popular Pinchuk Art Centre, founded in 2006, a colossal six-storey building that was the first private museum opened in the former USSR, which has had nearly a million visitors come through its doors. "There is only one queue in the country," Pinchuk told *The New Yorker* in 2009: "ours."

Collector:
Victor Pinchuk

Address:
1/3-2, "A" Block
Velyka Vasylkivska/Baseyna vul.
01004 Kiev
Ukraine
Tel +38 44 5900858
info@pinchukartcentre.org
www.pinchukartcentre.org

Opening Hours:
Tues–Sun: 12–9pm

U

206, 207 — *208*

United Arab Emirates

206 The Farjam Collection
*A voyage from ancient Islamic art to contemporary
Middle Eastern and Western art*

Collector:
Farhad Farjam

Address:
DIFC Gate Village 4
Dubai
United Arab Emirates
Tel +971 4 3230303
info@farjamfoundation.org
www.farjamfoundation.org

Opening Hours:
Sun–Thurs: 10am–8pm
And by appointment.

Farhad Farjam, a Dubai-based Iranian industrialist, started his collection when he was still a student in New York
in the 1970s. He had bought the first piece of his collection
of Persian miniatures for 2 000 dollars, the cost of a semester's tuition. This resulted in, well, a lost semester. "It was
a dramatic story for me that I never forget," he recalled
during a panel at Art Dubai in 2010. Today Farjam owns
one of the most important collections of privately held
Islamic art in the world, an undertaking he considers a **U**
social responsibility. Over the years Farjam has turned to
modern and contemporary art from the Middle East and
the West. The Farjam Collection today includes artists
like Mohamed Ehsai and Nja Mahdaoui, as well as western icons Andy Warhol and Jean-Michel Basquiat. The
collection forms the core of the eponymous foundation,
which has committed itself to the promotion of intercul-
tural dialogue.

207   Salsali Private Museum
*A platform for collectors in Dubai's
hub of creativity*

Located in the industrial area Al Quoz 1—Dubai's des-
ignated hub of arts and creativity—the Salsali Private
Museum, which opened in November 2011, is not just an
exhibition space for Ramin Salsali's collection of contemporary art. It is also a platform for collectors who want to
meet and exchange ideas, or to exhibit their own collections. "An art collection is an art in itself," Salsali says. "It
should reveal to its audience a story more significant than
any individual viewpoint." An Iranian consultant for the
petrochemical industry, Salsali started collecting when
he was a twenty-one-year-old student in Germany. Today
he owns over 300 works by Middle Eastern artists such
as Reza Derakshani, Mona Hatoum, and Shirin Neshat,
which sit alongside international stars like Arman, Niki de
Saint Phalle, Jonathan Meese, André Butzer, Fischli/Weiss,
Meret Oppenheim, and Daniel Richter.

Collector:
Ramin Salsali

Address:
Al Quoz 1, Road 8
Alserkal Avenue Complex/Unit 14
Dubai
United Arab Emirates
Tel +971 4 3809600
spm@salsalipm.com
www.salsalipm.com

Opening Hours:
Sat: 1–5pm
Sun–Thurs: 11am–6pm
And by appointment.

Dubai's art scene reflects the spirit of the city: contemporary, rich, and dynamic. In less than a decade **Dubai** has become one of the most prominent centers of the international art market—and for several good reasons: first, there's the key protagonist of the development of Dubai's local scene, Art Dubai, an enormously successful art fair, founded in 2007, which takes place every March at the hotel Madinat Jumeirah. Second, Christie's had already transformed the city into a Middle Eastern center for the international secondary art market by launching its first Dubai-based auction of international modern and contemporary art, in 2006. Other factors favorable to Dubai's art industry are the cosmopolitan character of the city and its prosperous economy. The business-friendly environment has facilitated the establishment of interesting art galleries, including Cuadro Fine Art Gallery and Opera Gallery, which have settled around the Dubai International Financial Centre (DIFC) Gate Village. Another gallery hub is the industrial area Al Quoz, where The Third Line, Green Art Gallery, and Gallery Isabelle van den Eynde are located. March is the best time to discover Dubai's art scene, not only because of Art Dubai but also events like Design Days Dubai, a fair devoted to various facets of design, and Sikka Art Fair, which focuses on emergent art from the United Arab Emirates, initiated by the governmental Dubai Culture & Arts Authority (DCAA). Every two years these events coincide with the Sharjah Biennial, organized by Dubai's neighbor emirate. As the entire region invests enormous resources in the arts, large institutions are emerging in the region, including the National Museum of Qatar or the Louvre Abu Dhabi, both designed by French architect Jean Nouvel. There's also the Guggenheim Abu Dhabi, designed by Frank O. Gehry, and the Performing Arts Centre designed by Zaha Hadid. Once the construction of these museums is completed, there will be even more reasons to explore this colorful region.

Silvia Anna Barrilà

208 Barjeel Art Foundation
Modern and contemporary art from four corners of the Arab world

Collector:
Sultan Sooud Al-Qassemi

Address:
Maraya Art Centre
Al Qasba
Sharjah
United Arab Emirates
info@barjeelartfoundation.com
www.barjeelartfoundation.com

Opening hours vary depending on exhibition. Please check the website for most current information.

The term "Arab world" comprises a vast territory spanning from the Middle East to North Africa, subsuming the Levant, Maghreb, Egypt, the Gulf Arab, and Iraq—places strongly characterized by their own history and culture. This internal diversity of the Arab world's countries lies at the basis of Sultan Sooud Al-Qassemi's art collection, which includes over 500 works by both modern and contemporary Arab artists, such as Shakir Hassan Al Said, Khaled Hafez, and Lara Baladi. Sultan Al-Qassemi spent over a decade amassing his collection, which was opened to the public in 2010, on the second floor of the Maraya Art Centre, in Al Qasba, the entertainment hub of Sharjah. **U** "What's the point in art," he asked the Abu Dhabi *National,* "if it is not shared?"

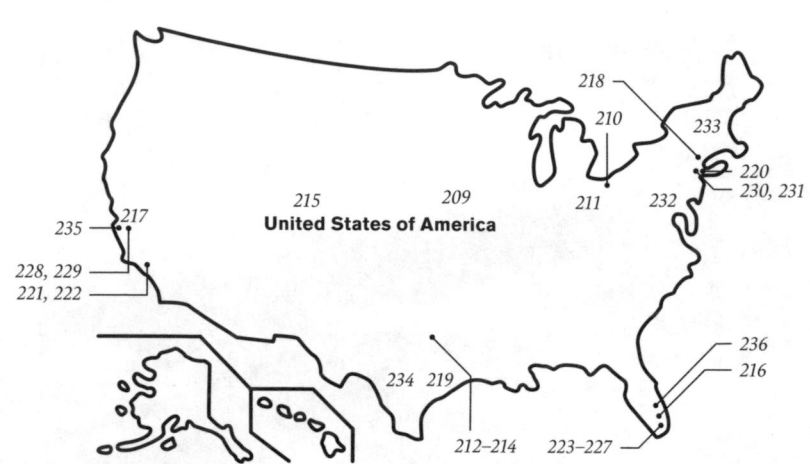

209   Clarinda Carnegie Art Museum
*A double-feature of contemporary art
in the heart of America*

Over eighteen months, in 2013 and 2014, Robert and Karen Duncan opened not one but two exhibition spaces in the American heartland. The couple has spent the past thirty years building a collection of over 2 000 works, by a varied cast of artists such as Kiki Smith, Bruce Nauman, Bernar Venet, Yinka Shonibare, and Sophie Ryder. Female artists are particularly well represented. While the Duncans have been open to by-appointment visits to their home to share these works, they recently decided to open up their holdings even further. Wanting to give back to their hometown of Clarinda they purchased the city's Carnegie Library, completely restored and refurbished it, and then turned it into an art museum for yet more works from their collection. It follows Assemblage, an exhibition space opened in 2013 near downtown Lincoln, Nebraska, together with fellow collectors Marc and Kathryn LeBaron, providing access on a by-appointment basis.

U

Collectors:
Robert & Karen Duncan

Address:
300 N 16th Street
Clarinda, IA 51632
United States of America
www.clarindacarnegieartmuseum.com

Opening Hours:
Wed, Sun: 1–4pm

210   Transformer Station
*International photographic art and
a unique collaboration*

Collectors:
Laura Ruth & Fred Bidwell

Address:
1460 West 29th Street
Cleveland, OH 44113
United States of America
Tel +1 216 9385429
info@transformerstation.org
www.transformerstation.org

Opening Hours:
Wed, Fri, Sat: 12–5pm
Thurs: 12–8pm

Fred and Laura Ruth Bidwell exhibit their collection in
a former transformer station six months out of the year.
Then they leave the exhibition rooms to the watchful eyes
of the Cleveland Museum of Art, which uses the atmosphere of the old industrial building for exhibitions that fit
the cool ambiance. This unique collaboration was decided
before the Transformer Station's February 2013 opening,
because both the Bidwells and the museum pursue the
same goal of bringing smartly curated contemporary art
exhibits to Cleveland. The collector couple's emphasis is on
photography, having purchased works by Jessica Backhaus,
Hiroshi Sugimoto, Philip-Lorca diCorcia, and Martin Parr.
They also offer a perfect link to the curatorial mission of
the museum by presenting historical positions like Walker
Evans and Lee Friedlander.

211   Pizzuti Collection
Meritorious midwestern assemblage of the now

Collectors:
Ron & Ann Pizzuti

Address:
632 Park Street
Columbus, OH 43215
United States of America
Tel +1 614 2804004
info@pizzuticollection.org
www.pizzuticollection.org

Opening Hours:
Thurs–Sat: 11am–5pm
And by appointment.

The Pizzuti Collection is one of the newest entrants onto
the American private museum circuit—one of the most
dynamic, too. Real-estate mogul Ron Pizzuti assembled the
estimated 2 000-work-strong collection over the past four
decades, starting with Karel Appel's *Circus People,* in 1974.
The print hung in the collection's inaugural exhibition,
in September 2013. Spread over a three-storey building,
which formerly served as the headquarters of an insurance
company, the Pizzuti Collection rotates at least once per
year. It features a wide range of artists from the collection, **U**
from established names like Carroll Dunham and David
Hammons to emerging exponents like Florian Meisenberg.
Pizzuti is particularly keen on works by Cuban artists, a
passion that began after a trip to the country in 2009. He
also recently launched a sculpture garden on the premises
with works by Tom Friedman, Thomas Houseago, and Jason
Middlebrook.

212 The Goss-Michael Foundation
*A must-see for everyone who loves
the Young British Artists*

The strong contingent of Young British Artists in Dallas, Texas, is due to the longstanding alliance between art dealer Kenny Goss and the pop singer George Michael. Both have great sympathy for Damien Hirst's marinated cadavers that deal with death and ephemerality, and for Tracy Emin's eroticized installations. Sarah Lucas's feminist statements also make an appearance in the collection. Since 2007 you can catch a glimpse of the overall criteria of the Goss-Michael Foundation, where the two enthusiasts have assembled roughly 500 works, including those by Gilbert & George, Op Art queen Bridget Riley, or provocateurs Jake & Dinos Chapman. Many works are from the 1990s, which were formative years, says the collector duo, for an entire artistic generation.

Collectors:
Kenny Goss & George Michael

Address:
1405 Turtle Creek Boulevard
Dallas, TX 75207
United States of America
Tel +1 214 6960555
www.gossmichaelfoundation.org

Opening Hours:
Tues–Fri: 10am–5pm
Sat: 11am–4pm

213 Nasher Sculpture Center
*A private collection of masterpieces every museum
dreams of owning*

Patsy and Raymond Nasher began obeying one command in the 1950s, and they have stayed true to it ever since: only collect sculpture. More specifically, by modernist artists like Henry Moore, August Rodin, Pablo Picasso, and Raymond Duchamp-Villon. These works are accompanied by masterpieces by Alexander Calder, Richard Serra, and Claes Oldenburg. Every single object in this collection is museum-worthy; taken as a whole, they show the development of an entire epoch. Since 2003 the Nasher Sculpture Center has presented its holdings in exciting contrasts and supplemented by matching new acquisitions. Built by architect and Pritzker-Prize winner Renzo Piano, the pavilion-like structure, situated at the end of a park in Dallas's arts district, allows for a perspective that sets the robust outdoor sculptures in a relationship with the fragile objects inside.

U

Collectors:
Patsy & Raymond Nasher

Address:
2001 Flora Street
Dallas, TX 75201
United States of America
Tel +1 214 2425100
www.nashersculpturecenter.org

Opening Hours:
Tues–Sun: 11am–5pm

214 The Warehouse
Two major United States collections in dialogue

Collectors:
Cindy & Howard Rachofsky
Amy & Vernon Faulconer

Address:
14105 Inwood Road
Dallas, TX 75244
United States of America
Tel +1 214 4422875
www.thewarehousedallas.org

By appointment only.

Cindy and Howard Rachofsky open their Rachofsky House, designed by Richard Meier, for events devoted to their charitable interests. But art lovers can find parts of the collection with works by Gerhard Richter, Lucio Fontana, Sigmar Polke, Piero Manzoni, Mario Merz, Kazuo Shiraga, and Atsuko Tanaka at a second address: since 2013 Cindy and Howard Rachofsky have shared a large hall called The Warehouse—divided into sixteen galleries—with fellow collectors Amy and Vernon Faulconer. Here the latter are interested in the art of Anish Kapoor, Bridget Riley, and James Turrell, among others. The result is an exciting dialogue of exhibits and, because collaborating collectors are rare elsewhere, a truly innovative experiment. **U**

215 The Dikeou Collection
Two artists collect artists they find to be important

The artists Devon and Pany Dikeou are less interested in establishing themselves than in making known the colleagues they deem important. Among them are established names like Momoyo Torimitsu, Vik Muniz, or Rainer Ganahl. Above all, the collection suggests a preference for subtle comedy, which can be found in the works of Dan Asher, Jonathan Horowitz, Anicka Yi, or Margaret Lee—not exactly what collectors of prestigious works are looking for. The Dikeou's exhibition hall, in Denver, matches their taste in art: an unrenovated high-rise building from the 1950s that has retained its retro charm. For the most recent acquisitions the house has now been expanded. Another novelty lies a few blocks away: Dikeou Pop-Up is a second address for young artists—and an enormous archive of vinyl records.

Collectors:
Devon & Pany Dikeou

Addresses:
1615 California Street, Suite 515
Denver, CO 80202
United States of America
Tel +1 303 6233001
info@dikeoucollection.org
www.dikeoucollection.org

Dikeou Pop-Up:
Colfax
312 East Colfax Avenue
Denver, CO 80203
United States of America

Opening Hours:
Wed–Fri: 11am–5pm
By appointment only.

216 Girls' Club
The name is the mission: to promote and rediscover female artists

With glamorous names like Beatriz Milhazes, Elizabeth Peyton, or the American concept-icon Barbara Kruger, you'll get noticed fast in the art business. But Francie Bishop Good and David Horvitz could name dozens of female artists who have been unjustly overlooked, which is why the American collector pair founded the Girls' Club in 2006. Here in this private foundation—comprised of spacious exhibition halls tucked behind a shimmering façade, designed by the fabulous architect Margi Nothard—the collectors show their holdings of women's art: the elaborate, cartoony paintings of Sandy Winters, or the stunning photography of Tracey Baran, who documented the inhabitants of a small New York town before her untimely death at age thirty-three, in 2008.

U

Collectors:
Francie Bishop Good &
David Horvitz

Address:
117 Northeast 2nd Street
Fort Lauderdale, FL 33301
United States of America
Tel +1 954 8289151
admin@girlsclubcollection.org
www.girlsclubcollection.org

Opening Hours:
Wed–Fri: 1–5pm
And by appointment.

217   Oliver Ranch Foundation
A sculpture park where art responds to nature

Collectors:
Nancy & Steve Oliver

Address:
22205 River Road
Geyserville, CA 95441
United States of America
Tel +1 707 8573975
www.oliverranchfoundation.org

Opening Hours:
Fri–Sun: Only guided tours
with prior registration. Group
tours upon request.

Driving through the countryside of San Francisco to visit the region's vineyards is no longer a hidden secret. But Nancy and Steve Oliver's sculpture park still is. In the mid-1980s the two decided to complement the picturesque landscape with art. The first sculpture was *Shepherd's Muse,* by Judith Shea, an allusion to sheep farming, the collectors' shared hobby. This was followed by sculptures by Miroslaw Balka, Fred Sandback, Richard Serra, and Bill Fontana. The fixed principle of the Oliver Ranch Foundation is that art must directly respond to nature. Each work is created in dialogue with the artist. The realization of a work often takes several years, as was the case with Ann Hamilton's accessible *Tower,* the centerpiece of the Olivers' collection. Visitors can take a seat on one of two curiously constructed staircases, while performances and plays are presented on the other.

218   The Brant Foundation Art Study Center
Important American art from the 1960s to the present

Collector:
Peter M. Brant

Address:
941 North Street
Greenwich, CT 06831
United States of America
Tel +1 203 8690611
info@brantfoundation.org
www.brantfoundation.org

Opening Hours:
Mon–Fri: 10am–4pm
By appointment only.

He sits at the source and is one of the first to know who the artists of tomorrow will be: Peter M. Brant—the owner of Brant Publications, chairman and CEO of a large paper manufacturing concern, and a coproducer of movies about important artists of the twentieth century, such as Jean-Michel Basquiat and Jackson Pollock. Over the decades, Brant has amassed one of the world's largest and most distinguished collections of American contemporary artists, including Andy Warhol, Julian Schnabel, and Keith Haring. His focus on American art stems from his concern with the American sense of life, which he finds in every work anew. The spectrum runs from the positive attitude of Jeff Koons to the provocative criticism of performer-sculptor Paul McCarthy. Appropriately, since 2009, a large part of the collection has been exhibited in something quite traditionally American: a former barn.   **U**

219 The Menil Collection
*An amazing collection with the format
of a metropolitan museum*

The legacy of the French-born pair is not only the imposing private museum with numerous individual galleries for works by Mark Rothko, Cy Twombly, or Byzantine art. Dominique and John de Menil began their collection in the 1940s and have amassed invaluable works of art over the decades: Fernand Léger, Henri Matisse, or Pablo Picasso mark the entry point of this incredible collection, and Jean-Michel Basquiat, Eric Fischl, Cindy Sherman, and Robert Gober belong to the list of later additions. Between the two groups hang the heroes of American postwar painting: Barnett Newman, Willem de Kooning, or Jasper Johns. Outdoor sculptures by Mark di Suvero or Michael Heizer complete the history of art in the twentieth century. Dominique de Menil, who passed away in 1997, had survived her husband for more than twenty years. She founded their museum in 1987.

Collectors:
Dominique & John de Menil

Address:
1533 Sul Ross Street
Houston, TX 77006
United States of America
Tel +1 713 5259400
info@menil.org
www.menil.org

Opening Hours:
Wed–Sun: 11am–7pm

220 Fisher Landau Center for Art
*International stars from the 1960s on, in one of
New York's most important collections*

It all started with a robbery: over half a century ago, a few thieves relieved Emily Fisher Landau of her jewelry. The insurance company reimbursed the victim, who then wondered just what exactly she should do with her fresh funds. She decided on art, becoming one of the most important collectors and patrons in all of New York City. Pablo Picasso, Fernand Léger, Piet Mondrian, and Jasper Johns all hang in Fisher Landau's spacious Manhattan townhouse—big, but not big enough for the entire 1 300-work collection. So in 1991 the Fisher Landau Center of Art was opened in a remodeled factory. Its focus is on works after 1960, works Fisher Landau bought directly from the artists at the start of their careers, the timely result of good instinct, good advisers, or both: Donald Judd, Jenny Holzer, Ed Ruscha, Kiki Smith, Cy Twombly, and Sherrie Levine are all here.

Collector:
Emily Fisher Landau

Address:
38-27 30th Street
Long Island City, NY 11101
United States of America
Tel +1 718 9370727
info@flcart.org
www.flcart.org

Opening Hours:
Thurs–Mon: 12–5pm

U

For many in the art world, **Miami** represents an annual December pilgrimage to Art Basel Miami Beach and its numerous satellite fairs. The thirteen-year-old exposition—now arguably on equal footing with its European progenitor, in Switzerland—certainly has more than enough dazzle to sate the visual and conceptual appetites of even the most enduring lover of art, not to mention its marathon of afterhours delights. But for that very reason, too, so much of what Miami has to offer can easily fall by the wayside. Principal among new additions to the city is the Pérez Art Museum Miami (PAMM), which opened its doors to the public during Art Basel Miami Beach 2013. First appearing as the Center for the Fine Arts (CFA), in 1984, then reincarnated as the Miami Art Museum (MAM), in 1996, the museum now barely resembles its previous iterations. This is due in no small part to the 131-million-dollar architectural gem in which it is housed, courtesy of Swiss architectural duo Herzog & de Meuron, one of contemporary art's favorite museum designers. The PAMM also happens to be part of the Miami Art Museums Alliance (MAMA), initiated to increase the city's international art profile in the fifty-one weeks of the year when Art Basel isn't in town and to coordinate programming across Miami's relatively nascent but ever-improving cadre of institutions. Miami also leads America in its number of publicly accessible private collections, all of which are well worth a look. But, the ever-more-popular field of street art is where Miami truly shines—especially in Wynwood. Late real-estate genius Tony Goldman began redeveloping this district of warehouses in 2009. While other cities have clamped down on street art and their developers—such as New York's former street-art mecca 5Pointz—and done their best to eradicate spray and stencil art, Goldman essentially legalized it, attracting landmark works by Shepard Fairey, Os Gemeos, Ryan McGinnes, and AVAF, among others.

Alexander Forbes

221 The Broad
A compendium of contemporary art in downtown L.A.

Collectors:
Eli & Edythe Broad

Address:
Los Angeles, CA 90012
United States of America
curator@thebroad.org
www.thebroad.org

Please check the website
for most current information
on the museum opening.

Eli and Edythe Broad's philanthropic efforts in the arts
are so extensive it can be hard to keep them straight.
Their gifts have earned them names on two museums—
the Broad Contemporary Art Museum at the Los Angeles
County Museum of Art (LACMA) and the Eli and Edythe
Broad Art Museum at Michigan State University (Broad
MSU). But the collectors are opening a more private affair
in late 2015, called, simply, The Broad. It's the first of the
three institutions to focus solely on the couple's private
collection and that of The Broad Art Foundation, which
they founded in 1984. Together, the over 2 000 works
by more than 200 artists, among them Jeff Koons, Kara
Walker, and William Kentridge, represent a veritable compendium of the very best contemporary art. Located in
downtown L.A., in a building designed by Diller Scofidio +
Renfro, The Broad sports two floors of exhibition space
and a vast vault in which to house the couple's immense
catalogue of works.

222 Frederick R. Weisman Art Foundation
The Who's Who of Modernism, from Surrealism to Pop

Collectors:
Frederick R. &
Billie Milam Weisman

Address:
265 North Carolwood Drive
Los Angeles, CA 90077
United States of America
Tel +1 310 2775321
tours@weismanfoundation.org
www.weismanfoundation.org

Opening Hours:
Mon–Fri: 10:30am and 2pm
Only guided tours with prior
registration.

It's as if Billie Milam and Frederick R. Weisman were
still moving about their mansion. Paintings by Abstract
Expressionists like Willem de Kooning or Mark Rothko
hang together with Pop Art works over the fireplace and
sectional sofas. Yet the collector couple had purchased the
1920s house only as an exhibition space. Weisman, the
son of Russian immigrants, and a passionate art buyer,
established a foundation in 1982 to preserve his esteemed
collection after his death. Now, guided tours through
the villa and adjacent gallery showcase the work that was **U**
most important to him: European Modernism from Paul
Cézanne and Pablo Picasso, Surrealists like Max Ernst, and
postwar art by Alberto Giacometti, Alexander Calder, or
Robert Rauschenberg. Way too much art for a mansion,
and all of it museum worthy, which why the forward-look-
ing collector founded several American museums before
his death, in 1994.

223   CIFO—Cisneros Fontanals
Art Foundation
Latin American art is not what you think
it is in this expansive collection

Anyone who equates Latin American art with colorful, mythical painting will be taken to school by Ella Fontanals-Cisnero's collection. Forty years of continuous collecting offers stellar insight into the abstract, geometric language of Jesús Rafael Soto or Lygia Clark. The centerpiece is a work by Julio Le Parc, whose hulking sculpture at Documenta, the *Continuel-Mobile,* was comprised of flexible metal discs that pinged scattered light about the room. It was stored in boxes for decades, but now it fits perfectly in a former department store that was transformed into an exhibition hall by the prize-winning architect Rene Gonzalez in 2005. Photography, video, and installation art form the 1 400-work collection, each given equal treatment. There's also an increasing amount of contemporary art—by Francis Alÿs or Ernesto Neto, for example—unrestrained by either geography or theme.

Collector:
Ella Fontanals-Cisneros

Address:
1018 North Miami Avenue
Miami, FL 33136
United States of America
Tel +1 305 4553380
info@cifo.org
www.cifo.org

Opening Hours:
Thurs–Fri: 12–6pm
Sat–Sun: 10am–4pm

224   De la Cruz Collection—
Contemporary Art Space
Emerging artists meet solid positions like Neo Rauch
or Thomas Houseago

Whenever Rosa and Carlos de la Cruz show up, art dealers get nervous. The American couple is part of the so-called group of "super-collectors," people who might never think their holdings are quite large enough: there's always room for one more work, preferably a large one by Thomas Houseago, Daniel Richter, or Neo Rauch. This quickly leads to the accusation of arbitrariness. But the fact is that the couple is quickly enthused over new movements and acquires them promptly for their museum, opened in 2009. This is how the work of the up-and-coming artist Dana Schutz or Jacob Kassay made it into the collection. With purchases of Manfred Pernice or Martin Creed, the de la Cruzes evidence their receptivity to complex theoretical works. Above all, they maintain an extensive program of lectures and workshops that allow people to inform themselves about contemporary art, free of charge.

U

Collectors:
Rosa & Carlos de la Cruz

Address:
23 Northeast 41st Street
Miami, FL 33137
United States of America
Tel +1 305 5766112
info@delacruzcollection.org
www.delacruzcollection.org

Opening Hours:
Tues–Sat: 10am–4pm
And by appointment.

225   The Margulies Collection
at the Warehouse
*Big-name photographers and sculptors
in curious combination*

Collector:
Martin Z. Margulies

Address:
591 Northwest 27th Street
Miami, FL 33127
United States of America
Tel +1 305 5761051
mcollection@bellsouth.net
www.margulieswarehouse.com

Opening Hours:
October–April
Wed–Sat: 11am–4pm

Old and new photography, from Helen Levitt to Cindy
Sherman; videos and installations by Sara Barker, Bill
Viola, or minimalistic light artist Iván Navarro count
among the interests of the real-estate tycoon Martin Z.
Margulies—a special niche not for everyone. His collection, which has been overseen by curator Katherine Hinds
since the 1980s, is situated in a former warehouse. There
you also find must-haves for any international collection:
Richard Serra, Donald Judd, Dan Flavin, Jannis Kounellis,
Michelangelo Pistoletto—all of whose presence gauges
one's own reputation. Margulies combines these with Surrealist sculptures by Joan Miró, or objects by Franz West,
artists separated by just a few decades but also by entire
artistic epochs. Such fissures, however, excite the collector
and uniquely mark his rotating exhibits.

U

226   Craig Robins Collection
A collection where art and design meet without angst

If anyone knows how art and design should be displayed together, it's Craig Robins. The real-estate agent founded Design Miami in 2005 as a companion to Art Basel Miami Beach and thereby managed to make a discredited Art Déco district chic and expensive once again. His collection, housed in his office building, brings together both fine art and fine design with consistency: paintings by Thomas Scheibitz, Kai Althoff, or Marlene Dumas meet classical furniture by Jean Prouvé, Charlotte Perriand, or Ron Arad, a contemporary design icon. Robins arranges the works with an eye toward form and content, both. It's not surprising that Cosima von Bonin or Mike Kelley are on the list of his favorite artists: both have extended their range to create sculptures that integrate furniture, plush, and even ambient music.

Collector:
Craig Robins

Address:
3841 Northeast 2nd Avenue,
Suite 400
Miami, FL 33137
United States of America
Tel +1 305 5318700
tiffany@dacra.com
www.dacra.com

Opening Hours:
Mon–Fri: 9am–5pm
By appointment only.

227   Rubell Family Collection/
Contemporary Arts Foundation
*The most resonant names in Western art are present
in this collection*

They are America's super-collectors, with museum-sized spaces, sponsors for exhibition projects, and a consistent and clear philosophy: for four decades Mera and Donald Rubell have only been purchasing art that speaks to both of them. They have agreed so far on over 1 500 works, including those by Bruce Nauman, Jeff Koons, Lawrence Weiner, Gerhard Richter, Richard Prince, and Keith Haring. Since **U** 1993 a part of their collection has been shown in a remodeled warehouse and adjacent sculpture garden. Another highlight is German photography, from August Sander to the Düsseldorf Becher School, including Thomas Ruff and Andreas Gursky. The Rubells know that their market power can influence the artists' careers—even if they collect solely out of passion.

Collectors:
Mera & Donald Rubell

Address:
95 Northwest 29th Street
Miami, FL 33127
United States of America
Tel +1 305 5736090
info@rfc.museum
www.rfc.museu

Opening hours vary depending on exhibition. Please check the website for most current information.

228 The Hess Art Collection, Napa
*Museum highlights from Europe and America in the
gentle hills of Napa Valley*

Collector:
Donald M. Hess

Address:
4411 Redwood Road
Napa, CA 94558
United States of America
Tel +1 707 2551144
info@hesscollection.com
www.hesscollection.com/art

Opening Hours:
Mon–Sun: 10am–5pm

Additional exhibition locations:
Salta, Argentina, p. 014
Klapmuts, South Africa, p. 164

He sold the family brewery. He successfully began a Swiss mineral water brand and sold it to Coca-Cola. From that day on, Donald M. Hess, the son of Swiss-American parents, was able to devote his time to his two true passions: wine and art. Hess owns vineyards and art collections in the Argentine Andes and the South African cape region. Prior, in 1978, he invested in California's Napa Valley. At Mount Veeder, it's not just about sampling the wine; the two-hour drive from San Francisco is worth making for other reasons: integrated into the rustic 1903 building is one-quarter of Hess's 1 000-work art collection, spread over two spacious storeys. Works by Francis Bacon, Franz Gertsch, Anselm Kiefer, and Per Kirkeby are true jewels: nowhere else in California can you see them in such quality and density.

Collectors:
Rene & Veronica di Rosa

Address:
5200 Sonoma Highway
Napa, CA 94559
United States of America
Tel +1 707 2265991
tours@dirosaart.org
www.dirosaart.org

Opening Hours:
Wed–Sun: 10am–4pm
Only guided tours with prior
online registration.

229 Di Rosa
Nature and art in almost equal standing

Since 1997 the collection of Veronica and Rene di Rosa has invited visitors to descend upon their vineyards and sprawling natural preserve. Everything here seems to be focused on the local: the large outside sculptures as well as the works housed in four elongated buildings were all made by regional artists. The painterly landscape is just as important to the collectors as the creatures that reside there. Artists like Mark di Suvero, Bruce Nauman, and Larry Sultan, or the painter Raymond Saunders have all spent time in California, which is why they fit seamlessly into the **U** di Rosa portfolio, as do artists less internationally known, including Mildred Howard or Joan Brown. Today the collection boasts over 1 800 works that can be visited year-round, in guided tours of no more than twenty-five people.

230 The Walther Collection—
Project Space New York
*African and Asian photo art in dialogue
with Western classics*

Having a second space in New York City makes sense, particularly for globally connected collectors like Artur Walther, founder of the Neu-Ulm-based Walther Collection, a high-quality German space opened in 2010 that specializes in contemporary and classic photography. For Walther, who has long lived on the Hudson, nabbing a space in New York City was entirely logical. Here he sits on the committee of the Whitney Museum and on that of the International Center of Photography; here he grooms his international contacts, from which his German location also profits. Since 2011, the Walther Collection has been located in 160 square meters in a historical landmark, the West Chelsea Art Building—ten floors of galleries and artist studios. The collection's cosmopolitan perspective includes African and Asian works, and its rotating three-month schedule offers both new discoveries and modern masters.

U

Collector:
Artur Walther

Address:
526 West 26th Street, Suite 718
New York, NY 10001
United States of America
Tel +1 212 3520683
contact@walthercollection.com
www.walthercollection.com

Opening Hours:
Wed–Sat: 12–6pm

Additional exhibition locations:
Neu-Ulm, Germany, p. 087

The **New York** art scene is thriving like never before. With this growth comes a shifting and expanding geographic landscape for the city's dealers, artists, and museums. A majority of the city's most important galleries remain—and are expanding—in Chelsea. David Zwirner now has a second gallery, as does Andrea Rosen. 303 is returning to its former home, on 21st Street, which will be located within a new Norman Foster-designed high-rise. And London's beloved Lisson Gallery is opening a vast space underneath the High Line, between 23rd and 24th Street. Others, like Casey Kaplan, who moved northeast to the city's Flower District at the beginning of 2015, after twenty years in Chelsea, are turning their backs on the neighborhood. For many, the non-stop increase in rent in New York's favorite gallery neighborhood has pushed them away. Others hope to rediscover the city's artistic heart—Chelsea and Soho were once artist neighborhoods too, after all. Today, the pulse driving New York's art scene is Brooklyn. The borough's mainstay galleries, such as Pierogi, Clearing, and Regina Rex, still add an experimental touch in the ever-more-gentrified neighborhood of Williamsburg. New spaces are popping up with feverish pace, especially in Brooklyn's further reaches. A cluster of impressive young galleries has settled at 56 Bogart Street, off the Morgan Avenue stop, in Bushwick. Others, like artist Dustin Yellin's nonprofit exhibition space and residency, Pioneer Works, have headed south to Red Hook, which, while still quiet these days, won't be for long. But it's not just the galleries that are moving. The Whitney Museum inaugurated its new High Line-abutting Meatpacking District location in spring 2015. Meanwhile, the Breuer Building—the Whitney's home for nearly fifty years—has been temporarily placed in the Metropolitan Museum of Art's hands, giving new wings to the museum's contemporary art department. The only real challenge to seeing unparalleled art in New York? Keeping up with where to go next.

Alexander Forbes

231   Zabludowicz Collection, New York
*The corner of Broadway and Times Square: the office as
an arena for international art*

Collectors:
Anita & Poju Zabludowicz

Address:
1500 Broadway
New York, NY 10036
United States of America
ny@zabludowiczcollection.com
www.zabludowiczcollection.com/
new-york

Office building visits by
appointment only.

Additional exhibition locations:
London, Great Britain, p. 102

At 176 Prince of Wales Road, in London, in a Methodist
church, a part of the 2 000-work collection belonging to
Anita and Poju Zabludowicz has been on display via rotating exhibitions since 2007. One of the collector couple's
recent exhibition addresses is located in the middle of
Times Square, in New York City: 1500 Broadway. In the
office of Tamares Real Estate, where Poju Zabludowicz
oversees his investments, exhibitions offer visitors what he
and his wife, Anita Zabludowicz, have gathered over the
years. Aside from temporary projects, there are group shows
spanning several floors that must assert themselves amidst **U**
the cool light of business offices. The rooms are open to
the public, but anyone who wants a more comprehensive view of the collection, featuring works by artists like
Jeppe Hein or Josephine Meckseper, is required to hop on
a jet and fly to Great Britain.

232 West Collection
Key names in international art meet new voices

Financial services professional Al West is a man of action. He doesn't wait for gallerists or curators to recommend emerging voices to him; he lures them in himself. In 2011, for example, he and his daughter, Paige West, asked artists to apply for the West Collection Art Prize. Everyone who downloaded the app, looked at the art, then gave an evaluation and became part of the extended jury. This kind of participation is continued in the public spaces of West's business, SEI Investments. Approximately 1 200 works are installed in SEI's main building and can be viewed by appointment. The collection has grown since 1996, now encompassing nearly 3 000 works, including those by Donald Judd, Richard Artschwager, Martin Boyce, and Candice Breitz. Many of the works are loaned to museums or curated travelling exhibitions.

Collectors:
Paige & Al West

Address:
1 Freedom Valley Drive
Oaks, PA 19456
United States of America
Tel +1 610 8837368
lee@westcollection.org
www.westcollection.org

By appointment only.

233 Hall Art Foundation
*Impressive presentations of art in an
eighteenth-century building*

Christine and Andrew Hall are not only longstanding collectors of art by Georg Baselitz. In 2006 the American commodity trader and his wife also bought the artist's former castle, near Hildesheim, Germany, to house works from their collection. More recently they bought and renovated Lexington Farm, in Vermont, an eighteenth-century structure that is now part of the Hall Art Foundation, where they show parts of their extensive collection. But unlike many of their peers, whose collected names read like a Who's Who of the international art scene, the Halls have decided to concentrate upon a few positions and prefer to collect them in depth. Here one finds notable Neo-Expressionist solo shows by the likes of A. R. Penck and Georg Baselitz, among other monographic exhibitions, including Neil Jenney's figurative paintings and Edward Burtynsky's photographs.

Collectors:
Christine & Andrew Hall

Address:
551 VT Route 106
Reading, VT 05062
United States of America
Tel +1 802 9521056
info@hallartfoundation.org
www.hallartfoundation.org

Opening Times:
May–November
Wed, Sat, Sun by appointment only.

Collector:
Linda Pace

Address:
111 Camp Street
San Antonio, TX 78204
United States of America
Tel +1 210 2266663
info@pacefound.org
www.lindapacefoundation.org

Opening Times:
Wed–Sat: 12–5pm

234   Linda Pace Foundation
The legacy of a patroness who promoted young art

Linda Pace was an artist. But she wasn't just that. From 1993 onwards she organized a scholarship and exhibition program for artists in the Texan city of San Antonio. The artists often went on to have fantastic careers. Artist Isaac Julien, whose films can be found in Pace's collection—alongside art by Susan Philipsz, Arturo Herrera, Mona Hatoum, and Gabriel Orozco—all called Pace an "artist-collector." The passionate patroness had procured roughly five hundred works of art before she died, in 2007. Pace placed a part of her sculpture collection in a park dedicated to her young deceased son. The publicly accessible terrain is adjacent to a new building of the foundation—Space—in which temporary exhibitions present works from the collection. The foundation continues to purchase works by emerging artists in order to continue Linda Pace's legacy.

Collectors:
Andy Pilara

Address:
Pier 24 The Embarcadero
San Francisco, CA 94105
United States of America
Tel +1 415 5127424
info@pier24.org
www.pier24.org

Online registration required.

235   Pier 24 Photography
Photography shines at this outsized venue
in heart of San Francisco

Collectors have long had a tenuous relationship to photography. It's a fickle medium: one difficult to preserve and with a relatively recently established market. But that hasn't dissuaded collector Andy Pilara, who is fairly new to the pursuit: his Pilara Foundation, on which Pier 24 is built, purchased its first photograph just over a decade ago. So entranced was Pilara with Diane Arbus's 2003 San Francisco Museum of Modern Art (SFMOMA) retrospective that he immediately embarked on assembling a col- **U** lection, which now boasts over 4 000 photographs. The collection's works are practically an A-to-Z of the medium's greats: from classics like Ansel Adams and Irving Penn to contemporary stars like Doug Aitken, Philip-Lorca diCorcia, and Jeff Wall. The works are stored and displayed on a rotating basis in what is perhaps America's largest photo-centric exhibition hall: a 2 600-square-meter space under the Bay Bridge.

236   Whitespace
*International art stars in a former warehouse
in Palm Beach*

The collector couple Elayne and Marvin Mordes has assembled works by established artist-teams like Teresa
Hubbard and Alexander Birchler, or Elmgreen & Dragset.
Their collection also includes international names like
Jonathan Meese, Thomas Houseago, Mat Collishaw, Christian Boltanski, and Anish Kapoor. The couple's treasures,
comprised primarily of sculptures and installations, are
housed in an unassuming warehouse in Palm Beach that
was previously used for the manufacturing of one of the
city's most in-demand products: dentures. Marvin Mordes
was a longtime board member at the Hirshhorn Museum,
in Washington. Since his death, his wife continues to ful-
fill the couple's mission: sharing knowledge and art with
others, and opening Whitespace's rooms upon request for
groups, private events, and, on Sundays, for all interested
art lovers.

U

Collectors:
Elayne & Marvin Mordes

Address:
2805 N. Australian Avenue
West Palm Beach, FL 33407
United States of America
Tel +1 561 8424131
info@whitespacecollection.com
www.whitespacecollection.com

Please check the website for most
current information.

A project like this can never be **complete.** Almost every month, collectors worldwide open new showrooms or make their private collections available to the public in a variety of ways. If you know of any private collection of contemporary art that is publicly accessible and not listed here, we would be delighted to hear about it. We would be equally pleased to hear of any plans you might have for opening your own collection to interested art lovers. Doing so will help us keep the *BMW Art Guide by Independent Collectors* up to date. Please write to us at: bmwartguide@independent-collectors.com

Silvia Anna Barrilà is a freelance journalist based in Milan and Berlin who specializes in the art market. Since 2008 she has been writing for the Italian financial newspaper *Il Sole 24 Ore (ArtEconomy24)*, as well as for *Icon, Panorama,* and for other international media, including *Damn, Auction Central News, Artinvestor, Monopol,* and *Art Asia Pacific.*

In this guide she wrote about collections in southern and eastern Europe: Greece, Hungary, Italy, Poland, Russia, Turkey, and Ukraine. She also covered several countries in Asia—Bangladesh, China, India, and Japan— as well as a few collections in Germany, the Netherlands, Qatar, South Africa, and the United Arab Emirates.

The journalist couple **Nicole Büsing** and **Heiko Klaas,** based in Hamburg and Berlin, have been writing freelance art journalism and art criticism since 1997 for a variety of national and international art magazines and newspapers, among which today include *Monopol, Artmapp, Artist Kunstmagazin, Dare, Zeitkunst, Artinvestor, Kunstmarkt Media, Photonews,* and *Next Level.* They also write catalogue essays for artists and institutions.

In this guide they focused on collections from Europe and South America—Argentina, Austria, Belgium, Brazil, Denmark, Finland, France, Germany, Iceland, Israel, Luxembourg, Mexico, the Netherlands, Norway, Portugal, Puerto Rico, Spain, and Switzerland—and on a few collections in Japan, South Africa, and the United States of America.

Alexander Forbes is a New York-based art writer and critic, who since February 2015 has served as News Editor for Artsy. He was based in Berlin for the previous five years, initially founding the *Berlin Art Journal,* an online publication with a focus on contemporary art, and later serving as the bureau chief for Louise Blouin Media's publications *Blouin Artinfo, Modern Painters,* and *Art+Auction* in German-speaking Europe. Forbes was *artnet News'* European Editor just prior to returning to New York.

His focus in this guide was on the collections in the United States of America, as well as on a few collections in Germany, Finland, and Norway.

Freelance art critic **Christiane Meixner,** based in Berlin, has served as editor of *Der Tagesspiegel's* "Art & Market" section since 2008; since 2013 she has also worked as an editor for *Weltkunst.* Additionally, Meixner writes for a variety of magazines and newspapers, including *Monopol, Frankfurter Rundschau, Kunstforum,* and *Zeit Online.*

Her focus in this guide was on English-speaking countries: Australia, Canada, and New Zealand—as well as several collections in Great Britain and the United States of America.

Anne Reimers lives in London. Since 2006 she has been a freelance arts journalist for the *Frankfurter Allgemeine Zeitung,* reporting on auctions, art fairs, and exhibitions in the British capital. An art historian, Reimers has been teaching cultural theory for nearly a decade and is currently Senior Lecturer for Visual Culture and Fashion Theory at the University for the Creative Arts (UCA), in Rochester, England.

Her focus in this guide was on the collections in Great Britain, as well as on a few collections in France and Norway.

City

City

* new in the Guide

Collection

Collection

Collection

Collection

Collector

Collector

Collector

Collector

Collector

BMW Art Guide by Independent Collectors

Editors
BMW Group, Munich
Independent Collectors, Berlin

Conception & Implementation
Independent Collectors, Berlin
Dorten, Stuttgart/Berlin

Project Directors
Katrin Mechler & Stephanie Schild,
BMW Group
Karoline Pfeiffer & Christina Werner,
Independent Collectors
Uwe Hiltwein & Yvonne Sussmann, Dorten
Sibylle Luig, Hatje Cantz Verlag

Executive Editor
Sylvia Dominique Volz, Berlin

Authors
Silvia Anna Barrilà, Berlin/Milan
Nicole Büsing & Heiko Klaas, Hamburg/Berlin
Alexander Forbes, New York
Christiane Meixner, Berlin
Anne Reimers, London

Additional Texts
Independent Collectors

Translation & Proofreading
R. Jay Magill & Tanja Maka, Berlin

Graphic Design
Bianca Wegner, Dorten

Typefaces
Arial by Robin Nicholas & Patricia Saunders,
The Monotype Corporation, Woburn
Akzidenz Grotesk BQ by Hermann Berthold,
H. Berthold AG, Berlin
LeMondeLivre by Jean-François Porchez,
Porchez Typofonderie, Clamart

Reproductions
Wagnerchic Digital Artwork, Stuttgart

Production
Nadine Schmidt, Hatje Cantz Verlag

Printed by
Offsetdruckerei Karl Grammlich, Pliezhausen

Paper
Invercote G, 180 g/m^2
Fly 06, extraweiss, 90 g/m^2

Binding
Josef Spinner Großbuchbinderei, Ottersweier

© 2015 BMW Group, Munich;
Hatje Cantz Verlag, Ostfildern;
Independent Collectors, Berlin, and authors

Published by
Hatje Cantz Verlag
Zeppelinstrasse 32
73760 Ostfildern
Germany
Tel +49 711 4405-200
Fax +49 711 4405-220
www.hatjecantz.com
A Ganske Publishing Group Company

Hatje Cantz books are available internationally at selected bookstores. For more
information about our distribution partners, please visit www.hatjecantz.com

ISBN 978-3-7757-3943-6 (English)
ISBN 978-3-7757-3942-9 (German)

Printed in Germany

Additional Contributors
Thomas Girst, Sina Honold, Katharina Knaus,
Hedwig Solis Weinstein

Art is a gift. When we look at a work, are pulled into and interact with it, we say a wordless "thank you" to all the artists that fascinate, inspire, and sometimes even change us. With this book, BMW and Independent Collectors wish to thank everyone who lives with art and who has opened their spaces to like-minded spirits from around the world. Our heartfelt thanks go to all the collectors who appear in this edition of the *BMW Art Guide by Independent Collectors*. Your support and confidence in our project are what have made this book possible. Our deepest thanks go also to our committed team of authors and editors, and to the many contributors in the Independent Collectors and BMW network. You never turned away from the challenge.

Thank you.